The Art of Software Modeling

Other Auerbach Publications in
Software Development, Software Engineering,
and Project Management

The Complete Project Management Office Handbook
Gerard M. Hill
0-8493-2173-5

Complex IT Project Management: 16 Steps to Success
Peter Schulte
0-8493-1932-3

Creating Components: Object Oriented, Concurrent, and Distributed Computing in Java
Charles W. Kann
0-8493-1499-2

The Hands-On Project Office: Guaranteeing ROI and On-Time Delivery
Richard M. Kesner
0-8493-1991-9

Interpreting the CMMI®: A Process Improvement Approach
Margaret Kulpa and Kent Johnson
0-8493-1654-5

ISO 9001:2000 for Software and Systems Providers: An Engineering Approach
Robert Bamford and William John Deibler II
0-8493-2063-1

The Laws of Software Process: A New Model for the Production and Management of Software
Phillip G. Armour
0-8493-1489-5

Real Process Improvement Using the CMMI®
Michael West
0-8493-2109-3

Six Sigma Software Development
Christine Tayntor
0-8493-1193-4

Software Architecture Design Patterns in Java
Partha Kuchana
0-8493-2142-5

Software Configuration Management
Jessica Keyes 0-8493-1976-5

Software Engineering for Image Processing
Phillip A. Laplante 0-8493-1376-7

Software Engineering Handbook
Jessica Keyes 0-8493-1479-8

Software Engineering Measurement
John C. Munson 0-8493-1503-4

Software Metrics: A Guide to Planning, Analysis, and Application
C.R. Pandian
0-8493-1661-8

Software Testing: A Craftsman's Approach, Second Edition
Paul C. Jorgensen
0-8493-0809-7

Software Testing and Continuous Quality Improvement, Second Edition
William E. Lewis
0-8493-2524-2

IS Management Handbook, 8th Edition
Carol V. Brown and Heikki Topi, Editors
0-8493-1595-9

Lightweight Enterprise Architectures
Fenix Theuerkorn
0-8493-2114-X

Outsourcing Software Development Offshore: Making It Work
Tandy Gold
0-8493-1943-9

Maximizing ROI on Software Development
Vijay Sikka
0-8493-2312-6

Implementing the IT Balanced Scorecard
Jessica Keyes
0-8493-2621-4

AUERBACH PUBLICATIONS
www.auerbach-publications.com
To Order Call: 1-800-272-7737 • Fax: 1-800-374-3401
E-mail: orders@crcpress.com

The Art of Software Modeling

Benjamin A. Lieberman

CRC Press is an imprint of the
Taylor & Francis Group, an **informa** business
AN AUERBACH BOOK

CRC Press
Taylor & Francis Group
6000 Broken Sound Parkway NW, Suite 300
Boca Raton, FL 33487-2742

First issued in paperback 2019

© 2007 by Taylor & Francis Group, LLC
CRC Press is an imprint of Taylor & Francis Group, an Informa business

No claim to original U.S. Government works

ISBN-13: 978-1-4200-4462-1 (hbk)
ISBN-13: 978-0-367-38957-4 (pbk)

Library of Congress Cataloging-in-Publication Data

Lieberman, Benjamin A.
    The art of software modeling / Benjamin A. Lieberman.
        p. cm.
    Includes bibliographical references and index.
    ISBN 1-4200-4462-1 (alk. paper)
    1. Software architecture. 2. System design. I. Title.

QA76.76.D47L536 2006
005.1'2--dc22   2006050075

Visit the Taylor & Francis Web site at
http://www.taylorandfrancis.com

and the Auerbach Web site at
http://www.auerbach-publications.com

Dedication

This book is dedicated in loving memory to my father.

Contents

Preface..xv

About the Author xvii

Notices...xix

Acknowledgments xxi

I ANALYTICAL FRAMEWORKS

1 The Art of the Model 3

Cognitive Resonance 5

Perception and Representation of Models 7

Learning and Reasoning...9

Beauty and the Beholder...10

Summary...12

Tips and Traps...13

Questions and Exercises...13

Exercise #1: Problems with Communication...14

References..14

Notes 15

2 A Systematic Approach..17

Formal Systems Analysis...19

Functional Decomposition 20

Scientific Method..24

Process Approach 25

Summary...28

Tips and Traps...29

Questions and Exercises...30

Exercise #1 System Analysis 30

References..31

Notes 31

3 **Observing Behavior**..**33**
 Observing Individuals 34
 Working in Groups...37
 Organizational Culture...38
 Investigating Legacy Computer Systems.................................. 40
 Environmental Considerations...43
 Summary 44
 Tips and Traps...45
 Questions and Exercises...46
 Exercise #1: Business Process Mapping 46
 Exercise #2: Organizational Mapping.....................................47
 Exercise #3: Team Construction 47
 References..47
 Notes 48

4 **Analytical Thinking**..**49**
 Analysis Patterns...50
  Pattern Structure...50
 Analytical Frameworks 54
 Adaptation and Application 56
 Summary 57
 Tips and Traps...58
 Questions and Exercises...59
 Exercise #1: Finding Abstract Themes....................................59
 Exercise #2: Creating an Analytical Framework 59
 References... 60
 Notes 61

II MODEL CONSTRUCTION

5 **Research and Investigation** **65**
 Recording Information 66
 Interviews 67
 Group Facilitation 70
 Independent Investigation...73
 Experimentation 74
 Organization of Research Information 75
 Summary 76
 Tips and Traps...78
 Questions and Exercises...78
 Exercise #1: Interviewing 79
 References..79
 Notes 79

6 Model Forms...81
Purpose and Form 82
Model Construction 85
Selecting Model Content 86
    Translating into the Model Form 86
        Static Structure..88
        Dynamic Behavior...88
        Interdependency 90
    Translating Jargon 90
    Tool Support 91
Summary 91
Tips and Traps...92
Questions and Exercises...92
Exercise #1: Domain Modeling..93
References 93
Notes 94

7 Data Validation 95
Team Review 95
Simulation 98
Direct Application 99
Test-Based Verification 100
Summary 100
Tips and Traps...101
Questions and Exercises...102
Exercise #1: Critical Review 102
References..102

8 Business Workflow Analysis...105
Business Environment..106
Business Model 107
Business Workflows 109
Business Workers and Actors 115
Business Entities (Domain Data Model)..............................115
Summary 116
Tips and Traps... 118
Questions and Exercises... 119
    Exercise #1: Identification of Business Actors and Workers 120
    Exercise #2: Business Workflow Modeling..............................120
    Exercise #3: Domain Modeling..120
References.. 121
Notes 121

9   Requirements Archaeology 123
   Preparation and Discovery...124
   Investigation 126
      Independent Study 126
      Interviewing...127
   Deciphering and Translation 128
      Audit Trail:...129
   Public Display..130
   Summary..131
   Tips and Traps 132
   Questions and Exercises...133
      Exercise #1: Translation of Structured Requirements 133
   References...134
   Notes 134

10 Modeling Software Architecture....................................135
   Functional View (Requirements) 137
   Static Structure View 138
   Component View (Implementation View) 142
   Dynamic View..144
   Deployment View 145
   Alternate Views..146
   Summary..148
   Tips and Traps 149
   Questions and Exercises...149
      Exercise #1: Framework Description................................150
      Exercise #2: Risk Analysis 150
   References... 151
   Notes 151

III PRESENTATION

11 Perception and Thinking..155
   Gestalt Theory 156
   Diagrammatic Reasoning 160
   Summary..164
   Tips and Traps...165
   Questions and Exercises...165
      Exercise #1: Iconic Representations 166
   References...166
   Notes 167

12 Composition..**169**
Line and Contour 170
Visual Balance 176
Information Balance 180
Emphasis 181
Shade and Color 181
Shade/Color Emphasis 184
Summary 185
Tips and Traps..186
Questions and Exercises...186
 Exercise #1: Diagram Construction........................187
References 187
Notes 188

13 Presentation..**189**
Presentation Flow 189
Presentation Techniques 193
Summary 195
Tips and Traps..195
Questions and Exercises...196
 Exercise #1: Observing Presentation Techniques 197
References 197
Note..197

IV APPENDICES

A Example Business Workflow: Execute Trade................................**201**
Brief Description..201
 Purpose 201
 Definitions and Acronyms....................................202
  Dependent Workflows 202
  Included Workflows.......................................202
  Extending Workflows 202
 Business Actors..203
 Business Workers..204
Workflow...204
 Basic Workflow: Execute Trade Ticket.....................204
 Alternative Workflows..207
  Scenario: Overnight Trade Instruction Letter (Mutual Funds).......207
  Scenario: Generate and Execute Terminating CTO.....................208
  Scenario: Trade Settlement 208
  Scenario: Post/Unpost Trade Ticket 209
  Scenario: Execute Electronic Trade.......................209

Exceptional Workflows 210
   Exception: Investor Oversold Shares or Other Trade Correction 210
   Exception: A Trade Ticket Does Not Post Correctly 211
   Exception: Trade Not Conducted before Market Closure 211
   Exception: Supervisor Denial of Trade 213
Improvement Possibilities 213
Special Requirements...213
Extension Points 213
Post-Conditions 213
Activity Diagram 214
Issues 215
Notes 215
Questions and Answers...215

B   Structured Requirement to Use Case 217
Brief Description...217
   System Requirements—Customer Care System 217
      Service Provisioning..217
      Customer Service 218
Translating into Use Cases...218

C   Answer Key and Discussion 223
Chapter 1...223
   Answers...223
   Exercise Discussion 224
Chapter 2...224
   Answers...224
   Exercise Discussion 225
Chapter 3...225
   Answers...225
   Exercise Discussion 227
Chapter 4...228
   Answers...228
   Exercise Discussion 228
Chapter 5...229
   Answers...229
   Exercise Discussion 230
Chapter 6...230
   Answers...230
   Exercise Discussion 231
Chapter 7...231
   Answers...231
   Exercise Discussion 232

Chapter 8 233

    Answers 233

    Exercise Discussion 234

Chapter 9 234

    Answers 234

    Exercise Discussion 236

Chapter 10 236

    Answers 236

    Exercise Discussion 237

Chapter 11 238

    Answers 238

    Exercise Discussion 239

Chapter 12 239

    Answers 239

    Exercise Discussion 240

Chapter 13 240

    Answers 240

    Exercise Discussion 241

Note 241

D   **UML 2.0 Overview 243**

Visual Software Modeling—UML (version 2.0) 243

    Package Diagram 244

    Use Case Diagram 245

    Structure Diagram 246

    Object Diagram 248

    Composite Diagram 249

    Component Diagram 250

    Deployment Diagram 251

    Activity Diagrams 252

    State Diagrams 253

    Communication Diagrams 254

    Sequence Diagram 255

    Timing Diagram 256

    Interaction Overview 256

Variations (UML Profile) 257

    Business Process Model 258

    System Analysis Model 258

    Database Entity Diagrams 259

Note 259

Index 261

Preface

In writing this book, I was heavily influenced by the writing and teaching of Gerald Weinberg ("Jerry" to his friends). As Norm Kerth remarked to me as we drove to the airport after the week-long Problem Solving and Leadership class, "Jerry's writing is more like a coal mine than a diamond mine—in a diamond mine you have to hunt and search for something of value; in a coal mine every shovel-full has value." To this end, I have tried to include in this book everything of value and nothing of waste. I have tried to present *The Art of Software Modeling* as an interesting and challenging work, worthy of a reader's time and consideration. Only you, the reader, can judge whether I have accomplished my goal.

Learning is a very difficult task. Change is never easy, and as learning requires change, the very act of reading this book represents a significant challenge. This book is about modeling—taking complex problems and forming an abstract framework in order to understand them. To aid you, I have decided to separate the material in this book into three parts. The first part deals with theoretical considerations of modeling—the "why." The second part deals with investigation and model creation—the "what" and "how." The final part deals with presentation of model information to others, so they may more readily learn the important details of the problem you have modeled. So, if you wish to design better diagrams, then start reading from Part III and move to Parts II and I. If you are interested in techniques for investigation and organization of complex information, then I suggest you start with Part II before moving to Part I and then Part III. Finally, you can simply read the book as I wrote it—from page 1 to the end.

Along the way, I have made a few assumptions about the type of person likely to read my words. I had in mind individuals who are responsible for the task of system analysis and design. Although they may go by many titles, these people are often responsible for setting the "vision" of the system and guiding its construction. Moreover, they typically are called upon to share that vision with several groups, including technical and non-technical stakeholders.

I believe that every model must satisfy the triumvirate goals of being correct, concise, and complete, which also has been my goal in writing this book. Additionally, by appealing to both the creator and consumer of model information, I hope to encourage the effective use of modeling techniques to improve the development process and the end product of a functional, useful, and maintainable system.

For me, *The Art of Software Modeling* is an ongoing process of learning and refinement. By definition, no model is ever complete; the more users of a model, the better it becomes. I also believe that the goal of modeling is to learn and teach, typically in that order. The modeler creates a model to learn the subject and then uses that model to teach others. I hope that you will learn from this book as much as I have in writing it.

Ben Lieberman
Denver, CO

About the Author

Benjamin A. Lieberman, Ph.D., serves as the Principal Architect for BioLogic Software Consulting. Dr. Lieberman provides consulting and training services on a wide variety of software development topics, including requirements analysis, software analysis and design, configuration management, and development process improvement. He brings over ten years of software architecture and information technology experience in various fields, including telecommunications, airline travel, Web e-commerce, financial services, and the life sciences. His consulting services are based on the best practices of software development, with specialization in object-oriented architectures and distributed computing, with a particular focus on Java-based systems and distributed Web site development (J2EE), XML/XSLT, Perl, and C++-based client-server systems. Dr. Lieberman has provided application architectural services to such companies as EchoStar, Jones Cyber Solutions, Blueprint Technologies, On-Command, Cricket Telecommunications (Leap Wireless), Cendant, Level(3), Galileo International, Duke University, and the University of Colorado. Dr. Lieberman is also an accomplished professional writer with a book and numerous software-related articles to his credit. Dr. Lieberman holds a doctorate degree in biophysics and genetics from the University of Colorado, Health Sciences Center, Denver, Colorado.

Notices

Portions of this work appear in the *IBM-RationalEdge* online journal, which is available from: http://www-128.ibm.com/developerworks/rational/rationaledge/.

Acknowledgments

I would like to acknowledge the influences that encouraged me to write this book.

To my wife, for her encouragement, understanding, and tolerance.
To my sons, for inspiring me to see the world through their eyes.
To my parents, well, for being the best folks a kid could ask for.
To my brother and sister, for always being there when I needed them.

I also would like to acknowledge the collected work of Gerald Weinberg in having a significant influence on my development as a software architect and a better person.

ANALYTICAL
FRAMEWORKS

Chapter 1

The Art of the Model

Models are now and always have been an integral part of the human experience. We create models of the world with information provided from our five main sensory inputs: visual, auditory, tactile, olfactory, and taste. These models inform us of changes in our immediate perception and also permit understanding of these changes in comparison to past events. As infants we develop sophisticated models of motion, shape, distance, time, and cause/effect in an effort to relate to the new and confusing world around us. Starting from a nearly clean slate we must build an internal understanding for every new experience. Thus, the idea of creating an *abstraction* of the world in an effort to understand complex ideas is inherent to human behavior. Taking conscious control of this behavior to capture, understand, and express complex information is the essence of the Art of Modeling.

As infants we also have a limited ability to express ourselves. We are limited to crying when startled or unhappy, and cooing when comforted. Although these simple forms of communication are sufficient to indicate the desire for food or to have one's diaper changed, they do not allow us to associate specific objects with other similar objects, such as the different colorful balls with which we wish to play. The development of language allows a greater level of self-expression; the ability to identify objects by name allows for the direct association of different kinds of objects. Eventually, this allows us to create abstract models to reason about complex concepts. George Orwell in his famous novel *1984* was very aware of the connection between language and the ability to reason about complex abstract ideas. In his novel, the development of "Newspeak" was an attempt by the government to limit creative thinking by altering and eliminating the words for undesirable concepts—such as civil rights and personal freedoms. As Orwell writes, "The purpose of Newspeak was not only to provide a medium of expression for the world-view and mental habits proper to the devotees of Ingsoc,[1] but to make all other forms of

**Figure 1-1 Impressionist Painting
(Claude Monet, Une Alle du Jardin de Monet, Giverny)**

thought impossible" ([2], p. 246). Although the idea that language can be used to control thought has been discredited, it is clear that language is critical to communication and represents the underpinning of all forms of modeling.

Human cognition is a complex combination of innate instinct and learned behavior, so a great deal of time is required to build up a robust worldview that can be used to relate new information to old [3]. Initially, these internal mental models[2] represent our ability to identify and associate concrete objects, but eventually they provide for more complex reasoning. For example, a person who attends a class on accounting principles may attempt to understand that subject in relation to previously learned behavior, such as balancing a checking account. In fact, abstract and impressionist painters often make use of this innate tendency by presenting a picture that can be interpreted differently by each viewer (Figure 1-1).

Our internal abstract models of the world are also critical to the communication of complex concepts with other people [4, 5]. For example, it would be impossible for a person from a hunter-gather culture who has never had contact with the modern world to understand the principles of refrigeration simply by describing the mechanics; it is completely foreign to their experience. To succeed, first you would need to have a shared communication medium (language, pictures, gestures, etc.). Once you can share ideas, you would then need to translate your understanding into ones that can be related to their internal models of the world: examples of food storage, the effect of cold temperatures on spoilage, and so on. In other words, you would need to align your model explaining a phenomenon to a shared experience with the intended audience [6].

A close alignment of one person's worldviews with another leads to a higher likelihood of understanding. This is one of the reasons that people form tight in-groups based on shared experiences [7], because of the comfort afforded by the reduced need to "understand" one another when communicating. The idea of "clicking" with another person is based on a shared understanding of a number of experiences, leading to a reduced effort to share information and a sense of familiarity.

For people involved in the creation of models for system analysis, these concepts are important when the model is intended for use by people other than just the modeler. By definition, when I create a model it will reflect my understanding of a subject. In order for my model to be useful to others, I need to ensure that I am capturing the right abstraction level and using a model form that meets the expectations and needs of the audience. For example, if I am modeling an automotive engine for mechanics versus engineers I should focus on engine elements for repair and replacement as opposed to the details of power generation.

To express these ideas, psychologists use the term *cognitive resonance* to represent the situation of matched internal worldviews between the modeler and the audience, and *cognitive dissonance* to describe a situation in which the presentation is disconnected from the audience's experience or expectation.

Cognitive Resonance

When a guitar string is struck, the string vibrates at a particular frequency and wavelength based on the string length, tension, and composition. If one looks closely, it is possible to see the string vibrating between the two endpoints of the fret pin and the bridge on the sound board. This vibration is transmitted through the air to our ears as a series of compression waves, which we perceive as sound. When these waves impact on another object that shares similar characteristics, a harmonic resonance will be imparted to the object. For example, if a second string is placed near the first and tuned the same way, the first string's vibrations will evoke vibration in the second.

In a similar manner, a model created for the purpose of communicating a particular subject should "strike a chord" with the audience. If this resonance is absent, the audience will have difficulty in understanding the content of the model (*mis*-sense), or worse yet, drawing incorrect conclusions presented by the model (*non*-sense). So, to create an effective model a modeler's primary responsibility is not only to accurately capture the subject information but also to present that information in a form that will be readily and correctly understood by the intended audience.

This is no simple task. We have all experienced teachers that have a good grasp of the subject but are unable to teach that information to students. By contrast, great teachers know how to package information in a way that captures the interest

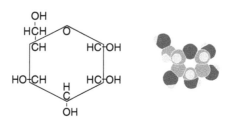

Figure 1-2 Two Chemical Representations for the Sugar Glucose

and excitement of the students. They bring the subject to life so that it connects with the students. In other words, the content of the lesson *resonates* with the students who have better lesson retention.

There are a variety of ways to construct models of information. Many of these models use symbology or some form of visual icons to represent complex and repeating concepts. This is done to group or "chunk" concepts so that they may be easily remembered and manipulated [8]. Some obvious examples are mathematical symbology or chemical notation (Figure 1-2). The topics of mathematics and chemistry are sufficiently complicated that complex constructs are necessary for explanation and prediction. Because of this complexity, these constructs would defeat most human understanding if they were presented in their entirety. Another example would be a map that was so detailed that to read it you would need to overlay it on the landscape it describes. Such a map would not be very practical for the purpose of navigation, where portability is critical. In both of these cases, a model that abstracts the key information and relationships is necessary. These kinds of models typically use some form of symbology "short-hand" to abbreviate basic concepts; this is very like the use of professional jargon to succinctly describe a complex idea.

If a model uses symbology or icons it is critical that the intended audience understands the meaning of these symbols. In Figure 1-2, the symbology is not clearly defined; thus, a viewer would have to be familiar with the representation of carbon atoms with a "C" (medium gray circle), oxygen with an "O" (dark gray circle), hydrogen with an "H" (light gray circle), and chemical bonds as lines or close proximity between letters (or adjacent circles). Similarly, a software Unified Modeling Language (UML) class diagram will not serve to further the understanding of someone who does not understand the notation and semantics of such a diagram (Figure 1-3; an overview of the UML is provided in Appendix D).

The recognition of symbols is often tightly coupled to the level of abstraction represented by the symbol. An icon that is of a familiar shape, such as the icons typically found in software systems to represent folders, files, controls, and so on, will be more readily understood than one that is an random collection of shapes and colors. Furthermore, society and culture will have a significant effect on the choice of symbology since some symbols will not be interpreted in a similar manner, and may in fact be interpreted as offensive by some members of the audience. This last point takes on increased significance when a development team is not collocated, as

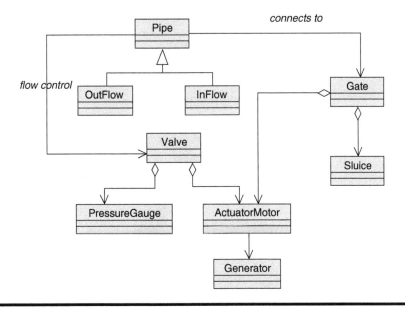

Figure 1-3   Example Unified Modeling Language (UML) Class Diagram

is the case with many outsourced projects. Later chapters will address these issues, and show how they affect the creation and presentation of system models.

Certainly, the search for symbology that is universally understood is not a new one. Plato's "Ideal Forms" represent an early attempt to identify the *eidos* (ειδος) or essential qualities for different objects and concepts [9, 10]. The details of this philosophical discourse are not relevant here, but some of the mechanisms for determining the *eidos*, or "likeness," of a particular object or concept will be useful as I present techniques for the creation of models in general, and software models in particular. The idea of an object's essential qualities and the kinds of relations that may be shared between different model elements will be further explored in Part II.

Perception and Representation of Models

A model can be defined as the abstraction of a complex system for the purpose of reasoning, simulating, analyzing, or communicating specific details of a subject. In this way, a model operates much like a magnifying glass lens; it focuses attention on items of direct concern while obscuring or omitting everything else (Figure 1-4).

For example, consider a scale drawing of a city. In this model, the street level details are obscured to permit a larger view of the overall city structure. This is an example of the concept of *abstraction* and how it is used to create a model. This brings me to the topic of model complexity, which can be summarized by the Golden Rule of Modeling:

A model expands one area

of
experience
at the

expense of others

Figure 1-4   The Effect of Modeling on Focus of Attention

Golden Rule of Modeling—A model shall be as complex as necessary; no more or less

Models may be considered "good" if they are suitable for their purpose. For example, a model of a jet plane with a scale of 1:1 (where one unit of measure on the model is equal to the same unit in real life, such as 1 inch:1 inch) may be exactly right for simulating the result of a crash, but is not very well suited to hang from the ceiling of my son's bedroom. So, for any system of sufficient size, the rule of thumb is that for anything too complex to entirely encompass in one's mind, it is necessary to sacrifice some accuracy in favor of understanding. Furthermore, as the human mind has a finite capacity to capture and retain information [8], reasoning about a complex topic requires breaking it down into smaller subproblems that can solved and rebuilt back into the whole.

There are many ways to create models (which will be further explored in Part II), but the selection of the best technique is a function of experience, research, education, and intuition. Experience is best thought of as encountering a situation similar to one in the past where, perhaps by accident, a workable solution was found. Education is where someone else has solved the problem and is willing to teach this mechanism directly or via some other communication mechanism. Research involves experimentation with a variety of approaches to determine the most appropriate one. Intuition is involved when trying to create a new model form for a previously unknown problem, and making guesses on what might work best for a given audience.

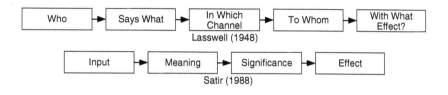

Figure 1-5 Two Models for Communication Flows between People [11, 12]

When building a model, it is often best to understand the intended audience before attempting to envision and create the model. Because there are many ways to represent a system, and a model is often intended for the purpose of communication, then the model should take into account an understanding of the intended audience, or there is a high likelihood of miscommunication. Because of this likelihood of confusion, when communicating ideas via a model, it is often useful to consider how information flows between people (Figure 1-5). Numerous theories have been developed to explain the process by which information is transferred from one person to another; each of these models has in common the need for a "communication channel" through which the information flows. Often this is verbal, as seen in a lecture hall or a meeting room. Frequently, visual communication is also used to convey information, as is the case with paintings and advertisements. However, regardless of the medium of exchange, there are two key aspects to communication: the generation of a message, and the interpretation of that message.

As mentioned earlier, individuals perceive and organize information through the use of mental models. However, no two people share the exact same experiences, so no two mental models are exactly alike. This can lead to errors of interpretation based on differences in perceptions. For example, consider Figure 1-6. What is in the center box?

Depending on which context is chosen (vertical or horizontal), the answer may be the letter B or the number 13. In fact, the contents of the box are simply a straight line next to a line with two adjacent curves. It is the mental models we have constructed that influence our interpretation of the symbology. To someone who cannot read or write (or uses different symbology for those operations), these figures are meaningless, and this example would represent a very poor model indeed. The take-home point of this figure is that model icons and symbology may be interpreted differently by different audiences, and should be considered when creating a model display.

Learning and Reasoning

Models serve as more than just a communication device; models are also central to perception, memory, learning, and reasoning. For example, the construction of mental representations in short-term memory is critical for our ability to process sensory information [3]. Reasoning is facilitated by the creation of possible solutions

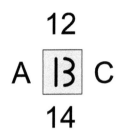

Figure 1-6 How Perception Is Affected by Context [13][3]

in the "working memory" to allow us to investigate different relationships between objects and events [14]. The use of mental "prototypes" to compare against perceived objects permits us to categorize the surrounding environment [15].

Cognitive Psychology is the branch of psychology that is devoted to the study of these aspects of human thinking. Cognition is the collected term that refers to our ability to focus attention[4] on a specific event, perceive that event via our senses, process the significance, and relate that information to previously collected information. Models, of all forms, are our way to deal with massive amounts of information with limited processing capability. We reduce the complexity of the perception problem by focusing attention to certain select inputs over others, and by "activating" on key features that are part of the subject of interest. For example, in the classic children's problem of finding specific shapes in a picture (e.g., *Highlights for Children,* published by Highlights for Children, Inc.) the desired simple object is hidden in a large, complex image. The child is shown the outline of the form and asked to identify its location in the image. The task is aided greatly by providing a template that the child holds in short-term memory while scanning around the image. The mental image is compared to perceived features in the picture until a match is found. Interestingly enough, the desired object is always in the *perception field* (or in other words, available to the child's processing systems), but not recognized until matched to the template object. Once the object is located, it becomes quite apparent as attention is "locked" on; after initial discovery, the object is then easily relocated in future searches. In the creation of models, this is critical in the creation of large, complex diagrams. The ability for a viewer to locate some key element of the diagram will be greatly aided by some form of distinguishing feature, such as color or shading, to call it out against the background of other diagram elements. This point will be further explored in Part III.

Beauty and the Beholder

The subject of beauty has intrigued people for millennia. Philosophers have argued frequently (and at length) for centuries on the qualities of beauty without forming any solid conclusions as to the source of our sense of beauty and "rightness" [10].

Figure 1-7   Hidden Pictures: Locate the Figures (Upper Right) in the Main Picture[5]

In more recent times, researchers in psychology, although not having any greater success in defining beauty, have formed theories that describe this aspect of human perception. Gestalt theory, from early research efforts in Cognitive Psychology, presents a set of principles for the organization of visual perception that have been shown to hold for most people [3, 16–18]. These principles are organized into general rules:

Factor of Proximity
Factor of Similarity
Factor of Uniform Destiny (Common Fate)
Factor of Objective Set
Factor of Direction
Factor of Closure
Factor of Past Experience

We will explore some of these rules in latter chapters, most particularly in Part III during the discussion on presentation of visual models. The Gestalt factors are based on studies that have shown that people search for the simplest possible organization of visual elements, which the early Gestaltist M. Wertheimer called the "Law of Prägnanz." Gestaltists held that the closer a particular organization scheme came to the "simplest" possible combination, the more likely this organization would be recognized by most people. Consider Figure 1-8; what groupings do you see? The majority of people would answer "four groups of two" instead of "one

Figure 1-8 Gestalt Factor of Proximity

group of eight." This is an example of the Gestalt principle of proximity, in which objects that are in close proximity are associated into a single group. This factor plays a part in diagram creation where elements may be grouped closely together to suggest some form of association.

In addition to the Gestalt principles, our sense of beauty is heavily influenced by familiarity, symmetry, and contrast between figure and ground. Humans seek structure and order in our environment, such that we will see patterns even in random arrangements, such as animals or other creatures in the arrangement of stars in the night sky. Objects that are placed symmetrically tend to be more appealing, and are perceived as being well balanced and in harmony with one another.

Many of the theories of Cognitive Psychology will be useful as we explore modeling in general, and system modeling in specific. We will return frequently to the Gestalt principles as we explore the creation, organization, and presentation of models. Theories on memory, attention, learning, reasoning, and problem solving will also be explored in the context of modeling. As should be apparent from this introduction, people are highly experienced in creating models as a natural part of perceiving the world; however, the creation of models for the specific purpose of reasoning about a complex subject, and the presentation of that reasoning to others, is a far more challenging task requiring practice and effort. In the chapters to follow, I will attempt to combine studies in psychology, art, and systems analysis into a single theme that illustrates the fine art of modeling.

Summary

1. All humans create models, starting from infancy when we need to understand the complex and confusing world into which we have been born. Over time, these "mental models" aid us in the understanding of language, and allow for the basis of human reasoning and understanding of complex concepts.
2. "Cognitive resonance" describes the ability to create a model that will closely align to the expectations of the audience. If a presentation does not resonate with the audience, it is not as likely to result in understanding and learning. A likely result of "cognitive dissonance" is mis-sense, or difficulty in understanding the content, and non-sense, in which the content is incorrectly interpreted.
3. Models often use symbology, icons (visual), or sound patterns (auditory) to represent complex subjects in a more compact form. This is done as an aid to human understanding, which has limited capacity to process information. However, if the symbology is not familiar to the audience, its use will defeat the purpose of the model. Recognition of symbols is directly related to the level of abstraction represented by the symbol or icon.

4. Models are similar to a magnifying glass in that a part of a subject is placed as the focus while the remainder of the topic is obscured or omitted. Thus, the key feature of a model is to reduce the complexity of a subject, via abstraction, down to a level that can be manipulated. Creation of models is a function of experience, research, education, and intuition, with the best modelers understanding how communication occurs between people.

5. Models also serve the purpose of facilitating learning and reasoning. Cognitive Psychology represents studies into the use of "internal models" for the purpose of perception, memory, reasoning, and learning.

6. The Gestalt school holds that there are a collection of rules about human visual organization. These rules include the idea that objects placed close to one another will be perceived as a group, as well as objects that are similar in form. The Law of Prägnanz is used to describe the level of "goodness" that a particular organization of elements will take.

Tips and Traps

Discovery of the expectations of an audience for a specific model is often a trial and error experience. When considering a model form, it is often best to create a prototype model from a small subset of the overall problem for presentation to the expected audience. This technique ensures that the model form that has been selected will meet the audience's need, preventing a great deal of rework if the model form is not appropriate.

Learning is often improved by limited duration exposure that is repeated several times. A one-hour session repeated several times is much better for long-term retention than a single three-hour session (e.g., interrupted study vs. "cramming"). In my experience, this principle seems to hold for model creation as well. Avoid attempting to create the entire model in one sitting; it is far better to include numerous spaces between information gathering and capture sessions.

Questions and Exercises

■ Question #1:
What is the purpose of human attention? Why does attention "wander"?

■ Question #2:
"Beauty is in the eye of the beholder." What does this statement mean? Is a sense of beauty innate in humans?

■ Question #3:
It was stated that models are for perception, reasoning, and communication. What other models uses can you imagine?

Exercise #1: Problems with Communication

In the far distant future you have been tasked with the job of the first contact with an alien species called the *Snoog*. This species uses scent as the primary mode of communication and has no understanding of verbal speech. Fortunately for you, a previous research team has determined that the range of scent for the Snoog is very similar to humans, and you have access to a machine that can replicate any desired sequence or type of odorant. Consider how you would go about introducing yourself and explaining the purpose of sound in human communications.

References

[1] Kellman, P., *Kinematic Foundations of Infant Visual Perception*, in *Visual Perception and Cognition in Infancy*, C. Granrud, Editor. 1993, Lawrence Erlbaum Associates: Hillsdale, NJ. pp. 121–173.

[2] Orwell, G., *1984*. 1950, New York: Signet.

[3] Eysenck, M., *Principles of Cognitive Psychology*. 2nd ed. Principles of Psychology, ed. M. Eysenck, S. Green, and N. Hays. 2001, Sussex, UK: Psychology Press.

[4] Mandel, T., *The Elements of User Interface Design*. 1997, New York: Wiley Computer Publishing.

[5] Morgan, J. and P. Welton, *See What I Mean?* 2nd ed. 1992, London: Edward Arnold.

[6] Schramm, W., *The Process and Effects of Mass Communications*. 1954, Illinois: University of Illinois Press.

[7] Brunvand, J.H., *Folklore : a study and research guide*. 1976, New York: St. Martin's Press.

[8] Miller, G., *The Magical Number Seven Plus or Minus Two: Some Limits on Our Capacity for Processing Information*. Psychological Review, 1956. **63**: pp. 81–97.

[9] Plato, *The Dialogue of Plato: Plato's Parmenides*. Vol. 4. 1997, New Haven, CT: Yale University Press.

[10] Satir, V., *The New People Making*. 1988, Palo Alto, CA: Science and Behavior Books.

[11] Lasswell, H., *The Structure and Function of Communications in Society*, in *The Communication of Ideas*, Bryson, Editor. 1948, London: Harper and Brothers.

[12] Meyhew, D., *Principles and Guidelines to Software Interface Design*. 1992, Englewood Cliffs, NJ: Prentice Hall.

[13] Kellog, R., *Cognitive Psychology*. 1995, Thousand Oaks, CA: Sage Publishing.

[14] Rosch, E., *Principles of Categorization*, in *Foundations of Cognitive Psychology*, D. Levitin, Editor. 2002, Cambridge, MA: The MIT Press.

[15] Koffka, K., *Principles of Gestalt Psychology*. 1935, New York: Harcourt, Brace and Company.

[16] Wertheimer, M., *Laws of Organization in Perceptual Forms*, in *A Source Book of Gestalt Psychology*, W. Ellis, Editor. 1969, London, UK: Routledge & Keegan Paul. pp. 71–88.

[17] Rock, J. and S. Palmer, *The Legacy of Gestalt Psychology*. Scientific American, 1990. December: pp. 48–61.

Notes

1. The socialist state of Orwell's world.
2. A mental model is defined as each person's internal perception of an idea or event—it is how we relate new information to our existing store of experience.
3. As an interesting aside, Michael Chonoles, one of my reviewers, noted that his son saw the McDonald's™ golden arches as the center symbol.
4. Here, attention is used in the psychological sense to represent the focus of the mental reasoning machinery on processing some form of sensory input (such as visual).
5. Reprinted with permission from Highlights for Children, Inc.

Chapter 2

A Systematic Approach

One major reason that models are created is to understand complex systems. This is particularly true in the software development field. By its very nature, a computer software system is created from a myriad of interacting parts that all combine to produce visible behavior. To understand and construct such systems it is necessary to deconstruct a large unmanageable problem domain into smaller domains that can be more readily addressed. This process of deconstruction is known as *Systems Analysis*, and was developed as a formal process in the early days of computer science during the 1950s [1–3]. This chapter presents a collection of approaches to the study of complex systems, including Formal Systems Analysis, Functional Decomposition,[1] Scientific Method, and Process Based.

There are three primary techniques to the analysis of complex systems: Top-Down, Bottom-Up, and Middle-Out. Top-Down analysis starts with a high-level description of the entire domain, similar to a road map, before moving down to the details. Bottom-Up analysis moves in the opposite direction by starting with the concrete details of the system and moving to a more abstract or functional descriptions. In contrast to each of these approaches, Middle-Out is often useful for dealing with existing systems that are poorly understood. Here the trick is to pick a start point somewhere within a small section of the system (e.g., a section of software code) and drill down to the implementation details while simultaneously discovering the functional system behavior.

For example, suppose you are presented with a poorly documented legacy software system. You have access to the user interface so the investigation could begin with the user functionality by inspection of the interface behavior—perhaps with an expert user as a guide; a top-down approach. Perhaps you wish to better understand the physical database data model before moving into the business logic that manipulates that data; a bottom-up approach. Finally, you could start with one section of the code base and determine the screens that it supports as well as the

Table 2-1   Overview of Analysis Approaches

Positive Aspects	Negative Aspects
Top-Down Approach	
Rapid construction of a high-level overview—immediate benefit for executive stakeholders	Time-consuming for construction of a useful model
Overall perspective, including synergy of system elements	Less obvious indications of modeling progress
Highlights data usage and control logic	More support and contact required with senior personnel
Bottom-Up Approach	
Localized effort, quick to find specific user needs	Neglects cross-boundary influences
Remains bounded within small area of the system	Significant rework with small system changes
Immediate benefit for implementers	Narrow, vertical viewpoint
Middle-Out Approach	
Well suited for existing systems	Need to investigate specific details and general principles simultaneously
Provides selection of a readily accessible starting point	Lack of immediate benefit for either sponsors or implementers

data that is manipulated; a middle-out investigation. See Table 2-1 for a listing of the positive and negative aspects for each of these approaches.

Before moving into a description of analytical techniques, I would like to take a moment to acknowledge the diversity of modeling forms. I recognize that there are many different diagram types for describing business enterprise systems—including Function Flow Block Diagram (FFBD), Integrated Definition models (IDEF0 to IDEF14), the Systems Modeling Language (SysML), DoDAF, and Zachman Frameworks. A detailed description of each of these model forms would require far more space than my publisher has allotted, so I will take the easy way out and instead direct interested readers to research these topics as a "homework" project. For the remainder of this book, I will focus on UML 2.0 (and its extensions) to illustrate various points; the principles in the following chapters apply to model creation regardless of modeling system. Appendix D presents an overview of UML 2.0 and several of the defined language extensions (referred to as UML Profiles).

Formal Systems Analysis

During analysis it is important to consider the following characteristics of systems:

- Purpose
  Intended use of the system
- Objectives
  Goals for system operation
- Synergy
  System total is greater than the sum of its component parts
- Trade-Offs
  Intentional or unintentional compromises to the system

A system is developed with a particular purpose based on the needs of the stakeholders who have requested or make use of the system. The system's objectives represent the desired behavior of the system to meet its purpose. A system exists such that all of the parts act synergistically so that the entire system operates toward the same goals. Every system has trade-offs that represent the limitations imposed by the physical context in which a system operates. For example, a radio represents a complex system comprised of multiple interacting components. The purpose of the radio system is to receive electromagnetic signals and translate them into sound waves. This purpose is supported by the functions of an antenna, internal circuitry, and speakers. Together, these components provide services that none can provide alone; moreover, in creating a radio system, the designer would not use these components to create a dishwasher (although a radio subsystem could always be embedded into the dishwasher system!).

Using the techniques of top-down/bottom-up/middle-out, one avenue for description of a complex system is to use formal system notation based on the concepts of Boundary, Interface, Component, Entity, and Dependency, as shown in Figure 2-1 [1, 4].

This technique works well with the three directed approaches noted earlier, because the modeler can begin by looking at the system boundary (Top-Down) or by working outward from the system components (Bottom-Up). As illustrated in Figure 2-1, icons are used to represent the various system elements such as the Interface (externally exposed services), the Controller (system logic), and the Entities (manipulated system elements) as the system details are captured and elaborated. These systems elements are grouped by Components to show cohesive behavior and connected by Dependency relationships to show communication between components and subsystems [1, 4]. Note, however, that a systems analysis approach is not identical to the software object-oriented (OO) design strategy, although they share features of logical encapsulation. Systems analysis can be thought of as reasoning about the structure of the problem, whereas OO is more geared toward the design of a solution.

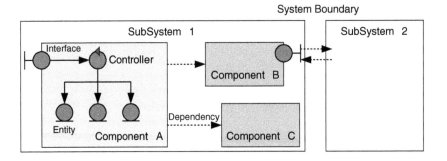

Figure 2-1 Formal System Analysis
(see Appendix D for more detail on this UML profile)

When using a system analysis approach, the system is broken into a variety of interacting components. Although this approach will simplify the overall system, it can lead to a problem in which the level of abstraction for each component doesn't match. What this means is that one component could be many times more complex than another, but they will appear to be similar in the model view shown in Figure 2-1. Care must be exercised to keep each level of the model linked to each succeeding level; a subsystem can have many components, which are in turn composed of components, and so on.

A simple example of this approach would be the analysis of a standard door lock. The *interface* would be the key-hole, the *controller* is represented by the tumblers, and the *entity* is the dead-bolt. Taken together, the *component* is the full locking mechanism, which has a structural dependency on the door and door-frame.

I have used this approach very successfully for the analysis of business problem domains intended for software automation. In particular, I found that casting the system requirements (assuming a new software system is under construction) into a system model with interfaces, controlling components, and entities maps well into a layered architecture implementation with presentation layer, business layer, and data access layer respectively corresponding.

Recommendation: The System Analysis approach is appropriate for new or existing systems that have well-defined external interfaces, and are open to direct inspection of the internal elements.

Functional Decomposition

Functional decomposition attempts to recursively segment a problem into the smallest possible subproblems, each of which is simpler to solve than the full problem itself. Many system analysts are of the opinion that functional decomposition is the technique by which system analysis is performed, rather than a standalone approach. Thus, this approach can be used in conjunction with a System Analysis approach, or by itself when there is no need to define formal interfaces, components,

Table 2-2   Overview of Aspects for System Analysis

Positive Aspects	Negative Aspects
Views a system as a whole composed of interacting parts (honors synergistic interactions of components)	Potentially time-consuming analysis for systems with a large number of small components
Captures the purpose and goals of the system	Assumes a well-organized system that can be organized into interacting components
Focuses on the interactions between system elements, providing for a breadth-first overview (one subsystem at a time can be defined)	Highly coupled systems (intertwined) are not easily broken down into components
Scalable to systems-of-systems (enterprise systems)	Requires direct inspection of the internal system elements

and entities. By this approach a complex, intractable problem can be deconstructed down to the most basic relevant pieces.

This approach has been a tried-and-true staple for the development of software solutions for as long as there have been computers and computer programmers. This approach was originally very well suited for software development because many of the small components (such as a sorting algorithm or a data structure) were reusable, thus saving very valuable computer storage space and processing capabilities. In more recent years, the ideas of Object Oriented Programming (OOP) have supplanted those of functional decomposition with a more system-oriented approach, as was shown in the component-based view in Figure 2-1. This avoids one of the major problems with functional decomposition, namely, the proliferation of multiple tightly coupled dependencies leading to fragile and difficult to maintain systems. However, a functional decomposition approach is still of value in many instances, such as in the actual implementation of an object, where the data and algorithms remain intimately coupled.

Another area of study where functional decomposition is used with great success is in the sciences. For example, the study of Biology would be nearly impossible without the ability to reduce the complexity of a living organism into less complex structures. A living cell is composed of multiple interacting subsystems including the structural components (cell membrane, cytoskeleton, organelles, etc.), dynamic components (protein manufacture, metabolism, nuclear replication, etc.), and interactive components (hormone production, cell surface proteins, etc.). Although each of these cellular components can be decomposed and studied independently using the proper molecular, biochemical, and genetic techniques, the findings must still be confirmed by observation of unaltered cellular behavior (see Chapter 7 for model verification techniques).

Table 2-3 Overview of Aspects for Functional Decomposition

Positive Aspects	Negative Aspects
Reduces the problem complexity into a hierarchy of atomic tasks (functions)	Can force segmentation of process and information (i.e., method and data)
Highlights areas of highest complexity (deepest decomposition graph)	Ignores the "whole" in favor of the parts (neglects information on system synergy)
Indicates areas of overlap and similar processing	Often leads to overly segmented systems with high levels of coupling

Thus, functional decomposition should be used with care since it neglects the synergistic information that is only present in the nondeconstructed whole (as seen in the System Analysis approach). However, this technique is very useful when approaching a complex system for the first time because it permits the division into more readily approached subsystems (each with a defined function), after which a more standard system analysis can be performed.

This technique is best used when rapid change to the system is not expected. This is because the structure that is created by the functional decomposition is highly interdependent, with the higher elements requiring interaction with many lower elements in the hierarchy. These dependencies will result in a proliferation of changes from highly reused low-level elements that affect multiple higher-level components, often in an unforeseen manner. This results in a highly coupled, fragile system that is prone to a large number of potential failures. Thus, this approach is not recommended for the construction of large, rapidly changing systems.

In contrast, one area in software development in which this approach *is* indicated is in the analysis of system user interaction flows. Because many business processes are readily reduced to a series of repetitive activities, these workflows may be rapidly discovered and captured using a functional decomposition approach. This information has traditionally been captured as hierarchically structured requirements (e.g., "the system shall perform … ") when applied to the development of software control systems. The introduction of use case analysis, which is a more "story"-based approach [4–7] in which these scenarios are described directly as Basic, Alternate, and Exceptional, provides for a more comprehensible collection of information that retains the context of the original workflows. However, each use case can be broken down into simpler scenarios and subscenarios that take advantage of a functional decomposition approach.

I have often used a functional decomposition approach when working with a systems integration problem (Figure 2-2). In one case, I was faced with seven interacting subsystems that needed to be coordinated to perform provisioning for

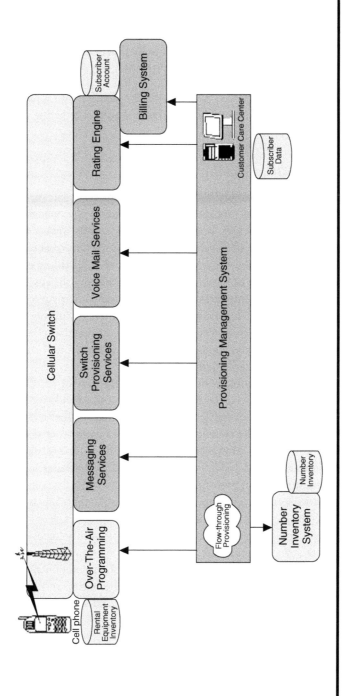

Figure 2-2   Interaction of multiple sub-systems for a cellular telephony product

a cellular telephony product. To understand these interactions, I first detailed the technical interfaces of each subsystem and the provided functionality. Then, I captured the business workflow as a series of individual steps cast as use case scenarios. Finally, I applied a systems analysis approach to order each subsystem interaction as part of the overall business flows. Here I used both functional decomposition and system analysis to gain a full understanding of the problem domain.

Recommendation: The Functional Decomposition approach is best applied to stable problems that are open to recursive subdivision into smaller interacting elements.

Scientific Method

Often a system will be inaccessible, such as with a proprietary software system or a highly complex biochemical process. In order to deduce the operation of such systems, a more indirect approach is required. The *Scientific Method* is one such approach that depends on the observation of a system in action (processing inputs and producing outputs), proposal of a hypothesis or theory regarding one or more internal operations, and a test of those assumptions by altering the environment of the system or system components and then observing overall changes to the system behavior. The indirectness of this technique often requires disturbing the system many times to deduce the internal workings. Basically, in practice, the conduct of science is similar to taking a large hammer to different parts of a well-tuned engine and observing the effect on engine performance.

The testing of software is often conducted in just this manner. A software quality assurance tester will take a completed closed system and provide specific inputs. The outputs of the system processing are then compared against the hypothetical behavior (e.g., based on the system requirements) to confirm or deny that the system performs as expected. However, as was noted in Table 2-4, the complete verification of all possible predictable behavior (especially error handling behavior) will be very time-consuming if performed manually.

Another area in software development in which this approach is frequently applied is in the implementation phase where the actual system code is under development. Designers will often experiment with multiple technologies to find the one that best meets the architectural and functional needs of the system under construction. Here the observation is that such a system component exists, the hypothesis is that the component is appropriate for the needs, and the test is to integrate the component into a small part of the system to verify that it will work as expected.

Recommendation: The Scientific Method is best used when the system under study is not open for direct study (i.e., requires indirect methods of discovery), and can be readily influenced by providing multiple inputs with observable output behavior.

Table 2-4 Overview of Aspects for the Scientific Method

Positive Aspects	Negative Aspects
Provides ability to study closed systems, for example, those unavailable for direct study of interacting components	Very time-consuming to verify all possible system behaviors by indirect experiment
Rigorous, repeatable verification of hypothesis	Requires multiple identical instances of a system that can be disrupted or modified
Provides for predictability of system behavior under different conditions	Requires a control or baseline to compare against the experimental result

Process Approach

Finally, a system may be studied based on its ability to respond to changing environmental stimuli. This approach can be considered similar to the Scientific Method, but differs in the ability to perturb the system. Here the focus of the study is on the effect of the environment on a system, rather than explaining the internal operations of the system itself.

Systems can be categorized as one of four process types:

Static system performs as designed with no feedback from the environment
Dynamic system attempts to maintain state but cannot ensure against uncontrolled environmental changes
Homeostatic system uses feedback to maintain a preprogrammed state
Cybernetic system adapts goals to changing environment

We can develop an organizational grouping for these forms by using three criteria [1]:

- Environmental Impact
  Effect of environmental conditions on the functioning of the system. If a system is independent of environment, the system is closed; if the output is influenced by changes in the environment, the system is open.
- Internal Control
  Internal capacity for a system to ensure continual attainment of system objectives
- Adaptability of Goals
  Reflects on whether goals of the system are fixed or can be changed depending on the environmental condition or state of system learning.

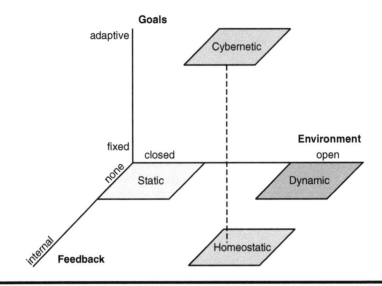

Figure 2-3   The classification of system behavior to external stimuli (extracted and redrawn from Athey, et al. [1])

A **Static System** is one that is not in any way responsive to external stimulus, and maintains a fixed set of system goals. For example, a wristwatch need not accept external input to maintain a consistent internal state of time keeping to one second/second. However, changes to external environment (humidity, temperature, etc.) will alter the system response.

A **Dynamic System** is one that has no means to internally ensure that the fixed system goals are met under unexpected environmental conditions. For example, a car moving down the road on cruise control at a set speed will have the throttle opened or closed as the speed increases or decreases as a result of terrain. However, because a dynamic system is unaware of an unexpected environment, a pilot flying at a constant apparent air speed of 200 miles/hour with a headwind of 20 mph will have a true air speed of 180 mph, so the system goals of the plane arriving on time are not likely to be met.

A **Homeostatic System** is designed to sample the external conditions in order to maintain the system state. For example, the temperature control system for a building (via the thermostat) uses the sensor inputs of external versus internal temperature to adjust the cooling/heat plant output for the resulting air mixture to

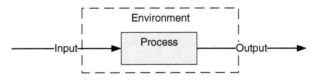

Figure 2-4   Dynamic system

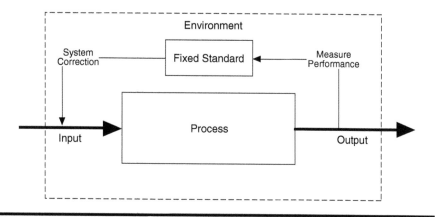

Figure 2-5   Homeostatic system

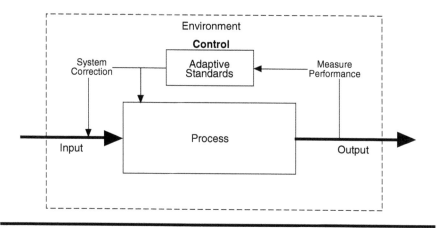

Figure 2-6   Cybernetic System

meet the preset standard thermostat temperature. All mammals have a similar biochemical process for ensuring a stable body temperature.

A **Cybernetic System** is designed to adjust the internal goal conditions (system objectives) based on external impacts. For example, given the thermostat example, a cybernetic system might detect that the reason for the temperature change is an open or broken window, which would tell the system that turning on the cooling/heat plant would be wasteful until the window is closed. The system goal is now changed to ensuring that the window is closed, which may be implemented by signaling an alarm. Cybernetic systems and feedback loops are often involved in human interactions and behavior [8].

Systems can be modeled as one of the four prototype reactive systems (simple, dynamic, homeostatic, or cybernetic). This identification may be useful in the selection of one of the other analytical techniques, described previously, to delve more deeply into the internal processing requirements for the system. As an example, the

Table 2-5   Overview of the Process Approach

Positive Aspects	Negative Aspects
Identifies and categorizes expected system behavior by inputs and outputs	Only valid on full working systems
Provides support for other analytical techniques	Requires knowledge of all possible inputs
A system-of-systems can be decomposed into the parts that are simple, dynamic, homeostatic, or cybernetic for further study	Useful only for systems with observable behavior
Prioritization of effort—modeling first simple, static system elements before the more complex dynamic, homeostatic, and cybernetic	Only defines the type of behavior; not the processing involved

Scientific Method may be used to determine how a thermostat operates by perturbing the inputs, or altering or removing parts of the system to observe the changes in behavior. If the internal elements of the heating/cooling system are available for direct inspection, the System Analysis/Decomposition approach may be useful to further segment the system into better understood components.

For the development of a mission critical software control system, such as a hardware embedded flight control system, it is essential to understand how the physical system is expected to respond to environmental stimulus. By classification of the system into one of the four system behavior groupings, the essential behavioral aspects of the system can be identified and captured.

Recommendation: The Process Approach is useful in the identification of expected system behavior, particularly complex reactive behavior. It is best used in conjunction with one or more of the other approaches described earlier.

Summary

1. Models are created to describe complex systems as an aid to understanding and reasoning. There are many ways to study a system including formal *System Analysis, Functional Decomposition, Scientific Method,* and *System Processes.*
2. Analysis of a system can be approached Top-Down, Bottom-Up, or Middle-Out. Top-Down approaches use a high-level description of the system under study to create a road map that directs a more detailed investigation. Bottom-Up starts with the concrete system elements and builds toward a full system understanding. Middle-Out begins at some convenient point in a small section of the system and works toward a full understanding and detailed description of that section.

3. Systems exist for an explicit *purpose* that is supported by a series of system goals or *objectives*. In addition, systems display *synergy*, where the complete system is greater than each individual part. Finally, systems must have *trade-offs* to account for compromises forced on system design because of environmental or other constraints.

4. Formal *System Analysis* often begins with a top-down approach to the study of a system. This form of analysis focuses on the *interfaces, controllers, entities, components, and dependencies* of a particular system. It is best utilized on existing systems open to direct inspection with well-defined inputs and outputs.

5. *Functional Decomposition* attempts to segment a problem into successively smaller and less complex elements. This approach focuses on the hierarchical aspects of a system that is composed of small reusable elements and the dependencies between these elements. This approach is best used with stable problems that are open to recursive subdivision into smaller interacting elements, and is often used as part of the System Analysis approach.

6. The *Scientific Method* focuses on three primary operations, *Observation, Hypothesis,* and *Test.* Observation of the unaffected system behavior is extended by hypothesis of a mechanism that is predictive of behavior under different stimuli. The theory is then tested by experimentation. To interpret the results, an unaffected *control* is frequently required for comparison. This approach is best used on systems that are closed to direct inspection but where the inputs are open to alteration and the system behavior/outputs are observable.

7. Study of a system via the *Process Approach* seeks to determine the behavior of a system under different environmental stresses. A *static system* is closed to outside influences and has a predictable internal structure. A *dynamic system* does not react to changing environmental conditions, but attempts to maintain preprogrammed state. A *homeostatic system* seeks to maintain equilibrium between inputs and a predetermined set of system goals by alteration of the environmental conditions. A *cybernetic system* acts to alter goal states under the influence of changing environmental conditions. A process-based analytical approach is often best in support of another form of study, such as formal *System Analysis*.

Tips and Traps

System analysis is a difficult skill to master. The most difficult aspect appears to be in selecting the correct level of abstraction for system components at each stage of the analysis. In selecting the correct level it is necessary to determine where the endpoints lie; for example, if studying a temperature control mechanism the highest level of abstraction is a heating/cooling system with a sensor, decision maker (thermostat), and an effector (heating/cooling plant). The lowest level would be the operational electronics and physical devices in the implementation. In Part II, the selection of levels of abstraction will be presented and discussed in detail.

The Scientific Method is also a difficult skill to master because most of the hypotheses are based on indirect observation of system behavior. In a software system, this is represented by "black-box" testing. To establish proper experimental techniques it is necessary to have some form of control that can be used as a baseline for interpreting the experimental results. For software performance testing, for example, a control would be the system with only a single user operating. This sets a baseline of performance for additional load tests. Additionally, only one aspect of the system should be tested at one time; this is known as *holding variables constant*. This technique requires highly accurate record keeping to track the results of the multiple experimental runs.

Questions and Exercises

- Question #1:
  Which of presented technique(s) would be most useful in determining the details of a software system deployment?

- Question #2:
  One of the hallmarks of experimental science is the high rate of experimental failure (e.g., negative results). Why is this then considered an effective analysis strategy?

- Question #3:
  Are software systems considered open or closed processes? When might they shift from one form to another?

- Question #4:
  Consider the following natural systems:
  - A river
  - A cloud
  - A rock
  - A forest
  What kinds of processes do these systems represent? (Hint: Many natural systems are aggregates of different forms of processes).

Exercise #1 System Analysis

Consider a living tree. Using the different forms of analysis create a thorough explanation of the behavior of a tree under different environmental conditions (e.g., drought, cold, heat, etc.). Your analysis should include why there are different tree forms, how trees survive in different environments, and the structures that form a prototypical tree. In what ways does a healthy tree differ from a sick one? Or a dead one? Or one on fire?

References

[1] Athey, T.H., *Systematic Systems Approach*. 1982, London: Prentice Hall.

[2] Langer, A.M., *The Art of Analysis*. 1997, New York: Springer-Verlag.

[3] Modell, M.E., *A Professional's Guide to Systems Analysis*. 1996, New York: McGraw-Hill.

[4] Jacobson, I., et al., *Object-Oriented Software Engineering: A Use Case Driven Approach*. 1992, Harlow, Essex, England: Addison Wesley Longman.

[5] Ecklund, E.F.J., L.M.L. Delcambre, and M.J. Freiling. *Change Cases: Use Cases that Identify Future Requirements*. In *OOPSLA-96*. 1996.

[6] Lieberman, B., "*Putting Use Cases to Work*". The Rational Edge, 2002. February.

[7] Leffingwell, D. and D. Widrig, *Managing Software Requirements, A Unified Approach*. 2000, Boston: Addison-Wesley. 491.

[8] Weinberg, G.M., *Quality Software Management: Volume I, System Thinking*. 1992, New York: Dorset House Publishing.

Notes

1. A reviewer of this chapter pointed out that Functional Decomposition can be considered a technique rather than an approach. My opinion is that studying a system by functional decomposition is a fundamentally different mental approach (leading to very different model forms) compared with the others, and therefore deserves to be separately described.

Chapter 3

Observing Behavior

This chapter is about observing the behavior of systems. Systems can be thought of as comprised of two parts, a static or structural part, and a dynamic or behavioral part. For example, consider an equity trading market. There is a physical location where the market resides (even "virtual" markets require some form of infrastructure to house the network servers and support personnel), and the operations that are conducted to perform transactions. The static part of a system is usually more accessible than the dynamic part, because the dynamic part is based on system operation—requiring long-term observation to understand all of the interactions. Thus, discovery of system behavior is often the more challenging task.

To discuss ways to observe system behavior, I will focus on two systems that are very common—business systems represented by individuals, groups, and organizations; and computer software systems represented by interfaces, data input/outputs, and processing rules. Business systems are often modeled to permit understanding of complex business interactions, and to permit optimization of operations. Computer systems are often modeled to ensure correct behavior, allow for redesign/maintenance, or to perform integration between multiple subsystems.

Systems, and especially computer systems, do not operate in a vacuum; there is always one or more groups who are expected to benefit from the operation of the system. These groups are comprised of individuals who have interactions with other groups in the enterprise and need to operate within a particular organization, such as a business, a research station, or a military task force. The environmental and cultural aspects of these organizations has a direct bearing on the nature of existing systems, as well as directing the needs for new system development.

So, a key element in the creation of system models is the ability for the modeler to observe a system in operation and record those observations for later analysis.

There are several methods by which this can be accomplished, including independent observation and interactive discovery. Independent observation assumes that the modeler intends to study a system without altering its behavior. An example would be recording business operations for automation by a computer-based system. It also may be applied to the study of group interactions between business teams (i.e., a form of "corporate anthropology"). In all of these cases, the observer is kept apart from the actions of the system or people under study so that records can be made of the unaffected behavior.

In contrast, interactive discovery involves the direct intervention of the modeler with the subject under study. This approach allows for a more direct study since the observer is involved with the group or system. Here, the observer is partaking in the actions of the team/group to better understand the significance or difficulty of those actions. In this chapter, I will discuss observing and modeling how the individuals and groups in a business organization perform their tasks, and I also will discuss modeling legacy software system operation, because this is often an integral part of the operation of a business.

Observing Individuals

There are many ways to model business operations. For example, a business implementing Total Quality Management (TQM) may use Six Sigma analysis to statistically measure the stability of a business process in support of product quality [6]. Alternatively, a business can be studied by modeling the tasks and processes performed by the individuals who comprise that business. Davenport and Short [7] define a business process as a "set of logically related tasks performed to achieve a defined business outcome." I will focus here on the study and capture of these tasks as performed by one or more people in a business setting.

Business workers, or just "workers," are at the core of any business process. Workers perform the tasks that comprise the business process, and so become the logical place to start for a business modeler. There are also business managers who are responsible for overseeing the completion of tasks and reporting on performance to the business leaders. All of these people are important to the business modeler, because each one plays a specific role in the operation of the business.

A business modeler (sometimes referred to as a *business analyst*) may be an internal company resource—say, from the information technology (IT) department, or she may be an external consultant hired to perform a specific analysis in support of a reorganization or automation project. In either case, although the same analysis is performed, the approach may differ. An internal resource should already have familiarity with the business overall structure, vision, and goals,[1] and the focus of the model may only be on one small part of the overall business process. Assuming that the project is for computer software automation/integration, the analysis should begin with the specific tasks that are intended for automation. These might include such repetitive tasks as document storage (e.g., filing), processing of forms, or other kinds of data manipulation. An external consultant, by contrast, must first understand the overall structure of the organization in order to understand the context of the current project. This usually requires starting with the executive or senior management to gain a "holistic" picture of the business prior to meeting with specific teams and individuals. In both approaches, the purpose and scope of the business model should be defined very early in the analysis effort.

My personal preference, once the purpose of the model is defined, is to seek out the individuals performing a task and observe two key aspects of their job: the data that is processed, and the actions performed on that data. The data that is manipulated is often found on paper or electronic documents (i.e., forms). This data is manipulated by work operations, which are a sequence of actions that have a basic path, possibly one or more alternate strategies and problems (exceptions) that need to be resolved. When observing an individual, I try to gain an understanding of how *they* view the job they are performing and what actions precede or follow. I capture this information as a series of actions arranged into flows (activity diagrams or flow charts are useful for this purpose), and then indicate where in each action the business data are manipulated. It is important for the modeler to be aware that each worker may perform multiple, perhaps even unrelated, tasks. Care should be exercised to recognize that a particular task is part of a separate workflow, and that the worker is operating in a different role. For example, a worker may be tasked with processing insurance claim forms, which involves entry of information into a legacy computer system. The worker may then, because she also happens to be an adjuster, approve the claim for payment. These are two different tasks that just happen to be performed by the same person. It is critical for a modeler to differentiate between a *task* and a *worker* performing that task. For a more complete example, see Chapter 8 and Appendix A.

Workers seldom perform an end-to-end business function. Instead, there are frequent *inter-* and *intra*group interactions that occur during the performance of a task. These interactions may be to gather additional information, to forward the results of one task to another, or to report problems that have occurred. Using the previous insurance claim example, a worker may receive a claim form for processing, but require information from the financial department on the claimant's current premium payment status. Alternatively, the worker may complete the claim entry into the legacy system, and forward the claim for approval to the manager of the financial control group. The business modeler should be sure to capture these interactions, either graphically or textually (Figure 3-1).

As always when working with people, some individuals will be more difficult to work with than others. This may be a result of many factors, including personality types (such as shyness), worries over job security, excessive number of task assignments, or simple dislike of being watched. Trust is key for all accurate observations, and particularly important in such cases. A modeler should always be careful to obey the following rules when observing individual behaviors:

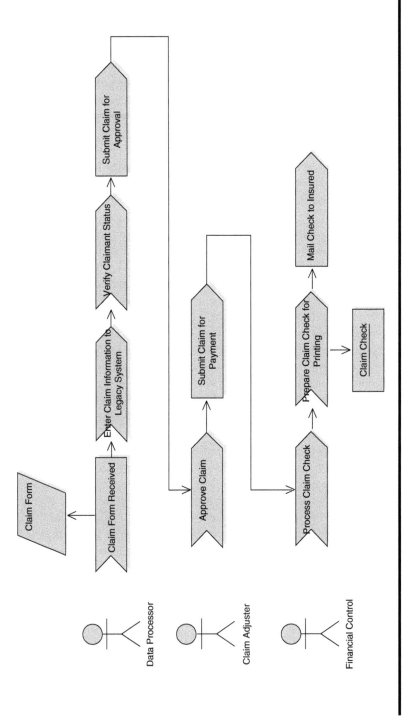

Figure 3-1 Capture of Multiple Worker Interactions Using an Informal Flow Chart

- Always ask permission before recording any activities; secretive observations invite mistrust
- Always introduce yourself and announce your intentions before starting work (e.g., "Hi, I'm Bob and I am collecting information on the company business process to support development of a new software system")
- Let the subject have control over the pace of the interview and follow their energy—this provides a higher level of comfort for the subject
- Always review your notes and findings with the subject before inclusion in the model or presentation of information to others—if the subject refuses to include something, be sure to find out why
- Never become argumentative or challenge a subject; seek support from management or find an alternate path to the required information
- Whenever possible, use a location that is most comfortable for the subject

Working in Groups

Understanding the target audience for a system or model is only part of the modeler's task. It is also important to understand how the system is used and the environment under which the system will operate. Interactions between groups tend to follow the N-squared Law of Group Interactions [3] which states the maximum number of interactions between individuals of a group will be $(N^2-N)/2$. Any model that requires review and approval by a large number of individuals will likely encounter this Law; even a group as small as six members may have 15 channels of communication that must be honored (Figure 3-2). Clearly, the Law of Group Interactions indicates that agreements will require a great deal of time and energy, and may still fail to gain consensus among all of the group members.

When reviewing a model for accuracy in a group setting, it is therefore best to limit the total number of individuals involved in submitting comments to between three and five. Informal review of models may take place between any numbers of individuals, but a time limit for comment and conflict resolution should be set in advance of the submission for review. There should be only one person with the final authority to approve the contents of the model, to avoid "review paralysis."

Understanding the number and kinds of interactions between groups and group members is also important to systems that are intended to facilitate collaboration. A collaboration tool intended to support teams must account for multiple team interactions and channels of communication. The modeler needs to be aware that some systems are created to facilitate the performance of repetitive tasks, whereas others are intended to support creativity. A system model for support of a group by the automation of repetitive tasks should focus on those operations that are most prone to error and that have the greatest benefit for cost savings. Alternatively, system models intended to support creativity should focus on the parts of the effort that are most laborious, such as the generation of free-form shapes in a drawing

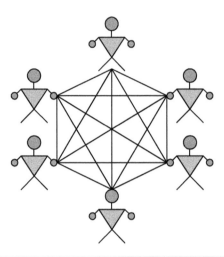

Figure 3-2   N-Squared Law of Group Interactions

program. By narrowing the focus of the modeling effort to the specific tasks that will be performed by the system, the modeler can better meet the needs of the intended user community.

Groups, like individuals, have dependencies on one another for materials or other forms of support. A service-oriented group (such as most internal information technology groups) will have multiple calls for those services from other groups in the organization. This may lead to overwhelming task loads, leaving little time to interact with a modeler performing system analysis. Moreover, the needs of such a group may conflict with the other groups in the organization. For example, a marketing group may want a new system with the ability to have highly configurable interface, whereas the support team may wish the exact opposite because they will be the ones to train and maintain such a complex system.

In addition to these intergroup dependencies, some groups also show an intragroup dependency on certain key individuals. These members are acknowledged as having specialized knowledge that is not shared amongst the other members of the group. Such individuals are often highly valued and are thus unavailable for supporting modeling or other analysis efforts. Where possible, the modeler should attempt to gain access to this information through other means, such as written documentation or collecting/correlating information from several individuals.

Organizational Culture

Every group of people develops their own sense of values and norms that define the characteristics of membership in that group [1]. The same is true for a group of people that form a company or association. Modelers must work within the confines of these cultural expectations, and so should be aware of the effect these cultures

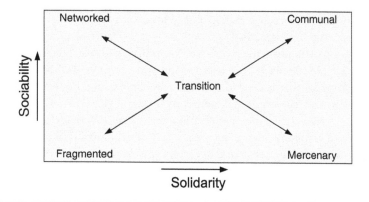

Figure 3-3   Corporate Culture—Five Basic Forms (adapted from Goffee and Jones [2])

have on subject individuals or groups. For business groups, the cultural norms are defined somewhat differently from a culture that forms in a society. For groups that comprise a business, there are five basic cultural forms [2]:

- *fragmented,* in which the group is comprised of loosely associated individuals, such as with most scientific research organizations
- *mercenary* organizations have a high solidarity with intense focus on the accomplishment of group goals, even to the detriment of the individuals of the group
- *networked* teams have a high sociability that leads to a strong sense of support for team members, even at the expense of group goals—many established firms show this culture type
- *communal* groups are tightly goal-focused, while retaining a highly supportive environment; a "we are family" approach found in many entrepreneurships
- *transitional* organizations are ones that are moving from one form of culture to another, either by purpose or by default (i.e., a communal culture is very difficult to maintain as a company grows)

Each of these cultural forms will have significant differences in behavior and response to the introduction of change. For a fragmented culture, the members have a high degree of individualism and so any model or system created to provide automation of tasks will likely need to be customized to meet each individual's specific needs. A mercenary culture, in contrast, will be focused on cost versus return for any modeling or construction effort; speed and indications of progress will be the most important aspects for the creation of a system model. The networked cultures are also interested in cost versus return but are more interested in a system that is usable and efficient. Thus, the model should be focused around the ideas of usability and suitability for the group as a whole. Finally, communal and transitional cultures may exhibit a need for *all* of these aspects, low cost, rapid development, and high usability.

Clearly, understanding these different forms of organizational culture is important to determine the needs and expectations of the group for whom the model is intended. A model that is created with the expectations of a networked culture in mind will not meet the needs of a mercenary one, and vice versa. This is especially true when the model is of the organization itself, that is, a model of the business workflows and company interactions. If the task of the model is to reorganize these workflows to increase efficiency and lower costs by eliminating personnel, there will be a challenge for the modeler to accurately capture the nature of the work. No one wishes to contribute to their own unemployment. Modeling in such environments must therefore, as was noted earlier, be undertaken in a sensitive and open manner; any other approach will lead to distrust and ill-will.

One final note on corporate cultures—in a sufficiently large company, multiple cultures may be found. "Large" in this sense is usually indicated by multiple, geographically separated offices and a total employee count of several hundred or more people. In such organizations, some groups may operate as a communal culture, whereas others exhibit fragmented behavior. Still others may be in transition from mercenary to networked because of management neglect or changing business environments. The modeler who is tasked with working among all of these disparate groups should be careful to acknowledge each group's special conditions and adjust the model and analysis approach according to the specific needs of each group.

Investigating Legacy Computer Systems

Most businesses have computer-based automation that is critical for operations. Often, these systems are poorly or inaccurately documented, and/or only understood by a few key individuals. In these cases, a system modeler may be asked to understand the current systems behavior in order to facilitate an integration effort, or perhaps a reengineering/replacement project. In order to create an accurate system model, the analyst will need to review any available system documentation, and learn the system behavior by observing the use and operation of such legacy systems. Two examples that include elements of this kind of analysis are provided in Chapter 9 and Chapter 10.

When investigating the behavior of a legacy system, I like to look at four key system aspects: Interfaces, Visible System Behavior, Data Processing/Storage, and Exception Handling. Computer systems built to interact with humans must have some form of interface through which the human operator can issue commands and the computer can display the computation results. In many modern systems, this is represented by some form of graphical user interface. This interface may be accessed in numerous ways including via a Web browser, application user interface, or remote access techniques (such as Microsoft Windows™ remote desktop functionality). Alternatively, the interface may be command line based, as are often found with Unix or Linux. Occasionally, both kinds of interface are available depending on the needs of the application in question (e.g., RedHat™ or Mac OS X™). Because these interfaces are visible to an end user, the system modeler can observe the system behavior either by direct use, or by observing a business worker performing specific tasks.[2] In addition to visual interfaces, most business applications also provide some form application programming interface (API) to allow direct machine-to-machine communication of information. When modeling a legacy system behavior, it is important to investigate the method of access (e.g., Web service) and data transmission format for these access points, because an application's API is usually central to an system integration effort.

System behavior represents any and all operations that are performed by the system in response to some input. Besides the visible result that can be seen on a screen or log file, there are any number of internal processing steps that are hidden. Depending on the needs of the model, such as system integration versus a complete redesign, these internal processing steps may need to be investigated. Usually this involves reviewing code rather than simply observing the system's inputs and outputs, and so requires a great deal more time and investigator skill. I have found that it is usually possible to identify 70 or 80 percent of a system's behavior from direct observation of the user interface, because many systems are built specifically to support business worker tasks. I capture this information into a model as a series of functional flows, using flow charts or UML analysis diagrams (see Appendix D for an overview of UML 2.0 Analysis Diagrams).

An integral part of system behavior is the processing and storage of information. In my experience, very few business workers are aware of the quantity and interrelationships of business data processed by a typical business's computer systems every day. However, these same workers, in aggregate, have access to most, if not all, of the business-critical data contained in a system. This information is frequently stored in some form of relational database (or other form of persistent storage), and is used to support business processes and reporting. A system modeler working to understand a computer system behavior should attempt to capture this information as part of the formal system model. I usually use a data domain model to capture the type and relationships of business data. Figure 3-4 shows two ways that I use to express system data and data relationships. The first technique uses a UML class diagram to graphically capture the business domain information. The second uses a text-based shorthand to describe the same information.[3] In both cases, the information shown could have been captured from a physical form containing the data, or from an electronic form that is shown on a screen or in a file.

The final computer system behavior of interest is how errors are generated and handled. Exception handling, as these behaviors are sometimes called, occurs when the system detects a process condition that is in violation with one or more

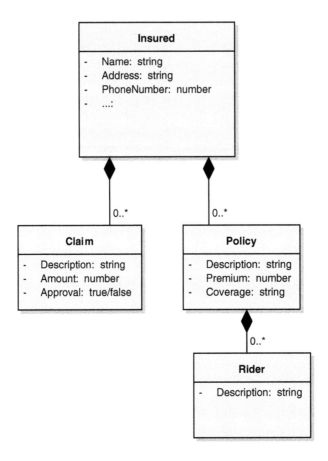

Insured = Name + Address + PhoneNumber + Policy [0..*] + Claim [0..*]
Policy = Description + Coverage + Premium + Rider[0..*]
Claim = Descripton + Amount + Approval
Rider = Description

Figure 3-4   Two Ways to Capture System Data: UML Class Diagram, and Textual Description

business rules. Data entry errors may be directly displayed to a user (referred to as data validation errors), others may occur as a result of some internal failure (such as a security failure on a user authorization request). Because this behavior is critical to understanding the business rules that are enforced by the computer, the modeler should spend time investigating and capturing as many system errors as possible. I have found that error handling in legacy systems is often added gradually over time, and in such a way that very few people understand all of the business rules that are embedded in the computer systems. To get at this behavior, I have found it effective to ask the following questions of workers as I observe them performing tasks:

- What can go wrong with this processing step?
- How does the system report the error?
- What kind of recovery is performed?
- Does the system seem to have conflicting behavior or inaccurate error handling?

I can then add this information as part of the overall system flows, usually captured as flow diagrams or described as a business use case.[4]

Environmental Considerations

Systems are not only intended for use by specific groups but also to be used within a defined environment. In other words, a system that is created to support a group will need to meet operating conditions in that group's setting. Computer-based systems operate in a diverse variety of hostile conditions, such as space-based systems. They also must be able to handle high mobility and fault tolerance as required by military operators. Some systems may need to have extensive security controls, such as those in financial or governmental settings. Other systems are mission-critical, such as are found controlling equipment in surgical rooms. Models constructed to describe such systems will have very different forms and levels of detail as compared to ones created for less demanding conditions.

Table 3-1 shows some of the possible environments in which a computer-based system may be deployed, and the main focus of the associated model. It should be noted that in some deployments several of these environmental aspects may be combined. It is a modeler's task to create the model to support the deployment of the constructed system. For example, a mission-critical system requires the modeler to focus intense attention to the handling of error conditions and automated system recovery. This is because the consequence of system failure may lead to severe injury or death.

An often overlooked aspect of the system environment is the need for configuration. Configuration settings may customize a system to a particular locale, as is the case with a remote site deployment, or they may be for personalization. System models should consider all of the conceivable system configurations when the system is in the analysis phase because this kind of information has a tendency to proliferate in an uncontrolled manner during system construction, leading to a system that is difficult to maintain and deploy. Web-based systems are particularly prone to this failing because they are perceived as highly flexible and configurable, even when the software design has not addressed these issues.

Environmental considerations are also important when considering the difference between development, testing, and production environments. The environmental constraints that are of interest to the software developer are not the same as those that concern a deployment manager. The modeler must understand the needs of each of these groups and create model views to provide specialized support (see Chapter 6 for a description of model forms, and Part III for presentation of models).

Table 3-1   Environmental Considerations for System Modeling

Environment	Example	Modeling Focus
Controlled Operations	Standard Business Office	System Functionality
Field Deployment	Limited Support Research Station	Stability, System Configuration
Mobile	Military Operations	Stability, Hardware/ Software Coupling
Hazardous Environment	Space Control Systems	System Recovery
Limited Physical Access	Hardware Embedded Systems	Error Handling, Recovery, Hardware/ Software Coupling
Mission Critical	Medical or Surgery Support	Failure Conditions, Recovery
Real-Time Operation	Flight Controls	Robustness, Stability, Performance
Legacy Integration	Mainframe Support	Interfaces, Functionality
Restricted Permission	Financial System	Security, Access Privileges
High Availability/ Reliability	Order Management	Error Handling, Stability
Timing Pressure	Deployment Delivery Deadlines	Architectural Trade-Offs

Summary

1. Software systems are generally created for a particular use group. The group behavior defines the needs that will be addressed by the software functionality. The purpose of the system is therefore intimately coupled with the ways in which the group will utilize the software system. A system model must capture this intended system behavior.

2. System modeling is often performed in a business setting in which a business process is proposed for automation. In this case, the principal source of information is the subject matter expert, who can be interviewed to learn the roles and tasks performed for a business operation. Less often, existing software systems are studied to support replacement or integration projects.

3. A modeler can study the actions of individuals either by indirect observation or by direct interaction. The modeler is interested in three questions: who will

be using the system, how will the system be used, and where will the system be deployed.

4. Groups interact with other groups, often in a supplier-client type relationship. Groups that are suppliers of services will often be unable to spare a great deal of time for the modeler, even if the benefits are substantial. Within a group there may be intragroup dependencies that are typified by dependence on a small number of individuals with critical knowledge. Modelers should be aware of these individuals and seek their support whenever possible.

5. Interactions between groups and group members will define how a system will be used. A system may be used to support informative, creative or repetitive tasks. The Law of Group Interactions notes that the larger the group becomes, the more difficult is reaching consensus on the needs the system is intended to support.

6. Groups, particularly groups in business, form cultural practices and norms that describe inclusion in the group. Business culture typically falls into one of five categories: fragmented, mercenary, networked, communal, or transitional. Each of these categories can be seen as positive or negative, with a direct consequence to the difficulty for a modeler to create a system model. Multiple cultures may be present in a single large business.

7. Existing software system behavior can be understood from the system interfaces, data handling, error management, and system behavior. Interfaces may be graphical-, batch-, or command line–based, and are an excellent window into system behavior. Data handling usually involves core business elements and can be captured using a data domain model. Error handling represents rules such as data validation or business practices. Business workflow documents (use cases) are well suited to capture of this information.

8. Systems are deployed with specific environmental concerns. The modeler should focus on the model's concerns with a full knowledge of environmental constraints. For example, a military deployment should consider how the hardware and software will interact as well as the reliability of such systems to mobile and hazardous conditions.

Tips and Traps

Operating in a negatively influenced corporate culture is a significant challenge for the modeler. It is often valuable to develop personal relationships with key people in the organization. Individuals with specific domain knowledge can facilitate success or ensure failure. The modeler should always maintain an open and honest posture when working with individuals, and avoid becoming involved in political or turf battles.

Some projects are doomed to failure from the start. It is important as an analyst and modeler to recognize these projects and steer well clear. Projects that have insufficient schedule, financial support, personnel, or access to key information sources are all indications that a project is facing an uphill battle from the word go. If there is no way to avoid the problem (or if it has reached a critical point) then the main challenge will be to secure sufficient management support to provide for at least partial success. For additional information on surviving these kinds of projects, I refer the reader to Edward Yourdon's delightfully titled work, *Death March* [5].

As noted earlier, a system's production environment may be confused with the development environment. Models created for the development team may conflict with the needs of the deployment and support team. Therefore, several forms of a system model may need to be considered in addition to different views, to support these diverse operations. Part II addresses the issues of creating multiple models and model views for differing audiences.

Questions and Exercises

- Question #1:
  What form of culture exists in your organization? Is there more than one form of culture at your company or organization?

- Question #2:
  Who in your group is considered "indispensable"? Why? If you were a member of senior management, would you consider the dependency on a few people risky to the business?

- Question #3:
  Many UNIX devotees have noted that "their" system is the most usable because the interface is powerful, specific, and highly customizable. Why is a command line–based interface not the standard for all computer operating systems?

- Question #4:
  What behavior differences should be noted in a system model of a gas versus electric stove? What kinds of failures can be expected with each system? How might the model capture the consequences of these failures?

Exercise #1: Business Process Mapping

You have been asked to form a team to study your company's business processes. You may have up to three additional members on your team and you have been given schedule and budget based on your own estimates of the task. What skills would you like on your team (e.g., direct business knowledge, modeling/architecture experience, team leadership skills, etc.)? Compile a list of skills and tools that are necessary to conduct a full business workflow audit.

Exercise #2: Organizational Mapping

- Make a map of the groups in your organization. Base your chart on the service/client model of group interactions:
- For each group that provides a service, list the service and show who depends on that service.
- For each group that is a client, note the number and criticality of the dependency on supplier groups.
- Note who the key individuals are in each group.
- Now compare your map with the organization chart of the business. How closely aligned are management's view of the business and the actual business functions? How might you reorganize the groups to reduce dependencies and increase efficiency?

Exercise #3: Team Construction

Your task is to create a five foot–tall building made only of standard playing cards. Form teams of two and decide on the best approach to this task. After your teams have completed the task, reform in teams of five to six people and repeat the assignment, this time building a suspended bridge made of tissue paper able to support a one-pound weight. Record the types of interactions between team members. Consider the following in your observations:

- Who assumes a leadership role? Are there challenges to the leadership?
- Who assumes a passive role?
- Do any members become frustrated and leave the group (at least mentally)?
- What form of group is created (Cooperative? Competitive? Argumentative?)?
- How long did it take to reach consensus on an approach in a small versus large group? What other differences occur between small groups and large groups?

References

[1] Oring, E., *Folk Groups and Folklore Genres: An Introduction*. 1986, Logan: Utah State University Press.

[2] Goffee, R. and G. Jones, *The Character of a Corporation*. 1998, New York: HarperCollins Publishers.

[3] Weinberg, G.M., *Quality Software Management: Volume I, System Thinking*. 1992, New York: Dorset House Publishing.

[4] Eysenck, M., *Principles of Cognitive Psychology*. 2nd ed. Principles of Psychology, ed. M. Eysenck, S. Green, and N. Hays. 2001, Sussex, UK: Psychology Press.

[5] Yourdon, E., *Death March: The Complete Software Developer's Guide to Surviving 'Mission Impossible' Projects*. 1999, Upper Saddle River, NJ: Prentice Hall.

[6] Harry, M., *The Vision of Six Sigma* (eight-volume set), *5th ed.,* Sigma Publishing Co., 1997.

[7] Davenport, T. and J. Short. "The New Industrial Engineering: Information Technology and Business Process Redesign," *Sloan Management Review,* 1990, pp. 11–27.

Notes

1. All businesses have goals, but oftentimes these are not readily apparent to the members of an organization. A business analyst should always seek out senior management to confirm the business purpose, vision, and goals, and include this information as part of the business model.
2. One of my reviewers suggests that the modeler act as an "apprentice" to the subject matter expert; this allows the modeler to learn the system as a user.
3. The UML containment association is shown with the black diamond attached to a line; the shorthand [0..*] indicates zero to many possible associations.
4. See Appendix A for an example of a business use case, including exceptional flow handling.

Chapter 4

Analytical Thinking

The construction of a suspension bridge is a massive undertaking. Architects and engineers who work as bridge builders are expected to safely span immense distances using a minimum of building materials and construction time. If these builders were required to recreate all of the necessary mechanical principles each time they approached such a project the construction of bridges would be prohibitively expensive in money, time, and risk of span failure because of oversight or error. Fortunately, people engaged in the construction industry can draw on a vast repository of physical properties, building techniques, and project examples collected over thousands of years in support of their efforts. Our hypothetical bridge architect can draw inspiration from such magnificent examples as the Golden Gate Bridge in San Francisco, the George Washington Bridge in New York, the Akashi Kaikyo Bridge in Japan, the Great Belt East in Denmark, the Tacoma Narrows Bridge in Washington State,[1] and other examples of the bridge builder's art. More, an architect can draw on the mathematical constructs and materials science that describe the properties of the materials and construction techniques used to create a new structure. Project management, supplier scheduling, material manufacture, and other aspects of the construction effort, are all supported by previous examples providing guidelines for the overall project development.

These collections of "prior art" and experience can be thought of as a set of formal and informal *patterns* from which to draw inspiration and guidance for new or unsolved problems. Patterns are defined as generalized solutions to specific problems in a defined context, with instructions on the application of those solutions [1]. Thus, a researcher faced with a new problem or observation can compare that problem to others that have been solved in the past. By consulting a catalog of patterns for the subject area the analyst may find one or more generalized solutions adaptable for use on the current problem. This reuse of prior successful approaches greatly increases the likelihood of success and helps to reduce overall project risk.

Previous studies and findings form a framework into which new information can be categorized and incorporated. Occasionally, genuinely unique information arises that leads to the creation of an entirely new area of research or the restructuring of an existing framework, but the vast majority of new findings can usually be fitted into the existing frameworks. Research techniques are frequently included in these frameworks to solve problems that don't necessarily fit any previous solution. For example, molecular biological research approaches originally were developed in areas of biochemistry, cellular biology, genetics, and virology. These collected techniques form a toolkit from which the molecular biologist may draw to conduct original research.

When modeling complex systems, it is of great value to be able to draw on both the solutions found by others, and the analytical techniques used to construct those solutions. In my work, I have found that my analysis approach is supported by three areas of previous knowledge. First is the training I received in reducing problems into manageable parts. Second are business analysis patterns that describe business domains at the level of business relationships. Finally, by a well-defined collection of "tools"[2] that I will refer to as an analytical framework. I have found that thinking analytically takes a great deal of practice and effort. However, when supported by a well-defined set of patterns and analysis tools, it is much easier to find examples of the current problem, thereby reducing the overall level of effort needed, and improving the quality of the final model.

Analysis Patterns

A design pattern is defined as a solution to a specified problem within a context. Architect Christopher Alexander is credited with codifying the concept of patterns such that they can be combined to form a larger structure known as a *pattern language*. These pattern languages show how one pattern connects to another and can be thought of as a collection of solutions organized "in such a way that you can use this solution a million times over, without ever doing it the same way twice" [2].

Pattern Structure

- A Name—describes the intent of the pattern
- Problem Statement—concise description of the problem
- Motivation/Forces—description of driving forces that require resolution
- Solution—instructions for solving the stated problem
- Discussion—relates the current pattern to other related patterns
- Known Implementations—examples of existing adaptations
- Related Patterns—previously defined similar patterns

The software development community has embraced this concept as a mechanism to capture and share analysis and design experiences with other practitioners

[3, 4]. In this way, an engineer has a collection of tested solutions to common problems available for study, rather than "reinventing the wheel" for each new project. Moreover, the use of patterns ensures a consistency that permits for rapid communication of ideas from one developer or architect to another. For example, the pattern of "Singleton," used to describe limiting access to a single object, is so well known that simply by naming the pattern other developers will immediately understand how that part of the system is constructed [4]. Similarly, a physician uses a specialized descriptive language for defined syndromes that permits the rapid communication of a diagnosis and treatment options to other physicians or care givers.

Analysis models for a particular domain also can be captured as patterns. Martin Fowler is credited with coining the term *analytical patterns,* which are similar to design-based patterns but are focused on the organization and capture of problem-specific information rather than as instructions for solving a problem [5]. Although the existing literature on this topic is scant, recent work has been conducted by Dr. M. Fayad and his students at the University of Nebraska. Dr. Fayad has suggested that the most stable form of these kinds of patterns are based on what he terms as "enduring business themes" (EBT) that represent the core behavior of a system [6, 7]. These themes are conceptual rather than physical, are common across a particular domain, and do not change when mapped to a specific implementation.

The determination of each element in the model is dependent on the selection of the level of abstraction for the pattern. The determination of the enduring themes of a kitchen requires the differentiation between the *physical elements* of the kitchen (e.g., pots, pans, stove, refrigerator, work-surfaces, etc.) from the *functions* of the kitchen (e.g., food preparation, food storage, etc.). The former represent the concrete IO elements while the latter are the enduring themes for a kitchen. One way to envision these differences is to realize that a kitchen can occur in different contexts such that a professional restaurant kitchen differs from a camp-kitchen in the implementation of the different themes (a refrigerator may be replaced by an ice filled cooler), whereas the purpose of elements are not changed (a propane stove still provides heat for cooking).

A recently published work by Arlow and Neustadt has presented a refinement and novel extension of Fowler's original work [19]. These authors take a somewhat different approach by introducing *archetypes* and *archetype patterns.* Their basic premise is that there are business archetypes—universal concepts that occur consistently in multiple business domains. Based on this idea, the authors propose a catalog of business domain archetype patterns. For example, the first archetype they identify is a **Party** (Figure 4-1). Common to virtually all businesses, a Party represents an identifiable entity that may have legal status, such as a customer, supplier, or client. Parties may enter into **PartyRelationships** with specific roles and responsibilities for each Party; for example, there is a **PartyRelationship** between a buyer and a seller of goods.

To support the diversity found in business environments, the authors also provide mechanisms to easily modify or extend the archetypes and archetype patterns.

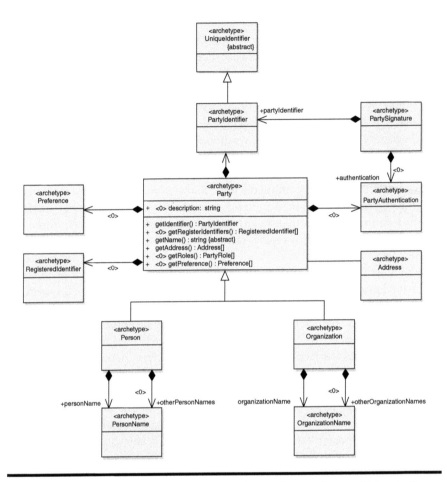

Figure 4-1 **Archetype pattern for Party (redrawn from Arlow and Neustadt [19])—the <0> stereotype indicates optional associations**

They describe a "principle of variation," which holds that different business require related, but slightly altered, versions of the same domain elements. They divide variations into three extension categories:

1. **Archetype variation.** This involves eliminating archetype options (attributes or methods) that are not necessary to the development model.
2. **Archetype pattern variation.** This refers to including/excluding optional archetypes while maintaining critical dependencies (e.g., a PartyRelationship always requires a Party).
3. **Pleomorphism.** This refers to the wholesale modification of part of a pattern while retaining the general theme. Usually this means making an abstract concept more specific (e.g., Product becomes UniqueProduct or IdenticalProduct).

Figure 4-2   Mind-Mapping for Puzzles (courtesy of the Buzan Organization)

Together, these extension mechanisms and the archetype pattern catalog provide a significant advancement in analysts' ability to approach complex, but common, business problems. Because the archetype pattern catalog is based on business domains—versus business rules, which are much more variable—the patterns are quite stable and require very little modification to be highly useful. Thus, an Analysis Pattern represents a description of a particular problem domain rather than a description of solutions to that problem. The elements and behavior of the system are captured so that different solutions can be considered and checked against the desired behavior of the to-be-constructed system.

The construction of Analysis Patterns is challenging because of the need to think in the abstract about a particular subject. The recognition that a core theme to a kitchen is food preparation rather than a stove, or that a Party may be a person or an organization is not an obvious one. Therefore, a set of analysis pattern examples, also known as an analysis pattern catalog [2, 9, 19], is under development as a guide for the steps to follow in the creation of analysis patterns. Fayad suggests that there are three primary categories for analysis patterns: Conceptual Patterns, Problem Analysis Patterns, and Building Patterns [8]. The conceptual patterns describe the concepts of enduring business themes and business objects, including instructions on determining these elements in a problem domain. The problem analysis patterns describe the segmentation of a problem into its component parts for study. The building process patterns discuss the actual pattern construction itself, including verification and application.

In addition to these more formal approaches, there are a number of more familiar analytical patterns that are used every day, even if they are not recognized as such. For example, writers often use the pattern of outlining to model story plot and character development before or during a book's creation. Libraries use the analytical pattern of cataloging and indexing information to model the organization and rapid location of information. Even the creative process itself can be modeled using "mind-mapping" dependencies to model the problem of free-form conceptual association (Figure 4-2) [10].

Patterns have proven a very effective way to capture domain knowledge for both the software problem and solution domain in the form of analysis and design patterns. At the time of writing, design patterns predominate over analysis patterns. However, I expect that problem domain analysis will eventually be supported by a diverse collection of analysis patterns. With the help of a catalog of analysis patterns, a modeler will be better able to rapidly create complete and accurate models, with less chance of error and oversight.

Analytical Frameworks

Over the course of my professional career I have noticed that when I conduct particular types of investigations I tend to use the same approaches, tools, and model forms again and again. For example, if I am asked to develop a set of requirements for a software project I will likely use case models, interviews, functional decomposition, and group workshops. By contrast, if I am asked to create a software system's architecture I will use a different set of "tools," including UML static/dynamic diagrams, analysis and design patterns, and systems analysis techniques. I have named these collections of model forms, patterns, and techniques *Analytical Frameworks*.

Analytical Frameworks represent a collection of tools, study techniques, analysis patterns, organization of information, and model forms intended to support the research of a particular subject. An analytical framework acts much like a "toolkit" for the modeler by providing a wealth of possibilities and examples to construct system models. By analogy, a woodworker is limited in the type and speed of furniture she can build based on the tools at hand. If the worker is limited to a few simple tools and the knowledge in her head, then it will be far more difficult and time consuming to create new pieces. However, if the same individual is provided a fully appointed workshop with multiple-purpose tools, with a full library of plans and example pieces, then the task of creating new pieces is greatly facilitated.

Table 4-1 Business Analysis Framework (see Chapter 8)

Tools	Modeling Software, Word Processing, Document Configuration Control
Patterns	Business Systems Patterns, Workflow Patterns, Business Organization Structures (e.g., matrix, hierarchy, divisions, etc.)
Model Forms	UML Activity, UML Business Case, Organization Chart, Zachman Enterprise Framework
Techniques	Interviewing, Observation, Document Study
Organization	Department Hierarchy, Business Functional Dependency Graph, Business Use Cases

Table 4-2 System Requirements Framework (see Chapter 9)

Tools	Modeling Software, Word Processing, Requirements Management, Document Configuration Control
Patterns	Requirement Engineering, User Interface Design, Root Cause Analysis
Model Forms	UML Use Case, UML Activity, User Interface Wireframe
Techniques	Interviewing, Usability Study, Group Workshops, Systems Analysis
Organization	Use Cases, System Functional Dependency Graph, Root Cause Contribution

Table 4-3 System Architecture Framework (see Chapter 10)

Tools	Modeling Software, Code Analysis, Code Profiler, Software Architecture Document template, Database Reporting Tool
Patterns	System Design Patterns, Architecture Patterns, Data Storage Patterns, Software Deployment Patterns
Model Forms	Structural Models (e.g., UML Class, Function Call Map), Dynamic Models (e.g., Algorithm Charts, UML Sequence, UML State, UML Activity), Data Flow Charts, Database Entity Relationship Diagrams, Enterprise System Models
Skills	Abstract Thinking, Critical Analysis, Organization/ Categorization, Note-taking
Techniques	Code Structure/Flow Analysis, System Behavior, Hardware Profiling
Organization	Functional Behavior, Component Dependency, Subsystem Dependency, Deployment Packaging

In a similar way, a system modeler is greatly aided by access to a set of proven analysis patterns, powerful analytical tools and techniques, and examples of effective model forms for the capture and presentation of information. Tables 4-1, 4-2, and 4-3 present outlines for three frameworks I have used in the analysis of business systems, discovery of software system requirements, and software designs. The application of these frameworks will be detailed in Part II during the exploration of specific model examples. In particular, Chapters 8–10 provide specific modeling examples in which these frameworks were directly applied.

Adaptation and Application

An analytical framework is only useful if the "tools" are familiar to the modeler. Continuing the woodworking analogy, the best tools are of no value without the creative application of a trained and talented artisan. The creation of effective and aesthetically pleasing models requires the adaptation and application of one or more frameworks to the analysis of a problem domain. This requires the selection of the most relevant framework, familiarization with the elements of the framework, and adaptation of the framework elements to the problem at hand.

Selection of a correct framework is based primarily on the experience of the modeler as each problem domain presents unique challenges that will need to be creatively handled. However, many problems are recurring in their general aspects, such that a framework that is closely related may be adapted for use. For example, almost all legacy computer systems will require some form of design rediscovery, if for no other purpose than to train new developers in the maintenance and extension of the system. Thus, the System Design Framework would be more applicable than a Business Analysis Framework. Alternatively, a new system may require the application of several frameworks, such as the System Requirements Framework and the Business Analysis Framework.

An analytical framework may require adaptation before it is usable in a particular context. Adaptation of a framework involves the inclusion of new patterns or organizational schemes to better match the needs of the subject. In this way, these frameworks can be extended and developed for novel problem domains. As new tools and techniques become available, and as new analysis patterns are discovered and codified, these can be added to the toolkit of the modeler and organized into a modified framework. If the level of modification is significant, it may indicate that an entirely new framework should be constructed.

The creation of a new framework may be as simple as cloning an existing framework and adding new patterns and examples. More complex frameworks, such as one that may be developed for the analysis and management of embedded systems projects, may require independent creation, with little in common with other existing frameworks. The elaboration of a new framework should begin with the consideration of the tools and techniques that may be applied to study of the domain. Existing techniques, such as interviewing or group facilitation, may need to be modified to support the new domain. Other tools, such as computer aided software engineering (CASE), may be provided to the modeler for specific tasks, such as organizing content for a federation of Internet Web sites. As time progresses, the framework may be extended to include multiple examples. Finally, at the conclusion of the project, the techniques and patterns that proved most useful can be formally captured as analysis patterns for use on the next applicable problem.

One final word is in order on spending too much or too little time in the analysis phase of a project. In most projects, there is a tendency to jump to the solution (which to many engineers is the interesting part) before an adequate job has been done on understanding the problem. To avoid this, the analyst should focus on generating models describing the "what" rather than the "how" (see the Tips and Tricks section). If the level of detail is correct, then there should be few requests for clarifications. The other primary project risk is *analysis paralysis* in which the modeler becomes too engrossed in the details of analysis to transition the analysis into design. To avoid analysis paralysis, a modeler needs to recognize when there are diminishing returns on the investigation effort. For example, a literature search for a research effort should be reduced after a majority of the references refer to already located information. Similarly, a software development project should commence once the architecturally relevant system information has been captured [11, 12]. There are a few exceptions to this general rule, such as the development of embedded systems in which the required hardware support must be developed concurrently with the controlling software [13, 14]. For these systems, it may be necessary to complete a more thorough analysis of the system before initiation of construction efforts.

The application of analytical frameworks, analysis patterns, and proven analytical techniques are of great benefit to the modeler by providing a solid starting point for system analysis. Because thinking by analogy (analogical) is a core reasoning strategy [15], all analytical frameworks should be based on existing examples that allow the modeler to view and apply proven techniques to the current problem.

Summary

1. Construction of large systems requires a solid understanding of the problem the system is intended to solve. Engineers and scientists are supported by a long history of previous works from which to draw inspiration. Similarly, system modelers can benefit from the application of analysis patterns and frameworks.

2. Analysis patterns have been developed in response to the need to abstract the elements of a problem domain in such a way as to capture the core themes and objects of the subject.

3. Analysis patterns are an evolving research area; few verified patterns exist. However, this formal capture of problem domain information has great promise to facilitate analysis and modeling efforts by providing guidelines and generalized examples to common analysis problems such as trading, inventory control, scheduling, and so on.

4. There are many common examples of informal analysis patterns including the techniques of outlining, indexing, sketching, summarizing, and note-taking. The use of analysis patterns greatly facilitates the collection and organization of information for use in solving complex problems.

5. Analytical frameworks provide a collection of tools, techniques, patterns, and organization examples. A modeler can adapt or adopt a specific framework to the needs of an appropriate subject, thereby reducing the effort of "reinventing-the-wheel" for each new project.

6. Selection of the correct analytical framework is dependent on the experience of the analyst; the most powerful tool still requires a knowledgeable operator.

7. Analysis frameworks can and should be modified as new tools, techniques, and patterns are discovered. The formal capture of these approaches into a framework allows continuous improvement as well as sharing of knowledge between colleagues.

8. Avoiding over-analysis or analysis paralysis is vital to the successful completion of a project. Key to this is awareness of diminishing returns for the investigation effort. Progress on a software construction project is measured by the successful completion of working components that meet the defined needs of the client.

Tips and Traps

As noted earlier, a major project risk is *under-analysis.* If insufficient time is taken to discover the nature of the problem domain before moving ahead with a solution, this results at best, in the right solution for the wrong problem! A clear sign of this condition is when the requirements gathering phase is cut short because the project is "falling behind schedule." Another indication is when the development staff starts to develop code before the architecturally relevant requirements have been defined (e.g., those that have a critical impact on the system such as security, performance, and external interfaces). To avoid this situation, the modeler should create many visual representations of their work, and to post these in highly visible areas around the workspace. This will help to show progress of the analysis effort as well as solicit discussion from management and development. The reader is encouraged to refer to the numerous books on the importance of requirement engineering; in particular Weinberg's four-volume set, *Quality Software Management* [16].

People are a primary resource for modelers. When approaching any new subject it is the interaction with the subject matter experts that will decide the accuracy and effectiveness of the resultant model. In my work, I have found that developing relationships with team members was as important and beneficial as all of the other sources of information (e.g. documentation, code, issue reports, etc.) combined. Thus, "people skills" are as necessary to a modeler as the correct application of an analytical framework. In fact, two of the most useful recommended techniques are interviews and group workshop facilitation. A successful modeler will need to be comfortable working both one-on-one with subjects and facilitating for small to medium-sized groups. See the references for recommended reading on this topic [17, 18].

Questions and Exercises

- Question #1:
  What are examples of information repositories? How has access to this collected information been of value?

- Question #2:
  What are some common analysis patterns in daily use? In how many different ways are these "informal" patterns applied?

- Question #3:
  Have you ever encountered a situation of over-analysis or under-analysis? What was the result? How might you have solved the problem using the benefit of hindsight?

- Question #4:
  How often are project retrospectives conducted in your organization? Are there valuable findings that would be useful to other projects? What is preventing widespread adoption?

Exercise #1: Finding Abstract Themes

Consider the following environments:

Home Garage
Auto Repair Shop
Long-Term Storage Garage
Harbor Ferry

What are the enduring themes for each of these locations? Create a model that describes the enduring business themes and business objects (perhaps as archetypes) for each location and then reconcile those lists to form a model that can be used to describe all four environments. Finally, consider other environments in which the analysis model may be effectively applied.

Exercise #2: Creating an Analytical Framework

Consider a recent project that was *successfully* completed. Create a list of all of the tools, techniques, and models that were created for that project. Organize this list into an analytical framework and create a short description on how and where this framework should be used. Now consider a similar project that was not successfully completed. Was there any part of that project that was of value, even though it was canceled? Include in your growing framework any formal or informal patterns that were helpful.

References

[1] Alexander, C., *A Timeless Way of Building*. 1979: Christopher Alexander.

[2] Alexander, C., *A Pattern Language: Towns, Buildings, Construction*. 1977, New York: Oxford University Press.

[3] Coplien, J. and D. Schmidt, *Pattern Languages of Program Design*. 1995, Reading, MA: Addison-Wesley.

[4] Gamma, E., et al., *Design Patterns*. 1995, Reading, MA: Addison-Wesley.

[5] Kerth, N., "Caterpillar's fate: a pattern language for transformation from analysis to design" 1995 (unpublished manuscript).

[6] Fayad, M., "Accomplishing Software Stability." Communications of the ACM, 2002. **45**(1): pp. 111–115.

[7] Mahdy, A. and M. Fayad, *A Software Stability Model Pattern*. In *9th Conference on Pattern Language of Programs (PLoP)*. 2002. Allerton Park, NJ.

[8] Hamza, H., *A Foundation for Building Stable Analysis Patterns*, in *Department of Computer Science*. 2002, Lincoln: University of Nebraska.

[9] Hamza, H. and M. Fayad, *Towards a Pattern Language for Developing Stable Software Patterns—Part I*. In *10th Conference on Pattern Language of Programs (PLoP)*. 2003. Allenpark, NJ.

[10] Buzan, T., *How to Mind Map: Make the Most of Your Mind and Learn to Create, Organize and Plan*. 2003, London, UK: Thorsons Publishing.

[11] Jacobson, I., G. Booch, and J. Rumbaugh, *The Unified Software Development Process*. 1999, Reading, MA: Addision-Wesley.

[12] Kruchten, P., *The Rational Unified Process, An Introduction*. 2nd ed., 2000, Boston: Addison-Wesley.

[13] Cantor, M., "Rational Unified Process for Systems Engineering, Part II System Architecture." The Rational Edge, 2003. September.

[14] Cantor, M., "Rational Unified Process for Systems Engineering, Part I Introducing RUP SE Version 2.0." The Rational Edge, 2003. August.

[15] Eysenck, M., *Principles of Cognitive Psychology*. 2nd ed. Principles of Psychology, ed. M. Eysenck, S. Green, and N. Hays. 2001, Sussex, UK: Psychology Press.

[16] Weinberg, G.M., *Quality Software Management*. Vol. 2. 1993, New York: Dorset House Publishing.

[17] Satir, V., *The New People Making*. 1988, Palo Alto, CA: Science and Behavior Books.

[18] Weinberg, G., *Becoming A Technical Leader*. 1986, New York: Dorset House Publishing.

[19] Arlow, J. and I. Neustadt, *Enterprise Patterns and MDA*. 2004, Boston: Addison-Wesley.

Notes

1. The first Tacoma Narrows Bridge was given the nickname "Galloping Gerty" because of the tendency of the bridge to sway and buck in a strong wind. This bridge eventually failed as a result of shortcomings in mechanical design that led to major changes in the ways in which bridges were constructed. The second bridge still stands today.
2. Here, I am talking about modeling forms, information gathering techniques, modeling software, and data organization. I rather like thinking about these various approaches as tools in my toolkit, which I can select for use on a specific task. The more tools in my kit, the wider the range of problems I can address.

MODEL
CONSTRUCTION

Chapter 5

Research and Investigation

All modeling begins with the research and investigation of a particular subject. Although approaches to investigation may differ, the intended outcome is the same—the creation of an accurate and useful model. Each subject presents a unique set of challenges to the investigator. Some topics will require the discovery of previously unknown information, as is the case with virtually all scientific research. Other topics require the rediscovery of previously known information that has fallen into disuse or has otherwise been lost, such as archaeological digs into ancient civilizations. Many will involve some aspect of both.

There are many tools, techniques, and approaches available to the modeler to uncover, record, and organize information related to a specific topic. One of the most difficult skills to master in modeling is how to *exclude* information from a model or representation. This is particularly true for written documents as there is a finite amount of attention span that can be assumed for any particular audience; exceeding that span means that the remaining information will not be considered or remembered. Thus, it is the duty of the modeler to anticipate audience need.

Research begins with the identification of information sources. Information sources for software systems often fall into three general categories: people, documents, and existing systems. Because Chapter 2 described approaches to systems investigation, I will not reiterate that information here. Instead, this chapter will consider some of the key tools and techniques for the research and investigation of complex problems using subject matter experts or documentation as a primary source of information. These techniques include interviews, group sessions, cooperative interactions (e.g., Joint Application Development—JAD), focus groups, and surveys.

After the initial subject information is gathered, this and all subsequent information should be organized according to some plan or category. As many research efforts will require days, weeks, or even months of data gathering, the information must be organized as it is discovered in order to fit it into the final model in an understandable and maintainable way. As will be discussed below, the organization of data is done by looking for similarity and differences; for example, use cases are formed by looking for cohesiveness between business flows and scenarios. Validation of model information is the final step of investigation; this will be discussed in detail in Chapter 6.

Recording Information

In the modern world of laptop computers and personal digital assistants, some of the tried and time-honored traditions have been lost. Of these, the ability to take accurate written notes using nothing more complex than a pen and paper has seemingly suffered the most significant decline. This is unfortunate because paper-based records have several advantages over their electronic counterparts.

First is the creation of a permanent record. Although electronic files also can have a long life span, a notebook on a shelf offers unparalleled rapid access to historical data. Notebooks more readily accommodate rapid sketching of figures or illustrations. A pen taking notes is far quieter than a keyboard, and, hence, less disruptive to an interview or meeting. Notebooks are easy to transport, do not require an external power supply, and are more durable than any laptop computer. They can be readily employed even in adverse environments with minimal precautions or concerns. Because they are bound, notebook pages will not become disorganized or lost.

This is not to say that there is no place for electronic-based recordings. Several new products have the capability to support many of the benefits of paper-based records. Of these, tablet computers using handwriting recognition and pen-based drawing support seem to offer the best of both worlds—quiet, handwritten notes with electronic storage and transport. Moreover, I often have combined the ability to take written notes with a screen projector to capture flow-based information in Activity diagrams.

Regardless of the recording medium, perhaps the most valuable aspect of note-taking is the emphasis that is placed on listening. If you are engaged in writing, it is very difficulty to also focus on speaking or interacting. Note-taking forces the investigator to focus on the key aspects of the conversation being recorded. Because an important part of modeling is the summarization of key points, by writing notes the modeler is taking the first step toward organizing model information.

Another approach to recording information is to use audio or video recording equipment. This is particularly valuable during focus groups or other facilitated group sessions to ensure that important conclusions are not overlooked. This technique has the advantage of accuracy—all conversations are recorded, including conclusions and tasks. The disadvantage is that many people are self-conscious about being recorded, especially video recordings, and may voice objections. A second disadvantage is that review of the recordings takes almost as long as the original meeting; by contrast, written notes force summarization of information as it is recorded. So, the use of recordings can be very powerful, but limited.

In school, many of us learned to keep our class notes in some form of bound notebook. We did this for the convenience of keeping all of the related information for a specific class together; the safety of a bound book means that pages are less likely to get lost, and it is efficient to have access to multiple subjects subdivided into separate sections. It is strange, then, that as adults many of us abandon these principles! During meetings notes are seldom taken or distributed to participants, critical information is captured on looseleaf pads that are misplaced or destroyed, and people's memory of conversations have omissions or misinterpretations. In short, many of us have become downright lazy about the capture of information.

An analyst cannot afford such laziness. Any errors in the capture of information can have dire consequences for the accuracy of the model. The key to avoiding mistakes is *active listening*. Cognitive psychologists are well aware of the benefits to memory and learning provided by "multimodal" capture of information [1, 2]. Information that is captured by the physical act of note-taking engages three separate perception systems—*hearing* the speaker, *feeling* the pen move across the paper (or tablet screen), and *seeing* the formation of words or figures. This combination of activities engages multiple parts of the brain in a manner that facilitates the active understanding and processing of information. Because very few people are now trained in dictation, the act of note-taking requires the analyst to record with care only the information that is truly important, thus keeping the discussion on target and avoiding drifting away to side issues. Finally, a well-captured set of notes can be verified immediately with the subject to ensure that there were not errors or oversights.

Interviews

One of the most powerful and widely applicable research techniques is interviewing. Interactions are often conducted in a one-on-one (or two-on-one) session between the modeler and the subject, with the eventual goal of knowledge transfer from one person to the other. As part of this process, the interviewer prepares a series of questions that are intended to solicit information with a minimum of bias or errors. The subject expert is provided guidance in formulating answers which are recorded by the interviewer.[1]

Unfortunately, the same people who are the most knowledgeable about a specific topic are also those with the highest demands on their time. The modeler is thus faced with the dual challenge of recording a complete and unbiased view of the subject's knowledge, while also using as little of the expert's time as possible.

Table 5-1   Context-free questions (from Gause and Weinberg [3])

Process Questions
Who is the client?
What is the solution worth?
What is the real reason for solving the problem?
Should there be a single design team?
Who should be on the team?
What is the time/money trade-off?
Where else can a solution be found?
Can we copy/learn from an existing solution?

Product Questions
What problem does this product solve?
What problems are created?
What is the expected environment?
What precision is required?

Meta-Questions
Am I asking too many questions?
Are these questions relevant?
Are you the best one to answer?
May I record your answers?
Have I asked all of the relevant questions?
May I return later with more questions?
Are you comfortable with the process?

As was noted in previous chapters, communication between two or more people occurs over a channel with the receiving party performing complex processing to understand the perceived information. This process provides ample opportunity for the introduction of errors into the recorded interpretation as the modeler attempts to relate the subject's information to their own past experiences. There are numerous possible sources of ambiguity:

■ Imperfect recall resulting in omissions
■ Misunderstood questions or answers leading to errors in interpretation
■ Improper level of emphasis leading to errors in determination of significance
■ Cultural/language differences between subject and interviewer
■ Lack of respect or status for interviewer (e.g., age bias)

As noted by Gause and Weinberg [3], "a problem is best defined as a difference between things as perceived and things as desired." To reduce errors caused by

Figure 5-1 Misinterpretation of Requirements [4][2]

these sources of ambiguity, and to avoid the introduction of biases from the interviewers, these authors suggest the use of context-free questions:

These questions are useful early in the discovery process to establish a working understanding between the subject expert and the interviewer. The intent here is to gain a *real* understanding of the problem domain prior to the exploration of possible solutions or model forms. Moving too quickly to a discussion of solutions introduces a *solution bias* that may prevent a more thorough investigation of the problem domain—leading to a correct solution to the wrong problem (see Figure 5-1).

As an aid to the interviewer during these initial discussions, Leffingwell and coauthors [5] recommend the preparation of a context-free question list before the first interview session. These questions can be written into a notebook and used as a guide during the conduct of each interview. They also suggest that research into the background of the subject experts will reduce the need to waste valuable time in asking questions, which can be obtained using other sources.

Interviews are best conducted in short, repeated sessions. It is almost always a good idea to pace the interviews around about one to two hours, with no more than two or three sessions in a day. This serves two main purposes. First, it limits fatigue in both the interviewer and subject. Second, it provides time for the interviewer to review and organize new information into the growing body of research. Studies have shown that retention of information is aided by these repeated, short sessions [2], thus making the final model more cohesive because the modeler will better understand the interrelationships of the information gained from the subject matter expert.

Interviews involve close interpersonal interactions between the interviewer and the subject. It is the responsibility of the interviewer to understand and adapt to the personal preferences of the subject. For example, some people are naturally reserved. Taking an aggressive approach with these people will cause them to withdraw, severely damaging any chance of building a good relationship between the subject and the interviewer. Conversely, others will be more engaging and welcome the chance to show their expertise. There is also the probability that the subject will be heavily pressured to produce on one or more projects and so will feel "harried" by any additional requests for time. Awareness of, and catering to, the subjects needs will aid the accurate capture of information.

The location of the interview is also critical to a successful session. Trying to interview someone in the middle of a busy office is a recipe for disaster. Whenever possible, it is always best to move to a neutral location to conduct the interviews, such as a conference room or closed-door office. Interruptions are also a frequent source of distractions, which can be solved by moving the interview off of the job site entirely (and turning off the ubiquitous cell phone). Unless it is critical that the subject be observed/interviewed in their normal work location (such as may be the case for the analysis of business workflows), it is usually best to set up a convenient, quiet, and distraction-free environment to conduct the interviews.

After a good conceptual understanding of the problem is gained, it is often useful to explore potential model forms for the capture and organization of the information. For example, software requirements are often modeled using both use case and structured hierarchical requirements [5–8]. This provides a good opportunity to validate the interview recording and interpretation by restating the information in a different form. Refinements, corrections, and additions to the emerging model can be performed at this stage as new insights or overlooked information is considered by the subject matter expert. An emerging model should be validated in stages to reduce the likelihood of rework and provide a more accurate final product. See Chapter 7 for more information on the validation of model information, and Thayer [9] for more information on the interview process.

Group Facilitation

Group facilitation can be thought of as an extension of an interview into a larger setting. However, there are significant changes to the approach that should be carefully considered. The first consideration is membership in the meeting—who are the right people to include? My experience is that there is a practical limit of between five and seven active participants in a discovery or review session. This is in agreement with the idea that a meeting with more members will either be too chaotic to control (recalling the N^2 Law of Group Interactions from Chapter 3) or limit participation of certain members. As a nod to the political reality in most organizations, people excluded from the discovery sessions may be invited to reviews or asked to contribute written information.

Table 5-2   Responsibilities of Meeting Attendees (from [3])

Facilitator Responsibilities:
Establish Agenda
Establish Meeting Policies (interruptions, breaks, etc.)
Outlaw Personal Attacks
Enforce Schedule
"Park" Unrelated Issues for Future Discussion
Avoid Distractions
Confront Surplus Attendees
Ensure All Materials are Available before Meeting
Arrange for Food/Refreshments

Scribe Responsibilities:
Record All Relevant Findings
Publish Meeting Notes
Capture Brainstorming Efforts
Support Facilitator as Required

Attendee Responsibilities:
Contribute Constructively to Meeting Goals
Avoid Personal Attacks and Arguments
Avoid Interrupting other Attendees
Arrive Prepared!

Meetings of any size should be facilitated by an agreed-on moderator. This provides for clear designation of authority to police the meeting (setting discussion time limits, defusing disagreements, avoiding distractions, etc.) as well as leadership for the discovery effort. The facilitator will be responsible for establishing the agenda, handling logistics (location, scheduling, refreshments, and breaks), and limiting participation to invitees by confronting surplus people [3].[3] The facilitator will *guide* discussions rather than *direct* them. This approach limits bias and generates a more inclusive and creative environment.

In addition to the facilitator, a second key individual in any sizable meeting (e.g., greater than three) is the *recorder* or *scribe*. This individual is responsible for the capture of key discussion points and information generated by the meeting attendees. In addition, the scribe is responsible for publishing meeting notes back to the group for review and annotation. As such, the recorder will rarely participate directly in the session but instead will focus on assisting the facilitator in preparing for, conduct of, and review of the group session. Occasionally, the facilitator also must act as the scribe; this dual role is not recommended because the facilitator tasks are much more active and trying to perform both roles is usually to the detriment of one or the other. Wherever possible, a member of the group should be given this assignment if no one else is available to perform the recording task.

Group sessions are typically held for one of three purposes—extended interviews, idea brainstorming, and team review. *Extended interviews* are similar to one-on-one sessions in that the facilitator prepares a series of questions that are answered by the group in collaboration. This approach typically provides for more robust answers since multiple viewpoints offer a greater opportunity for complete coverage of a specific topic. However, there is also a greater risk of off-topic conversations and disagreements exploding into arguments. It is the responsibility of the facilitator to rein in such nonproductive behavior.

Brainstorming is another powerful discovery mechanism. The term "brainstorming" originated with Alex F. Osborne in the 1950s as a way to rapidly generate and organize ideas. The technique involves two phases, a generation phase for the origination of creative ideas and thoughts, followed by a reduction phase for reducing redundancy and to focus on the most potentially useful ideas [3]. The generation phase is guided by imagination and creativity bounded by a few necessary rules:

1. No criticism or debate
2. Aim for quantity
3. Time-bounded limits for generation
4. Allow for combination and mutation of ideas

The facilitator should show considerable patience during lulls or quiet periods. Often the participants are simply pausing to catch their mental "breath"—as the saying goes, good things come to those who wait. As ideas are generated it is the scribe's role to record and post them as quickly as possible. A white-board and 3" × 5" Post-it® are a good "low-tech" way to accomplish this task.

The reduction phase is used to winnow down the total number of ideas and to assign some form of priority to the remaining points. There are four principal mechanisms to accomplish this goal: voting on each idea with acceptance thresholds (requiring multiple votes per attendee); blending and removal of redundancy; application of specific filters to increase focus and reduce scope; ranking or scoring based on a categorization theme.

The final typical form of group discovery session is the *team review*. The primary purpose of these sessions is to validate and confirm the findings that have been captured and modeled. The facilitator presents the model information while the scribe records comments and criticism. Reviews should be held in a nonjudgmental way with suggestions and corrections put forth to improve the accuracy of the data and effectiveness of the presentation rather than as an attack on the group or modeler. All areas of the model, content, presentation, and form are up for review and criticism. I have found these sessions can be quite the humbling experience as my brilliant and beautiful model is reduced to so much scrap. However, the end result of such sessions is often to produce a stronger, more accurate, and more usable model.

In addition to these common forms of group meetings are several other forms of group meetings that are used for special cases. Joint application design (JAD) refers to the process of involving the end user in all aspects of the development effort. Typically, end users are interviewed for their needs, which are then translated into requirements and produced by the development team in isolation. The JAD approach benefits from the close cooperation between the target users of a system and the developers of a system, thus reducing errors and omissions at the earliest (and least expensive to fix) step.

Another special form of group meeting is the *survey*. This technique is not a meeting per se; instead, it represents the polling of a large group of people to find commonalities between different demographics. For example, a newly developed Web site that wishes to offer discounted prices on merchandise would be interested in polling as wide a group of potential customers as possible. However, it is not practical to gather all of these people together in one place. Instead, a written survey (either paper or online) can be distributed to the target audience, collected, and analyzed for trends. The downside to this approach is that it is time-consuming and possibly misleading if the respondents are not truthful, or if a significant number of people refuse to respond.

To address this last point, it is possible to gather a representative sampling of a population to form a Focus Group. These groups are carefully chosen to represent a significant potential market for a product or service. The Focus Group is then interviewed as was described above, with the hope that the findings will be more accurate and timely than is provided by a random sampling or survey.

Independent Investigation

Independent investigation involves the review of existing artifacts (documents, reports, experimental results, code files, etc.) to gain information about a specific topic. This may be done for a variety of reasons. The most common is limited access to subject matter experts. By definition, someone who is highly knowledgeable about a critical business topic will be in high demand; the value of this approach that the need for direct interaction with subject matter experts is reduced. Moreover, by doing your "homework" before an interview or group session, there is less time spent on background. In addition, study of existing artifacts may lead to discovery of neglected or otherwise overlooked sources of information. The downside to this approach is that many documents are obsolete or inaccurate, experimental results are based on faulty or poor quality data, or code files are not used by the current system.

To begin this form of investigation the researcher first must locate and identify potential information sources. The types and quantity of written information will depend on the organization and the nature of the study. In the following chapters, I will show common sources of information for business workflow modeling, requirements archaeology (rediscovery of "lost" system requirements), and documenting software architectures. Each of these investigations will employ different project artifacts as primary data sources. Business modeling will look at procedures and business plans, requirement rediscovery will study documents describing system behavior and use cases, and software architecture modeling will utilize code artifacts and system performance reports to understand system construction details.

Documentation represents a key source of information. However, documents tend to become inaccurate or obsolete over time, so the investigator should work chronologically backward starting with the most recent information. This can be determined from the document itself (if a date is included somewhere in the document content) or from the file listing (if the electronic source is available). Also, the authors of recently created documents may still be around to answer questions and reduce ambiguity or resolve conflicting information, which will help to eliminate wasting time on inaccurate documents. Documents with no acknowledged author should be treated with suspicion and used with care to validate the contained information.

Another source of information about a software system is the actual source code. Fortunately, this is rarely necessary to determine system functional behavior, but it is required study in cases in which a legacy system is being replaced, modified, or integrated. The analysis and review of software code artifacts presents several challenges to the system investigator. The first is dealing with the sheer volume of code files. A modern software system may be composed of hundreds of thousands or even millions of lines of code. Knowing where to search for needles in such a large haystack is daunting to say the least! Second, the ability to read and understand the code is complicated by the seemingly endless number of programming languages available for implementing software systems. Assembler, COBAL, FORTRAN, C, C++, C#, Java, Perl, Lisp, Python, Eiffel, Smalltalk, and a number of others are all in common use or are still serving as part of critical business systems.

Fortunately, many common programming structures are found in all languages (loops, branches, subroutine calls, variable declarations, etc.) and so the task of learning a new language is reduced to recognition of keywords and syntax. There are also numerous tools available to analyze code structure and dynamic calling behavior. The introduction of UML has greatly facilitated the analysis and modeling of code-based system information. Many of the currently available automated modeling tools can display graphically code structures for many different programming languages.

Information about a subject also may be found by researching marketing materials, system specifications, slide-show presentations, e-mail trails, Web-based discussion boards, issue tracking systems, and even from your local library! In short, information about a subject under study can be found in many forms and in many locations, even places you might otherwise not think to look. The key to investigation is knowing the reliability of the source, and the relevance to the subject at hand.

Experimentation

Experimental research is a powerful approach to gain information about a poorly understood system. Long a mainstay of modern science, experimentation with an operational software system is often impossible, particularly when the system is business critical and no test version is available. However, experimentation still serves a valuable purpose for functional, volume, and performance testing. It is also a good way to gain familiarity with the functioning system by allowing the investigator to see the interaction of different system components. Experimenting with something is often the best way to learn how something works (e.g., trial and error).

Experimentation is useful when faced with an unknown software system, when the first step is to understand the purpose of the system. Is the system built to support nonuser interactions (batch processing), task performance, or customer relations management? This is particularly true when the system in question has become an integral part of the company business process but has been around so long that no one is entirely sure about all the functionality or the original requirements.

A good starting point for this form of experimentation is to determine the availability of a set of test cases. The test cases should outline the functional behavior that is visible to a system operator. By following the protocols described in the test scripts, an investigator will be able to capture much of the information required to construct an activity map of the observable system behavior. Even an incomplete testing set will often prove a very useful starting point for system analysis.

In the event that test cases are unavailable, a system user manual will often suffice to provide guidance on system behavior. User manuals are critical for the training of personnel on most systems so it is common for at least *some* form of documentation to exist. Although a user guide does not provide the same level of detail as is available in a test case, it will, nevertheless, provide a great deal of information regarding the *expected* system behavior. In this case, it is up to the investigator to experiment with *unexpected* inputs to determine the system handling of exceptional cases. A complete functional map (e.g., flowcharts or activity diagrams) can be created to detail information regarding both types of system processing.

Organization of Research Information

The organization of information can be an extraordinarily difficult task. Simply consider the effort involved in maintaining the Library of Congress indexes[4] to get an idea of the importance of categorizing and arranging large sets of complex information. As Jesse Garrett notes in his discussion of Web site content organization, "The challenge isn't creating a structure, but creating the right structure" [10]. Regardless of the amount of information, or the end purpose for the data, some form of organization will be required to form a meaningful, understandable, and ultimately useful model.

There can be many ways to arrange the same information (Figure 5-2)—so many, in fact, that only a small cross section can be presented here. However, I have found that the categorization strategies in Table 5-3 work well for many modeling efforts.

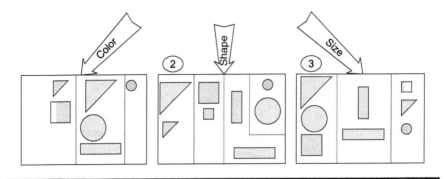

Figure 5-2 Organization of figures by different categories

Besides placing information into a more easily manipulated structure, organization also highlights areas where there are gaps or omissions. With a random collection of information, it is difficult to see where something is missing. A typical example of this is requirements analysis. Unless a careful job of research and information organization is done, critically important information may not be captured, leading to expensive mistakes that are not discovered until the system is in testing or production.

Without some form of organization, is also difficult to know when you are reaching the point of diminishing returns on research. Sooner or later, the time comes to finish research and start creating the model. My rule of thumb on finding this point is when I find myself revisiting information in different sources that has already been captured. At this point, I know that I have likely covered the currently available information, and I can confidently move forward to validating my information (Chapter 6), and choosing a model form (Chapter 7).

Summary

1. Research and investigation is necessary to all modeling efforts. The appropriate techniques for collection of data will vary depending on the subject and level of detail required.
2. When recording information, the use of an appropriate bound notebook is invaluable. Although seemingly archaic, handwritten notes provide an opportunity to record critical information, promote active listening, and forms a permanent record of investigation findings. Electronic aids, such as audio/video recordings, handwriting recognition, and scanners, can also be very effective in the capture of information.
3. Interviews are a principal and universal technique for the capture of information about a subject. The subject matter experts are invited to answer questions posed by an investigator in such a way that knowledge transfer is accomplished. Context-free questions should be used to prevent the introduction of interviewer bias or other forms of data distortion.

Table 5-3   Ways to Organize Information

Type of Category	Description
Hierarchy	This form of organization uses a tree-based structure to show a parent-child type relationship. This works well with information that has clear distinctions between each organizational level, as is typified by a family heredity tree, or a company reporting structure.
Taxonomy	Taxonomy uses attribute similarities between data elements to form groups. These groupings may form a tree (as in a hierarchy) but often form more loosely connected graphs. The many kinds of living organisms are organized by this approach.
Topic	Information organized around topics works well for data that has little apparent internal relationship. Newspapers group "world" events that may be about an election in Peru or a bullfight in Spain.
Task	Task or workflows are another way to form organizational groups. Tasks use the natural divisions and dependencies in a business workflow to form groups of related business functions.
Chronology	Timelines are a common way to organize sequential activities. Historical events are the classic example, but timing of system events also may be captured using this form.
Geography	Similar to time-based organization, location-based organization is common with information about position, for example, the physical installations of a telephony company.
Ownership	This organization form is based on one data element having an "ownership" relationship to another. Data models of business objects frequently can be organized by which elements own or use each other; for example, a bank account will "own" the balance, currency type, account type, and so on, but would only have an association with a "customer."
Dependency	Similar in form to ownership style, organization by dependency looks for elements that require others. An example would be workflows that operate in a particular order to produce a product or service.
Index	Information that can have multiple ways of grouping (such as a book in a library being grouped by title, or author, or topic) can be rapidly accessed by forming an index.
Metadata	This form of organization uses abstraction to create labels for specific data elements. Metadata is often used with the indexing organizational form.

4. Group facilitation is used most often for one of three reasons—extended interviews, brainstorming, or team review. The roles of facilitator and scribe are critical to the success of a group meeting and should always be performed.

5. Independent Investigation is useful in situations where access to subject experts is limited, and other data sources are available. Review of documents should be performed in reverse chronological order with the most recent documents reviewed first. Software analysis based on code artifacts should take advantage of the many automated tools available on the market. Other information sources include marketing materials, e-mail trails, and Web discussion boards.

6. Experimentation is sometimes the only mechanism available to discover information about a poorly documented system. This is particularly true for the discovery of system error handling, as the handling of system exceptions is often a design afterthought.

7. Information captured during an investigation should be organized and summarized to ensure completeness, and facilitate model creation. Many times, the discovery of a "key" aspect of the system will facilitate the organization by topic, ownership, hierarchy, or some other categorization.

Tips and Traps

Remember that many problems are recurring; someone somewhere has probably already solved a problem that is very similar to the one that you are facing. When initiating an investigation, it is a good idea to visit the local library to do background work on the subject. This will provide the modeler with some background information on the topic and aid in the development of a sound investigation.

A model is only as good as the data that is used in its construction. Always verify documentation with a subject expert if there is no other way to validate written information (e.g., via direct observation of the system or experimentation). Once incorrect data has been saved in a model, it becomes exceedingly difficult to locate and remove.

Questions and Exercises

■ Question #1:
Scientists often use multiple notebooks to track different kinds of information such as a daily journal of experimental protocols and a more formal recording of results and conclusions. How might several notebooks be useful to capture and organize model information?

■ Question #2:
Interviews are often conducted in the subject's workspace; why might this be a bad idea? What environmental factors are present that could make an interview less effective?

- Question #3:
  How often do you use your local library for research about business topics? If the answer is "infrequently" or "never," why so seldom?

Exercise #1: Interviewing

The task is to conduct an interview to gain information on how one goes about preparing a typical evening meal. Create a series of context-free and context-sensitive questions (e.g., "Do you more often create meals from scratch or from prepared ingredients?"), and form into groups of two to conduct an interview with your partner. Begin the interview with an introduction of yourself and your reasons for taking the subject's time. Limit the interviews to no more than 10 minutes and record the findings for presentation and class review. Be aware of assumptions made by the reviewer and the subject, and watch for knowledge gaps that may exist. Note also the differing levels of detail captured by each group. Switch partners and repeat the process with a different topic (e.g., preparing for bed).

References

[1] Gardner, H., *The Mind's New Science*. 1985, New York: Basic Books, Inc.
[2] Eysenck, M., *Principles of Cognitive Psychology*. 2nd ed. Principles of Psychology, ed. M. Eysenck, S. Green, and N. Hays. 2001, Sussex, UK: Psychology Press.
[3] Gause, D.C. and G.M. Weinberg, *Exploring Requirements, Quality before Design*. 1989, New York: Dorset House Publishing.
[4] Alexander, C., et al., *The Oregon Experiment*. 1975, Oxford: Oxford University Press.
[5] Leffingwell, D. and D. Widrig, *Managing Software Requirements, A Unified Approach*. 2000, Boston: Addison-Wesley. 491.
[6] Cockburn, A., "Goals and use cases." Journal of Object Oriented Design, 1997. September: pp. 35–40.
[7] Jacobson, I., et al., *Object-Oriented Software Engineering: A Use Case Driven Approach*. 1992, Harlow, Essex, UK: Addison Wesley Longman.
[8] Lieberman, B.A., "Requirements Archaeology." The Rational Edge, 2002. November.
[9] Thayer, R.H., *Software Requirements Engineering*, 2nd Edition, ed. R.H. Thayer and M.D. Dorfman. 1997, Danvers, MA: Wiley-IEEE Computer Society.
[10] Garrett, J.J., *The Elements of User Experience*, 2003, Boston: New Riders Publishing.

Notes

1. Occasionally, it is useful to have two interviewers meeting with a subject matter expert. This allows one to act as a scribe and record all of the information produced, while the other member of the team focuses attention on the subject.

2. CREDIT LINE: "Figure, p. 44", from THE OREGON EXPERIMENT by Christopher Alexander, copyright © 1975 by Christopher Alexander. Used by permission of Oxford University Press, Inc.
3. "Surplus" mean people who were not invited but decided to "drop by"—such as directors, VPs, or other senior company people. The challenge is to ensure the meeting will be successful, while avoiding the appearance of exclusion.
4. Just for reference, the Library of Congress is the largest library in the world with over 17 million books, 95 million maps, and manuscripts, photographs, and films. For more information, visit http://www.loc.gov.

Chapter 6

Model Forms

Models can take on many forms. The form chosen to represent the subject should reflect the underlying data structure, use a consistent style, and account for presentation of the end result. Over time, modelers in specific domains have developed standard model forms to facilitate model creation and to ensure a uniform notation and semantics. For example, hydraulic engineering uses a very different set of symbology and semantics (how the symbols are arranged and connected) compared to charts for ocean navigation. Each of these model forms, however, share similarities in the techniques used for model creation. Information is translated from the subject matter expert's jargon and nomenclature, encoded into the model form's notation, and mapped to the structural elements of the domain (the "things" that are manipulated), or the dynamic behavior of the system (the "actions" performed).

Selection of an appropriate model form is typically a matter of experience and training. In my opinion, a modeler should be familiar with many different model forms, rather than specializing in just one. This permits a more broad-based experience base, which means that the modeler can adapt or adopt a particular modeling form that is the best for the topic, rather than simply using the tool of greatest familiarity.[1] This doesn't mean that you should go out and learn every modeling form ever devised. Rather, some time should be spent reviewing different modeling forms that are appropriate for the domain, even though most of your experience may be with one particular model form. For example, even if your main software engineering model is the UML, it is still worthwhile to know other forms such as Entity-Relationship Diagrams (ERD) for database design or the Zachman Framework for enterprise modeling.

Every model will necessarily be influenced by the modeler's personality and experience. It is therefore also important for a modeler to understand his or her own biases and account for these differences when translating information into a

Table 6-1   Examples of Model Forms

Purpose	Form
Prediction	Macro/Micro Economic Model, Weather Forecasting
Education/Communication	Language (Written/Spoken), Icons
Construction	Architecture Building Plans, Software Development UML Diagrams
Investigation/Reasoning	Mathematical/Logical Symbology
Navigation	Library Indexing, Charts/Maps
Emotional Response	Dance Notation, Music Score, Chording Charts
Descriptive	Gestalt Rules of Perception

model form. These biases can result in models that are overly complex and difficult to interpret or models that are too vague to be useful. Indeed, all models that are intended to communicate something to other people—which is the purpose for a majority of all models—should be concise, correct, and clear.

Purpose and Form

Every model should have a clearly identified purpose that describes the intended use. As shown in Table 6-1, there are many different reasons people create models, including creating models to describe models (known as "meta-modeling"[2]). Ideally, a model will serve exactly one purpose, such as building blueprints describing the construction of a building.

Because communication channels (Chapter 1) are used to pass information between people, each model form takes advantage of a specific mechanism [3, 4]. These channels are represented by the five known human senses, especially the sense of sound and sight. Although most models use a single presentation mechanism (e.g., visual diagrams), some models will employ multiple channels at the same time—for example, a lecture with spoken language and photographs; or during a wine tasting event, where products are described and categorized through a combination of smell, sight, and taste.

A great number of model forms have been created to take advantage of human vision, most likely because tremendous range of differentiation is possible based on the shape, color, and texture of diagram elements. The most common form of visual model is a text-based representation. Examples include musical scores, scripts for screen/stage plays and novels, this book, and virtually all software development documents. Many models combine visual diagrams and textual descriptions:

■ Software Development
■ Chemical Formula
■ Civil Construction Blueprints
■ Dance Movements Chart
■ Business Models (budget, marketing, etc.)
■ Icons (traffic control, information signs, etc.)

With a purpose and form clearly established, a well-constructed model also should have a central *theme* that is representative of the subject under study. Compare this to the way a plot is presented in a novel; the plot provides the central information that guides the reader along. For a model, the theme serves to set the boundary for what gets represented in the model and what gets excluded. As an example, if the model purpose is air traffic control and the form is visual aircraft tracking via display screens, then the theme may be the color coding of aircraft by type and condition (take-off, landing, climbing, descending, flight path) with textual descriptions of speed, direction, altitude, and so on. Because the terrain over which planes are flying is usually not relevant to the air traffic control tower, this information would be typically excluded (or filtered) from the model.

Finally, each model view[3] should focus on a specific information aspect that I will term a "pivot." The pivot provides a category on which the rest of the view information depends. A pivot should be selected from the model information that is most important to the view. For example, in a musical score, the pivots are the time signature (beat) and key signature (pitch). The remaining information on scale, volume, lyrics, and so on is gathered around these two central ideas. In a UML use case model, the pivot may be a specific area of functionality, such as Mutual Fund Trading in a financial services model or Billing in a telecommunications model.

Time is often used as a pivot point for model views. Examples range from historical timelines to the more subtle astronomical charts in which time is a central theme but is overshadowed by the description of stellar object positions [5]. Another common pivot, position, is often used as central organizing point for geographic models, such as a road atlas (Figure 6-1) or coastline navigational chart.

Finding the pivot for a model view is a challenge. Because the view will key off this organizational point, it is worth spending a significant amount of time experimenting with different pivots to find the best one. As a rule of thumb, a pivot should be one of the common abstractions shared by all information in the model. Typically, as the model information is organized, these abstractions are the ones used to fit information into a category structure, such as those presented in Chapter 5, and represent commonalities between different aspects of the data.

A final point to consider before the creation of a model is the model's *context*. All models exist within a greater context that represents the environment for information presented in the model. For example, a car in the context of a highway would be modeled in a significantly different manner from a car sitting in a showroom. The information elements critical to the highway context are speed, position,

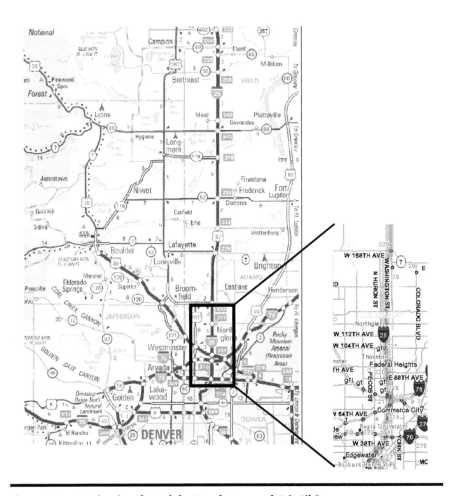

Figure 6-1 Navigational Model—Road Map and TripTik®.
Source: American Automobile Association

road composition, traction, weather conditions, fuel consumption, engine temperature, and so on. By contrast, a showroom context for the same vehicle would consider color, amenities, reliability ranking, design, fuel efficiency, and price far more relevant aspects (particularly to the salesperson!). Similarly, for software development the context of the project will determine the relevant details that should be highlighted; a data analysis model in the business domain context will be focused on the data elements and relationships of the problem domain, whereas the same data model in the context of a database implementation will be more interested in presenting construction details such as the size and type of each data element, primary/foreign key relationships, data integrity validations, and so on.

Model Construction

So, you say, how does one go about creating a model? I'm glad you asked.

Model construction consists of the principal steps for *choosing* a model form, *organization* of information for that form, *selection* of relevant information, and *translation* of that information into the model form. These steps may be performed sequentially, but more often they are followed iteratively or even in parallel. The choosing of a model form is sometimes dictated by the target audience, who may not have great technical experience with complex model notation. Others will be chosen based on the nature of the information that is modeled, such as with engineering blueprints. In other cases, there may be several forms that serve in a similar way, such as for software development. As was noted earlier, the greater the modeler's familiarity with multiple forms, the better the chance that the most appropriate form will be selected for the model. Experience and experiment are often the best way to find a good model form; experience with forms that have worked for similar projects in the past, and experimentation with multiple candidate forms to find the one that works best for the intended audience.

The organization of information was discussed in the context of research (Chapter 5), but for model creation, a different organizational structure may be required. This is because the needs to organize research information, such as to determine missing information or to track progress, differs from the need to present that information in a model. For example, research involving an automobile inventory system for a car dealership. The analyst might use the research technique of interviewing and group sessions to gather information on inventory control for the dealership. She organizes the information based on who participated in the interview, to facilitate complete coverage of everyone who should have input, and review of the gathered data. This information is reorganized by functional area before it can be presented to the development team, because the model form of a use case scenario or functional decomposition will be less coherent if organized around the subject experts.

At the risk of stating the obvious, the speed at which a model can be created will be directly influenced by the experience of the modeler with the model topic and the model forms selected for use. This aspect of modeling—namely, learning—is always present when a modeler is presented with an unfamiliar project. It is important that the modeler and project sponsor both understand that learning is a nonlinear process,[4] and that all projects will require some form of learning, when planning schedules for model creation. To aid this learning process, I often begin my models during the process of investigation, rather than waiting until I have met with all of the principal groups. This allows me to try out multiple model forms on the intended audience and to force early organization/selection of captured information. By using an iterative creation process, in which the model is created and presented in stages, I have found that the end product is much better because the content is reviewed by the intended audience at the time the model is created. Alternatively, if the area of investigation and modeling is very familiar to the modeler, then the actual model creation can be delayed until after much of the model content has been collected.

Selecting Model Content

Information selection is a key determinant in the success of a model. Models should only contain the information that is relevant for the model purpose to avoid becoming cluttered. The filtering of model information involves the difficult task of choosing which information should be included into the model, and which should be excluded. Unfortunately, I have not yet discovered a clear set of rules that can be used to filter model information. The following guidelines may be useful, however, in aiding the modeler's selection of relevant information:

- **Key Abstraction**—key abstractions are the common themes around which all of the model information is based. Information that is not directly related to those themes is a good candidate for exclusion (example: business work-flows or inventory control)
- **Cohesive Behavior**—system elements that operate as a unit should be modeled as such; elimination of one part usually results in an incomplete model (example: telephone switching systems require lines, directory numbers, central offices, etc.).
- **Dependency**—similar to cohesive behavior, system elements that depend on other system areas should be included in the model, even if they have very different internal behavior (example: billing and service provisioning).
- **Required by Model Form**—model forms may require certain information in order to be semantically correct (example: a UML Sequence diagram requires messages between objects)
- **Definitions**—Information that is needed to define terms or system elements should be included to aid the model viewer

Translating into the Model Form

Finally, the collected information needs to be translated into the model form notation and semantics. This is not a simple mechanical task, as information organization has a dramatic effect on model presentation. A model form that captures the idea of system behavior (e.g., flowchart, timing graph, enterprise network, etc.) can be created at many levels of detail: too abstract and the model is not useful, too detailed and the model is confusing. Again, the purpose of the model will drive the level of detail used during the translation step. There are three major model sections to consider when translating into a model form: *Static Structure, Dynamic Behavior, and Interdependency*. Static structure refers to the system elements (e.g.,

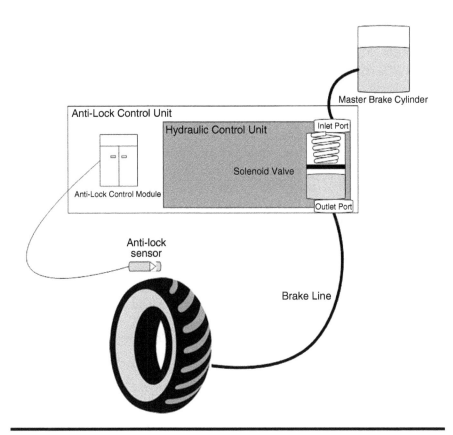

Figure 6-2 Antilock brake control unit overview

the "things" of the problem domain). Dynamic behavior is how these elements interact; the rules, events, messages, and order of operation. Interdependency tracks how different system areas depend on one another for support.

As an example of the process of choosing a model form and translating information, I will choose a reasonably familiar system—the antilock braking system of a car. This device is a combination of mechanical and embedded software systems that monitors each wheel of a car when the brakes are applied. If the system detects that one or more wheels are slipping, as might occur on wet or icy roads, the system reduces braking pressure to that wheel until traction is regained. This permits the driver to maintain steering control and avoid "lock-up." My first step is to identify the purpose of the system, and the intended audience so that an appropriate model form is selected. Because the purpose of this model is to show how a model is created,[5] I will avoid using model forms intended for a specialized audience, such as engineering diagrams of the antilock brake electrical or hydraulic components. Instead, I will use a more ad-hoc model that describes a high-level overview of the system elements (Figure 6-2).

Static Structure

The structure of the system contains four principal components: the antilock control module (ALCM), the antilock sensor (ALS), the hydraulic control unit solenoid valve(s) (HCU), and the master brake cylinder (MBC). Each of these units participates in the system behavior but has very different associations. The ALS is connected to the ALCM by electrical wires, while the MBC, HCU, and wheel brake unit are connected via hydraulic lines. The ALCM is powered by the car electrical system, which is excluded from the model as not immediately important.[6] Similarly, there are a number of pumps and additional control units associated with the brake system that have been excluded from this model.

Each component of this system has a particular role:

- Antilock Control Module—responsible for controlling the flow of brake fluid through the Hydraulic Control Unit, based on sensor data from the Antilock Sensor
- Antilock Sensor—responsible for measuring the rate of slippage during braking; also responsible for reporting on the system's functional state
- Master Cylinder—holds a reservoir of hydraulic fluid that is pumped to the Wheel Brake
- Brake Fluid Pump—maintains pressure in the braking system; actuated by application of the brake peddle
- Hydraulic Control Unit—contains several Solenoid Valves that are used to control the flow of hydraulic fluid from the Master Cylinder to each of the Wheel Brake units
- Solenoid Valve—operates in three modes, "open" to allow hydraulic fluid to flow freely to the Wheel Brake, "closed" to stop the flow, or "released" to allow fluid to flow back to the Master Cylinder
- Wheel Brake—attached to each wheel, and used to slow the vehicle by applying friction when hydraulic fluid enters the unit, usually by pads moving against a disk or drum
- Brake Line—used to transport hydraulic fluid from the Master Cylinder to the Hydraulic Control Unit, Wheel Brake, and back again

Dynamic Behavior

The dynamic behavior of the antilock system describes how each element operates, and when the behavior is triggered by internal or external events. For this part of the model, I have chosen to use a sequence of events diagram[7] to show critical events in the system operation (Figure 6-3).

The diagram shows the initial brake activation, followed by two events, the detection of wheel slippage (and consequent operation of the antilock system), followed by detection of wheel grip (and consequent reversal of antilock system).

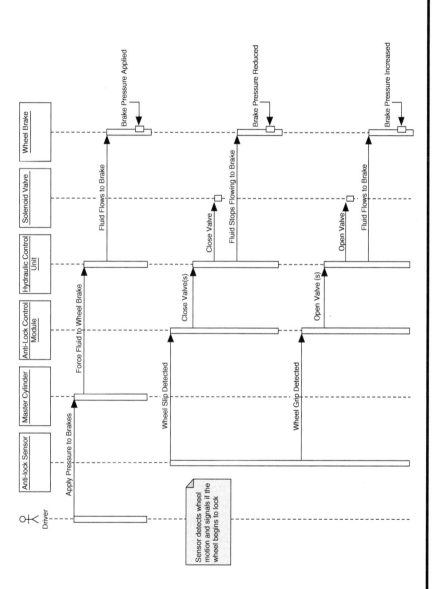

Figure 6-3   Sequence Diagram of Antilock Brake System Operation

There are other interactions that could be captured in a similar manner, such as the state of the system when the brakes are released.

Interdependency

Clearly, there are multiple interdependent behaviors associated with the antilock system, including some that have been excluded from the current model:

- Sensor and Controller signaling depends on electrical system
- Hydraulic system depends on the electrical system (pump and actuators)
- Wheel brake depends on vehicle structural components
- Hydraulic components depend on pressure sensors
- Warning lights (to indicate correct system startup and operation) depend on electrical system

Interdependent behavior can be listed, as shown here, or shown graphically using some form of dependency graph. A fairly common form is to list the system components in boxes and draw lines with arrows between them to indicate the system dependency.

It is important to consider which dependencies are shown and which are simply acknowledged, just as it is important to note structural elements and dynamic behavior. Dependencies between system elements are often overlooked, or implicitly stated rather than explicitly listed. This can lead to modeling errors in which a critical dependency is overlooked, leading to mistakes in planning or construction.

Translating Jargon

Model creation is the point where jargon or other domain specific terminology must be defined. Virtually all technical fields develop a jargon that allows practitioners to rapidly and accurately communicate complex ideas to other similarly trained experts, as with engineering, science, law, and medicine. Modeling such information requires that technical terms be understood by all model viewers. Otherwise, there is a high risk of miscommunication and confusion, leading to the failure of the model because it won't be used if it is not understood.

In the earlier example, I was very careful to translate the abbreviations and define each of the components. Abbreviations, acronyms, and other shorthand devices are encountered frequently in technical research. No assumption should be made that all model viewers share a common understanding of acronyms or terms. For example, the letters DNA can mean Deoxyribonucleic Acid to a biologist but Distributed Network Architecture to a software developer. Therefore, all acronyms should be defined on first usage (as is the case with the example), or defined in the model description, or glossary.

Tool Support

A final word on tool support for model creation—if the selection of the correct model form is necessary to the success of the model, then the correct selection of tools is necessary for model maintenance. A hand-drawn model can be accurate, concise, and correct, but it will be very difficult to incorporate modifications over time. Consider the cost of blueprint drafting before the invention of CAD (computer-aided design) systems. *Any change* required the complete redrawing of the model view (the blueprint). This was time-consuming, and it encouraged errors to creep into the diagram, which required careful review and checking. However, a tool is only as good as the skill of the operator. Someone lacking in modeling experience will not produce a high-quality model simply by using an expensive tool.[8] It is, rather, the combination of experience, technical expertise, critical thinking, and tools that work together to produce useful, maintainable models.

Summary

1. All models should have a defined *purpose* that guides the selection of model *form*. There are many purposes that are met through modeling including prediction, education, investigation, construction, and models describing other models (meta-models).

2. Models must take advantage of one or more sensory mechanisms to communicate information, for example, touch, scent, taste, sound, or sight. Each model *form* is developed to utilize one or more of these perception mechanisms. Human vision is a primary mechanism for information gathering and so has been used for a variety of model systems.

3. After the determination of model purpose and the selection of an appropriate form, next is to develop a guiding model *theme*. The theme sets the boundary for information inclusion or exclusion from the developing model.

4. Complex models will often need to use one or more model *views* to present the information. These views should be created with a *pivot* around which the view will be based, such as time or physical position. As a rule, the view pivot should be based on the common abstraction shared by all elements shown in the view.

5. Models necessarily exist within a greater context that represents the environment for all of the information captured in the model. The context will have a strong influence on the presentation, as will the emphasis placed on particular model information. For example, a database implementation will be focused on persisted data and data relationships, whereas an object model is more concerned with the temporary relationships created/destroyed during program execution.

6. Models are constructed by selecting a model *form*, identifying the *structural* elements, detailing the *dynamic* behavior, and listing system *dependencies*. Structural system components have roles and responsibilities to the system, which is performed by the dynamic interactions and messages sent between

elements. Dependencies may be either internal to the system, or on other external systems.

7. All jargon must be defined in the model to avoid confusion over the meaning of terms.

Tips and Traps

Although the discovery of elements for a particular system is usually not difficult, the determining of the correct level of abstraction to describe these elements and the relationships between them can be quite tricky. For example, consider the following system elements:

- Stove
- Knife
- Bowl
- Pan/Pot
- Lid
- Cutting Board
- Refrigerator
- Cabinet
- Dish
- Cutlery

How should these elements be arranged? Should a Dish be considered in a relation with a Cabinet? Does the Knife have a relationship with the Cutting Board, if so what? When determining the correct relationships between elements it is useful to consider the purpose of each element to the overall system (e.g., what is its function?). There are many temporary relationships (such as a Dish placed in a Refrigerator to temporarily store prepared food), that only exist for a specific period of time (or condition). An element may be entirely dependent on another for its function (a Pan/Pot and its Lid). Finally, when an element shares common attributes with another element then there may be an abstraction that can be used to describe the relationship (e.g., Amana, Wolf, and Coleman are all Stoves). Note also that some elements may participate in more than one form of relationship.

Questions and Exercises

- Question #1:
  How many different models can you envision? Consider models that you use in day-to-day functions (such as fashion or vehicular driving laws). Why are these models useful?

- Question #2:
  Table 6-1 lists a number of different model forms. What other forms can you envision? How might these models be used?

- Question #3:
  Time and Position are two common pivots for model views. What are other possibilities?

- Question #4:
  What would be the context for a business transaction model? What is the context for a model represented by a screenplay?

- Question #5:
  What would be a key abstraction for a sports franchise? What about the business side of the organization?

- Question #6:
  Can you think of any other types of relationships that can occur between elements? Should the ability to create and destroy other elements be considered a relationship?

Exercise #1: Domain Modeling

Create a domain model describing the elements of a bicycle. Define each separate part of a bicycle (e.g., tire, inner tube, spokes and rim as part of the wheel) with the appropriate relationships and attributes (e.g., the attributes of a sprocket are the gear ratio, weight, and composition). The model should describe how all of the elements work together to perform the overall task of vehicular transport. Be sure to have a pivot based on a particular information focus for each model view, such as steering or propulsion. Create a model view catalog of all model views.

References

[1] Lieberman, B., *Putting Use Cases to Work*. The Rational Edge, 2002. February.
[2] Leffingwell, D. and D. Widrig, *Managing Software Requirements, A Unified Approach*. 2000, Boston: Addison-Wesley. 491.
[3] Morgan, J. and P. Welton, *See What I Mean?* 2nd ed. 1992, London: Edward Arnold.
[4] Schramm, W., *The Process and Effects of Mass Communications*. 1954, Urbana: University of Illinois Press.
[5] Tufte, E.R., *The visual display of quantitative information*. 2nd ed. 2001, Cheshire, CT: Graphic Press.

[6] Evans, E. *Deconstructing the Domain: A Pattern Language for Handling Large Object Models.* in EuroPLoP. 1999.

[7] Silverston, L., *The Data Model Resource Book, Vol. 1: A Library of Universal Data Models for All Enterprises.* 2001, New York: John Wiley and Sons.

[8] Menard, R., *Domain Modeling: Leveraging the Heart of RUP for Straight Through Processing.* The Rational Edge, 2003. June.

[9] Lakos, J., *Large-Scale C++ Software Design.* 1996, Reading, MA: Addison-Wesley Publishing Company.

[10] Mattsson, M., *Object-oriented frameworks, a survey of methodological issues.* Licentiate Thesis, Department of Computer Science, Lund University, 1996.

Notes

1. By analogy, this is similar to using a wonderful, perfectly balanced hammer to drive a screw or cut a board. Using the right tool for the job, even imperfectly, is usually preferable to using the wrong tool perfectly.
2. The Unified Modeling Language (UML) uses just this kind of meta-model in a self-referencing manner.
3. *Model views* are a subset of the model information that is presented for a specific audience. I will have more to say on views in Part III during the discussion on model presentation.
4. This means that it is impossible to predict exactly how long it will take to understand the topic well enough to build a useful model. However, the closer the current problem matches a previously encountered one, the faster the learning process becomes.
5. You may have noticed that this example is a form of meta-modeling.
6. Obviously, without power the ALCM will not function; however, as the focus of the model is on the antilock system components, inclusion of the full automotive power generation system would introduce unnecessary model complexity.
7. Readers familiar with UML will recognize this diagram as a Sequence Diagram.
8. I am reminded of the old saying that "a fool with a tool is still a fool."

Chapter 7

Data Validation

Models are created by people and people make mistakes. For this reason, it is necessary to validate both the contents and the utility of a model. As has been noted in previous chapters, models should be complete, correct, and concise to be effective. Accuracy and completeness are necessary attributes of a correct model, whereas utility and maintainability are attributes of an effective model. To ensure that a model has these attributes, a thorough review and verification procedure should be conducted. There are at least four good techniques to validate a model: team reviews, simulation, testing, and direct application.

If a model is constructed in stages (e.g., iterative development), then the verification also should occur in stages. Models consisting of multiple levels of abstraction, such as one that has many detailed views, also can be verified in steps by testing how well the model is comprehended at each of its defined levels. As the model's detail emerges, the organizational power of the next higher abstraction layer is tested to see if all of the new data is still expressed effectively. If the key abstraction is poorly defined or ill-chosen, then some of the relevant data will not integrate smoothly; elements will seem "forced" to fit in an inappropriate category. An excellent model is one that has a certain elegance of form—all of the model elements are found in their proper place. A model has achieved its purpose if a reviewer need not ask questions of the modeler or subject expert that cannot be answered directly by the model itself.

Team Review

Reviews are one of the best techniques for confirming information contained in the model. Team reviews may be conducted in both a formal or informal setting, and either localized or distributed [9]. A formal review is established by an arranged meeting of modelers and reviewers. The goal of such meetings is usually to accept or reject part or all of a specific model's contents. Meetings of this nature are usually rather complex to schedule and so often are held only at critical project points. The meetings are conducted by a mediator and recorded by a scribe as was described in Chapter 5 for group meetings, but here the mediator's role is to ensure that the model is thoroughly considered. At the conclusion of the meeting, the results and suggestions are published and specific tasks for modification or rework of the model are assigned.

As an alternative to a formal review with a moderator, models may also be reviewed by walkthrough. In this form of semiformal review, the modeler takes the lead role in the meeting and presents his/her model to the rest of the team. The team members then ask questions or make comments, with the modeler incorporating the comments into the final model. In this form of informal review, which is more geared toward the model author than the team needs, the modeler is presenting the model so there is a bias toward the sections of the model in which the modeler is most interested. This subtle bias is not present in a formal review with a moderator, because the model is presented independently of the creator. Author-run reviews are excellent in getting direct feedback to the author, who can use the information to make corrections and additions.

Informal review sessions are usually conducted more frequently among the team members with the end goal of providing continuous feedback to guide model development. These meetings may occur over lunch, in hallways, at workstations, or in other casual settings. Both informal and formal review should be used as frequently as possible during the model development, and not just at the end phase of a project when the model is submitted for acceptance.

Another key aspect to reviews is that they are intended to *find* problems rather than fix them [9]. By this I mean that a review session is not a design session; faults that are found with the model should be noted and then corrected after the meeting finishes. This problem often occurs when technical reviews are conducted (such as an architectural model for software development, or the review of a device blueprint), rather than during specification reviews (e.g., system requirements). If the meeting participants begin to suggest fixes to the model, then the meeting will likely derail into a debate session rather than a review session. In a formal review, it is the moderator's task to prevent this digression. In informal reviews, it is up to all of the participants to be responsible for policing their own behavior.

Team reviews also may be held in a distributed format. Although this approach is significantly less efficient than a local group meeting, it may be the only avenue available to solicit input from a geographically dispersed team. Such is the case with user interface reviews for software systems where the end users are located at sites separated from the development effort. In these instances, the review team should be increased to eight to ten people, compared to the three to five members considered optimal for a group review session [3]. The larger number of reviewers

Table 7-1   Review Questions

Stakeholder Needs

Have the correct stakeholders been identified as consumers of the model?

Are there any individual or group concerns that have not been considered?

Are there sufficient model views to meet each stakeholder's needs?

Are the model views well organized to permit rapid access to information?

Does the model form adequately satisfy the purpose of the model?

Model Construction

Are there sufficient mappings between views to guide reviewers from one
   view to another?

Have all assumptions been noted and justified?

Is there a glossary of terms and a consistent nomenclature?

Has all unnecessary redundancy been removed?

What are the strengths and weaknesses of the model?

Is there a consistent organization of information (adherence to form)?

Model Contents

Is the model internally consistent
   (e.g., no conflicting/ambiguous information)?

Is the information current and complete?

Do the defined views have a pivot?

Does the model have a consistent theme?

Is the presented information accurate and contain no distortions?

Has any relevant data been overlooked or incorrectly interpreted?

accounts for the reduced response rate as a result of oversight, neglect, conflicting priorities, and so on. Reviews of this nature are also best conducted on a focused, critical section of the model to maximize the return value.

When conducting a review session, it is often helpful to use an *active* style [4]. This involves the direct participation of all review members, rather than permitting a more passive role for the reviewers while the model presenter does most of the talking. This is accomplished by having the presenter/facilitator ask questions of the reviewers rather than the other way around. Some questions that can be posed are listed in Table 7-1.

By having questions asked of reviewers, there is a strong encouragement to think and reflect on the nature of the model. This in turn will encourage a thorough and critical examination of the model form and contents, leading to a stronger and more useful final product. For more information on reviews and walkthroughs, refer to the works of Weinberg [5] and Weiger [9].

Simulation

Validation of a model via simulation involves the creation of a set of environmental conditions to test the theories and assumptions that underlie the model. There are many models that can be verified in such a manner. A familiar example would be an aircraft flight simulator. Here a pilot may safely practice emergency procedures without risk to life or property. A well-designed flight simulator allows for training and experimentation of emergency preparedness procedures in a controlled, safe environment.

Other forms of simulation can be used when there are no dire consequences in the event of model failure. One such involves the validation of computer user interfaces (e.g., graphical user interface or GUI) via usability testing. A candidate set of interfaces is simulated by one of two forms—a "click-through" model that permits viewing of scripted behavior, and a "wire-frame" model that provides a view to illustrate the static layout of Web page elements [6]. The first form facilitates conducting of user-experience interviews permitting the system user to comment on system behavior. The second form is useful when discussing the value of design trade-offs of different screen arrangements. In either case, the user interaction model is validated before the full system is constructed.

Another example of model validation through simulation can be found for models of business workflows. For these model types, it is useful to simulate a new or existing workflow. In this form of simulation, a worker is asked to perform all of the steps for a particular business operation without actually conducting (or committing) any real business activities. A captured workflow model or one developed to improve a current business process can be tested and corrected without placing actual customer accounts or orders at risk.

Finally, a potential software design model can be simulated by prototype development. Prototypes are a time-honored approach to prove a design assumption. If a design choice is questionable, for example the selection of a particular application server that may cost hundreds of thousands of dollars, then the possible choices can be tested by creating a small simulation (e.g., a minimally functional program of core, complex system flows) and hosting the prototype on different application server platforms. A series of performance tests can then be conducted to select the best choice for the current need (Figure 7-1).

Naturally, these results and conclusions are only reliable if the simulation is an accurate representation of reality. At first glance, this would seem a paradox—we are using a model of reality to validate another model of reality! Fortunately, a simulation can be independently checked for accuracy either by inspection (e.g., review by domain experts), by mathematical proof (e.g., financial or engineering models), or by testing using a previously established and validated model as a control. If a suitable simulation is found and confirmed, then this technique offers an excellent and inexpensive way to perform model validation.

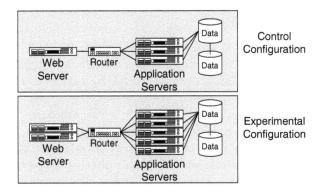

Figure 7-1 Performance Experiment for Web Server Configuration

Direct Application

One of the most conclusive ways that models may be verified is by *direct application* of the model. Needless to say, such models require the ability to be "executed" or otherwise exercised on an actual problem. This technique is also best utilized on a model that is built in stages illustrating key features of a particular solution. Such is the case with most models describing the construction of software systems. A best practice for system construction is to establish a baseline structure (also known as a reference or candidate architecture [4, 7, 8]). The model describing this structure is validated by implementation into a functional, albeit incomplete, system. If the model fails to define an adequate solution, it is still early enough in the project for corrective action.

Other model forms can be validated through execution, including business marketing models. The purpose of this form of model is to describe the likely response for a particular customer population to an advertising campaign. However, because a full campaign may involve many millions of dollars, a smaller "test market" may be selected to verify key assumptions regarding customer buying habits. If the test case meets expectations, then full funding may be approved for the project. Note that a group review theme (i.e., "focus groups") may be combined with this approach to provide a more accurate result.

The main drawback to the direct execution approach for model verification is that not all models can be safely executed in a production (i.e., "live") environment. A nuclear reactor control model would be far too dangerous to test on a real reactor system. For such models, a form of simulation as described previously is a much less risky way to validate the model.

Test-Based Verification

Another time-honored way to validate a model is via testing. Although similar in many ways to prototype development, validation through testing goes one step further by requiring more rigorous acceptance criteria. For test-based validation, there can be *no* test cases that are in conflict with the model; the model must either be modified to account for the discrepancy or discarded as inadequate. This approach is often used in research to provide support for theoretical models. Because these models are constructed to be predictive, they can be directly tested by experimental procedures based on those predictions. Many scientific theories have failed to meet this high standard and as a result have been abandoned.

Testing is often used in software development to verify that the functionality has been delivered as specified in the requirements. The testing is of the software model, rather than the requirements model, because it is the delivered functionality that is being verified against the original requirements. For this form of testing to be effective, it is necessary that the source for the test model (e.g., requirements) be as accurate as possible. Typically, requirements are reviewed by one of the team review techniques as described above, whereas system testing is performed by direct use of the system in a suitable testing environment.

This form of verification also requires access to an unchanging baseline for comparison of the obtained results known as a *control or baseline*. Without internal controls, it is often impossible to judge the effects of test manipulation. For example, consider a unit test in which a developer is attempting to verify that a particular section of code performs as expected. If an error is found, only one change should be made before the test is rerun. This is done to hold *variables constant* so that only one variable in the test is changing. This is a requirement for all forms of experimental testing. The reason is quite simple: the more variables that are allowed to influence the result, the more complex becomes the interpretation. In the worst case, a proliferation of dependencies will make determination of a root-cause impossible.

Even with these limitations, experimental validation is the strongest of all system validation forms. Because the model must explain all of the test results, there is no room in the model for error or ambiguity. Even the direct execution of the model is not as powerful a technique for ensuring that a model is robust and complete.

Summary

1. Model validation and verification is a necessary part of model construction in order to assure that the model is effective and correct. Well-built models will embody an elegance and simplicity of form while maintaining a high degree of accuracy.
2. Model verification may be conducted in at least four ways: by review, by simulation, by direct application, and by test.

3. Reviews can be conducted in a formal or informal setting. Formal reviews are complex to arrange but highly effective and require a smaller number of participants compared to distributed reviews. Informal reviews may be conducted with a minimum of preparation by walkthrough, and so permit rapid feedback to modelers. Active reviews are a very effective mechanism for group review sessions, in which the moderator asks questions of the reviewers to solicit critical examination of the model.

4. Simulation offers an inexpensive and effective mechanism for the validation of model assumptions. Simulation permits the safe and controlled testing of a model using real-world parameters and conditions. However, the simulation must be verified as correct before its use as a test basis. Simulations have been successfully used in many environments in which a direct test would be dangerous or impractical and in which model failure would have dire consequences.

5. Direct application of a model is a proven technique for model validation but is best performed in stages. A best practice of software development is an iterative approach, in which at each stage the development model is checked and verified to ensure correctness.

6. Experimentation represents the most rigorous form of model testing because of the high standard placed on the model to explain all results. In addition, this form of verification requires both a system that is open to manipulation, and a set of requirements (controls) against which the test results can be compared.

Tips and Traps

Review sessions often can feel like a shark tank at feeding time; the attacks come fast and furious with little regard to the possibility of injury. Although a critical review of a model's contents and form are expected, the manner in which those remarks are presented can make the difference between help and harm. The reviewers should be cautioned to focus on the work rather than the workers and to provide a solid reason for every comment. A response such as, "Well, I just don't like it," should only be allowed if the reviewer can support this position with details (e.g., color selection, organization categories, etc.).

Everyone likes to take pride in their work. This is especially true of models that are created to illustrate radical change. One of the most difficult tasks a modeler has is to disprove a dogmatic position that has become entrenched; the more the position is challenged, the stronger the adherents cling to the existing structure. When conducting verifications or validations of these kinds of models, be especially careful to present the evidence in a nonconfrontational manner; after all, there may be more than one possible interpretation for the model information. All conceivable views should be considered and debated before a final conclusion is reached.

Questions and Exercises

- Question #1:
  There are *at least* four verification techniques. Can you identify others?

- Question #2:
  Are formal group reviews more effective than informal reviews? Why or why not?

- Question #3:
  Some distributed reviews take the form of a questionnaire. What are the advantages or disadvantages of this approach?

- Question #4:
  One of the major problems with simulations is the omission of critical real-world parameters. How might a simulation be constructed that is complete? Is it possible to have a simulation that is *completely* accurate to the real world?

- Question #5:
  I have stated that experiment-based verification is more powerful than direct application of a model. Do you agree with this statement? What evidence can you provide for the opposite view?

Exercise #1: Critical Review

Select a recent technical article for review and analysis. Form a review group with a moderator and conduct a critical review session to illustrate the merits and failings of the article. When conducting the study, consider the following questions about purpose, form, and content:

- Has the author written the article with a consideration of the expected audience?
- Is the form of the article effective in meeting the needs of the reader?
- Has the information been presented in a clear and concise manner with examples?
- Are there critical omissions? Redundancy? Irrelevancy?

Prepare and present the group's findings to other groups for their assessment.

References

[1] Tufte, E.R., *Visual Explanations*. 1997, Cheshire, CT: Graphic Press.
[2] Tufte, E.R., *The Visual Display of Quantitative Information*. 2nd ed. 2001, Cheshire, CT: Graphic Press.

[3] Weinberg, G.M., *Quality Software Management: Volume 2, First Order Measurement.* 1993, New York: Dorset House Publishing.

[4] Clements, P., et al., *Documenting Software Architectures.* 2003, Boston: Addison-Wesley.

[5] Freedman, D. and G.M. Weinberg, *Handbook of Walkthroughs, Inspections, and Technical Reviews: Evaluating Programs, Projects, and Products.* 3rd ed. 1990, New York: Dorset House.

[6] Meyhew, D., *Principles and Guidelines in Software Interface Design.* 1992, Englewood Cliffs, NJ: Prentice Hall.

[7] Jacobson, I., G. Booch, and J. Rumbaugh, *The Unified Software Development Process.* 1999, Reading, MA: Addision-Wesley.

[8] Kruchten, P., *The Rational Unified Process, An Introduction.* 2nd ed. 2000, Boston: Addison-Wesley.

[9] Wiegers, Karl E., *Peer Reviews in Software: A Practical Guide.* 2001, Boston: Addison-Wesley Professional.

Chapter 8

Business Workflow Analysis

In the next three chapters, I will present some common system modeling problems using examples from Business Workflow Analysis, Software Requirements Archaeology, and System Architecture Documentation. Each of these areas requires the modeler to interact with different groups of people whose modeling needs vary widely. An executive looking for gains in workflow efficiencies is quite different from a software engineer looking to maintain a 30-year-old computer system. Thus, the purpose, form, theme, and views for each of these models should be considered separately. The techniques used for investigation, however, will have a great deal of overlap.

Business modeling is primarily concerned with the operations and workflows that are found in all business organizations. Frequently these workflows are redundant or inefficient, but as no one is entirely sure exactly how the full business works, changes cannot be implemented without fear of massive disruption. For example, consider a rapidly expanding package delivery service. The business is expanding from a local "rapid" delivery service to a national one. The CEO dictates the business need to deliver more packages with fewer workers. The "obvious" solution is to automate the currently manual processes for sorting packages to delivery trucks. To ensure that the business system is meeting the stakeholder's needs (in this case the CEO), a first step is to identify the business vision that describes the business goals, and the environment in which the business operates. This is followed by discovery of the system components, and finally by the formation of the business workflow model.

Business Environment

The vision statement is a key artifact in detailing core business drivers for a company. This artifact defines and describes the basic business strategy the company will follow. The lack of a clear vision statement can be taken as an indication that the company may not have a clearly defined business goal, or at the very least has not articulated that goal to all employees. When performing business modeling the first step should be to ascertain the core business niche the company fulfills.

> Vision Statement—A clear, declarative statement of the company's strategies, goals, market niche, and customer base

The core business niche for a company can be defined in terms of the customer served and the services/products provided by the company. The nature of the customers, the services delivered, and the level of competition present in the market are all valuable information for the business analyst. The nature of the business can be discovered by asking questions similar to the following:

- Who are the business's customers? Are any groups more important than others? Knowing the core customer base provides critical information on the business drivers for the company. For example, if the core customer base is teenage boys, then the business drivers likely include time to market, novelty, and an action-based marketing focus (a few pretty girls doesn't hurt either).
- What services or products are provided to these customers?
  All companies exist to provide a product or service to their customer base. These services/products define the scope of the business and to a large extent the mechanisms the company will use to produce and provide these services to their customers.
- How is the company structured to provide those services?
  The structure of the company will be directly related to the services or products it provides. A toy manufacturer will have a production facility to create the toys, shipping departments to package and deliver the product, and marketing departments to advertise and sell the product. A computer consulting company may have a group of analysts to determine requirements, architects to structure the system, programmers to create code, and testers to ensure the code performs as desired. Thus, each company is structured differently to most effectively provide for their specific customers.
- Who are the primary competitors? How many are there?
  The type and number of competitors will define one of the primary difficulties that a company will face. Time to market pressures, need to adapt to changing market conditions, and customer base maintenance are drivers heavily affected by business competition.

- How large is the company?
  A company's overall size (as measured by the number of employees) also will affect the complexity of the business model. Larger companies typically have developed more complex workflows than smaller ones. Moreover, in smaller companies multiple workflows are often performed by the same person, which can lead to confusion to the analyst trying to separate the person from the task (see discussion later).
- How geographically distributed is the company?
  The more geographically distributed a company, the more difficult it will be for each part to interact with another effectively. The business analysis model should account for these difficulties in communication and any dependencies that exist between physically separated groups.
- What regulations/laws are applicable to the business?
  All companies are responsible for complying with state and federal regulations with regards to their business practices. Many of these companies also must comply with safety or financial security practices (e.g., banking regulations). It is of the utmost importance that any irregularities be noted and brought to management's attention.
- What types of problems does the business face?
  All businesses face challenges, even if they are those of rapid growth! Identification of the current set of company difficulties and the risk associated with those difficulties will aid in identifying critical business areas.

After this initial business discovery phase, the modeler will be better prepared to research the business systems and to organize that information into a concise business model.

Business Model

There are numerous ways to study a business process. The business process stability can be measured by a Six Sigma statistical analysis [1,2]. A manufacturing process can be modeled by indicating the processing steps and machine interaction [3]. For this business model example, I have adapted the Business Model extension to the UML developed for the Rational Unified Process™ by IBM-Rational Corporation. This model form is based on several key business components as described in Table 8-1. The model icons that represent these key model elements are shown in Figure 8-1. Please note that although this example takes advantage of one particular implementation of a business model, there are a number of tool vendors that support business modeling using similar icons and semantics.

The model is formed by showing the interactions between the core elements. The flows are typically initiated by an External Business Actor, a person or system that requests service of the business system. This request is handled by an internal

Table 8-1 Description of Business Model Components

Business Component	Description
Business Case	Task performed by business workers to accomplish business goals
Business Workers	Those people who are performing one or more workflows in a particular role
Domain Entity	Business objects that are manipulated by one or more workflows
Roles	Categories of workers who perform a business function, for example, driver, sorter, loader, and so on
Business Actors/Systems	People or systems directly affected or benefited by the performance of a workflow
Business Stakeholder	A person or agency that has a direct influence on the development or performance of workflows (e.g., CEO, Governmental Regulatory Agency, Workers' Union)

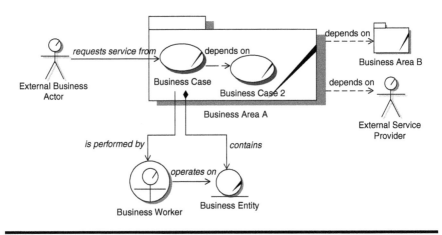

Figure 8-1 Business Modeling Icons and Relationships

Business Case that describes each step of the workflow, including the basic path, alternate paths, and exceptional conditions.[1] The business case flow is the one most often performed by a Business Worker, a person responsible for providing a specific set of services to the External Business Actor. Business Workers manipulate Business Entities that represent the information or product the business is providing to the External Business Actor.

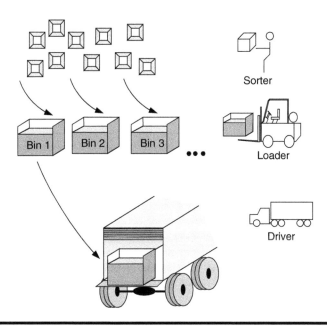

Figure 8-2   Overview of Workflows for a Package Delivery Service

Businesses are often divided into specialized groups represented by a Business Area. Some Business Areas are capable of providing direct service to the External Business Actor, such as a customer service operations group. Other Business Areas, such as accounting or marketing, provide support services or specific expertise to the performance of a business task. These dependencies are indicated in the model with the use of a dependency link (the UML dotted arrow). Often there is also a dependency on some external source of information or services; these are shown in the model as External Service Providers.

Together, these model elements permit the capture of the core business processes and dependencies. As detailed later and demonstrated in Appendix A, this technique is very powerful for the capture and presentation of business processes.

Business Workflows

Business components are best identified and captured by interviewing workers on specific aspects of their jobs (as discussed in Chapter 5). Using a package delivery service example, one interview might be with a package *Sorter*. The Sorter's role is to ensure that a package designated for delivery to a specific geographic "zone" goes down one of the available chutes to a waiting storage bin. Once a bin is full, a *Loader* then places the full bin on a truck that is designated for that particular zone. The *Driver* will confirm the shipment and drive the truck on its delivery route. The workflows and workers are summarized in Figure 8-2.

Table 8-2   Business Analysis Analytical Framework

Tools	Modeling Software, Word Processing, Document Configuration Control
Patterns	Business Systems Patterns
Model Forms	UML Activity, Business Case,[2] Organization Chart
Skills	Facilitation, Note Taking, Information Organization
Techniques	Interviewing, Observation, Document Study
Organization	Department Hierarchy, Business Functional Dependency Graph, Business Use Cases

Clearly, this simple model will not suffice to describe the details for the interactions between each worker and the specific tasks each worker must perform. It does, however, provide a good starting point to indicate the areas that will require investigation, and it suggests some of the key business elements and workers.

In this model, there are at least three key worker roles—*Sorter, Loader,* and *Driver.* There are likely to be other roles that are missing from the current model. Perhaps there are *Supervisors* who periodically review Sorter accuracy. Who brings the packages to the Sorter in the first place? Does the Driver deliver directly to the customer? If not, who takes the bins out of the truck at the delivery distribution center? As you can see, during investigation and discovery the number of roles and responsibilities for the business model often grows beyond the initial set of workers and workflows.

At this point, we can begin to apply some of the guidelines from the analytical framework for business modeling (Table 8-2). The framework suggests a number of techniques for identifying workflows including interviewing, observation, and document study (as described in Chapters 3 and 5). The model forms that are recommended are UML activity, and business case diagrams as well as the organization's management chart.

During the discovery phase, the most useful model view is likely to be the Business Use Case. This model form provides two main benefits. First, it is a visual tool to aid discussions with business workers. Second, it permits the capture and organization of workflow information. This model form also can be utilized effectively to chart the investigation's progress by creating a business case catalog and tracking the elaboration of each business case.

To elaborate the relevant business cases, the first step is to identify the unique workflows that are performed by each worker (Figure 8-3). I like to use a middle-out approach, in which I begin my investigation by interviewing a particular role, such as the worker performing the role of Sorter. When determining worker roles, it is a good idea to focus on the *role* rather than on the person performing the role. I have occasionally encountered documentation that says something to the effect

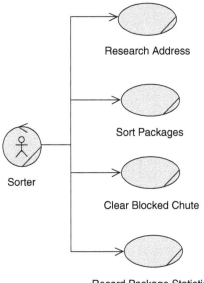

Figure 8-3   Package Sorter Business Case Diagram

that "after the form is received it is given to Samantha for approval." If the document reader is unfamiliar with Samantha's role (or she has left the company and another individual is responsible for that role), then this description is confusing at best and useless at worst. Thus, instead of using the name "Samantha" in the workflow description, the role of *Approver* is defined. The business organizational chart or human resources department often will have a list of such role names, but these names may be misleading and should be reviewed carefully with the subject expert before inclusion into the model.

After worker roles are defined, the next step is to establish workflow boundaries. The business use case boundary can be best established by modeling the workflow activities. For this task, the most useful tool is a flow-based model form, such as flowcharts or UML Activity diagrams (see Appendix D for a description of the UML 2.0 Activity Diagram). Either form is effective, but I prefer the UML diagram semantics, as they provide a more robust way to describe the actual activities and their relationship to each other; especially for complex interactions such as parallel processing, time-critical handling,[3] or workflow synchronization. Figure 8-4 shows a comparison of Flow Chart semantics versus UML Activity diagram semantics. Both techniques are effective model forms; for business modeling, the selection of one over the other is often a matter of modeler choice and experience.

The goal of workflow analysis is to identify discrete performance steps—those actions that have a well-defined starting and ending place (as illustrated in the activity or process boxes in Figure 8-4). As a general rule of thumb, an *activity* is one in which the worker can "take a coffee break" without fear that the workflow

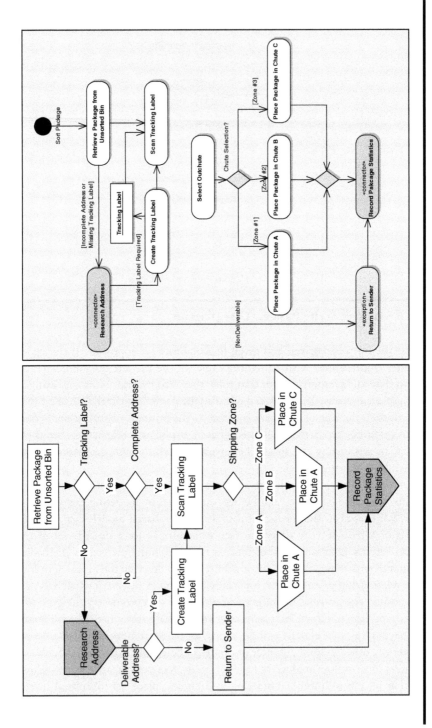

Figure 8-4 Flow Chart vs. UML Activity Diagram of Sort Package Workflow

would be compromised in some way. Other indications are places where decision points exist selecting the next step in the workflow. Such branch points might be *binary* (yes/no) or *n-ary* (multiple branches) and indicate a point at which selection of the next activity is dependent on some work entity quality, such as the presence or absence of a tracking label on a shipping order or some other business criteria.

The steps in an activity are usually only relevant to that workflow (such as placing a package in a particular chute). Occasionally, however, there will be cross-over between workflows, as happens in Figure 8-4 with the "Research Address" workflow or the "Record Package Statistics." In this model, I have chosen to present these workflows separately because of the complexity involved. In these instances, a workflow may be referenced as shown in either flowchart or activity diagram model form. As a side note, the decision to include a workflow directly or by reference is determined by the complexity of the workflow to be included and the complexity of the current workflow. As a general rule, an activity diagram that has less than three activities can be directly included into the diagram (even if it occurs in several workflows), whereas anything more complex may be captured as a separate diagram and referenced.

A second important aspect to the capture of workflow details are alternate and exceptional paths. In Figure 8-4, a package with no delivery address needs to be returned to the sender, clearly a common, albeit undesirable, action. During an interview, a subject sometimes will provide a great deal of information on common pathways while neglecting or ignoring problem handling processes. Because these exceptional paths are critical for a complete understanding of the workflow, it is important for the analyst to capture a summary of the workflow as described by the expert. I like to prompt the interviewee to consider processes for unexpected, but reasonably possible, conditions (such as a package jamming in one or more chutes, or recalling a misdirected package).

Once an outline of the basic workflow steps is complete, the detailed activities are captured. Usually at this stage of the analysis the identification of business objects becomes necessary. Business objects are represented by any paper or electronic form, physical objects (e.g., packages, bins, chutes, trucks), and information gathered from or sent to other workers. This information can be gathered and added to the emerging model either in the form of notes attached to the visual models, or via descriptions in the documented Business Use Case. As is noted in the Analytical Framework for this topic (Table 8-2), the Business Use Case is recommended as a principal documentation form. Appendix A of this book contains a completed business workflow document as well as the context within the larger business model.

As was discussed in Chapter 5, many companies have some form of workflow documentation in their company records. However, these documents are seldom in a uniform format, are typically inaccurate, out of date, and have many critical omissions. Nevertheless, they remain a valuable source of information for the analyst to research. As suggested in Chapter 5, the analyst should review the most recent documents first, followed by older materials. A thorough review of historical

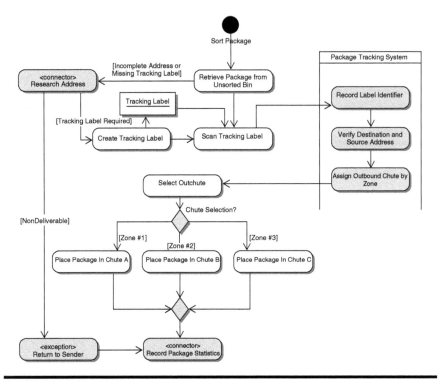

Figure 8-5   Swimlanes in Business Workflows

documents may illustrate areas of exceptional behavior that was overlooked in the interview process, or provide additional context around the purpose of somewhat mysterious workflows.

Finally, a workflow analysis would be incomplete without a detailed description of automated systems (e.g., computer systems). As shown in Figure 8-5, activity diagrams utilize the idea of "swimlanes" to provide a boundary point between on set of workflow steps and another. These boundaries can be between workers, workflows, internal systems, or external systems. Virtually all modern businesses use some form of computer-based automation and support to critical workflows, from simple letter writing to complex satellite control systems. Nearly every significant business operation requires some form of computer support. Consequently, as a workflow's details are elaborated, the computer systems that are employed by the worker should also be captured. As shown in the diagram, a swimlane has been used to differentiate the different aspects of an automated package Tracking System. The workflow activity "Scan Tracking Label" accesses the Tracking System to perform the listed steps (although not all steps require manual user intervention). The workflow is rejoined at the "Select Outchute" step and continues from that point. This diagramming technique is very useful for distinguishing the boundary points between the business worker and all other associated or utilized systems.

Figure 8-5 shows the use of swimlanes in an activity diagram to illustrate interactions between activities performed by a worker and one performed by an automated system. Interactions between multiple workers also can be illustrated in this manner.

Business Workers and Actors

In review, Business Workflows are initiated by *Business Actors* and performed by *Business Workers*. Business Actors initiate workflows by interacting with Workers or automated business systems. Activities are then performed by manual operations or by automated processing. A business worker is defined by the specific role and set of workflows they perform, such as a worker in an "accountant" role performing a workflow called "audit." As mentioned earlier, a single individual may take on multiple roles. If an interviewee describes multiple unrelated tasks, then this is a good indication that there is more than one role being described.

During the discovery phase of the modeling effort, the business workers will be easier to find than the roles. Although the titles of each business worker is a good indication of the type of work they are performing, a single employee may assume multiple business roles, even ones that they are not formally recognized as performing. It is the responsibility of the modeler to identify these different roles by noting that workflows are not all related to the performance of a single business function. Someone who is acting in a "management" role to assign tasks to a group of workers also may assume the role of "quality assurance agent" if they inspect the output of each worker.

Business Actors often provide information to the company through several mechanisms. Two of the most common are written forms and computer-based forms. The data that is included in these forms will comprise one or more business objects as described earlier. A Business Actor is always looking for some service of value; the relationship that is formed between the actor and the business system will be defined by these needs. Therefore, when capturing a description of each external actor, it is useful to describe each one in terms of the needs that the business is providing.

External actors that are computer systems will desire a special form of service from the business, usually via an automated computer interface. For these types of actors, the best technique is to capture the technical details of the interfaces, such as the data structures that are passed and the functional subsystems that are accessed.

Business Entities (Domain Data Model)

As was discussed earlier in this chapter and also in Chapter 5, a key abstraction for business modeling is the identification of fundamental business objects. Such objects comprise both the physical materials manipulated by workers and the logical data utilized by the business in day-to-day operations. Many physical business objects can be readily identified as the "things" that are handled by workers during the performance of a task. For example, in a warehouse, the physical objects would include shelves, boxes, forklifts, and so on. Logical elements are often more difficult to identify and sometimes are captured in written or computer-based forms processed by workers.

Logical data elements are kinds of business objects that are related to *mechanisms of control* required by all organizations to track important business events, such as customer orders, shipments, deliveries, transactions, historical records, and so on. Often this information is provided to the worker by a Business Actor (customer order), but much of the business information is generated internally to the organization (accounting records). When capturing this information for the formal business model it is important to note when a form contains multiple logical elements. Consider a standard business service application form; there will be a sizeable amount of information contained in the form. This may represent independent but related data on customer personal information, financial status, preferences, business priority, account activity, and other data relevant for the business to provide services. The business modeler should recognize these relationships and capture them into a logical domain model.

Figure 8-6 illustrates a domain model constructed to describe one aspect of the air transportation business. This segment of the model describes the elements, attributes, and relationships for the business domain entities that describe the creation of an air travel reservation. Each piece of data is critical to the business task of reserving and tracking a commercial aircraft before and after a particular journey is traveled. Although this model is for commercial transportation, a model developed for flight-based package delivery would contain similar information relevant to that business context. This form of model view is particularly useful when attempting to automate a business process because the data elements will be used to form the basis for system objects and stored database tables.

Note that for many business analysis projects this level of detail is not required and a more abstract level that simply notes which workflow uses which printed form may be of greater interest. In these cases, the information on the physical form can be directly noted on the workflow(s) in which it is utilized (Figure 8-7).

Summary

1. Every model is created to meet a specific purpose. Business models are intended to provide information on workflows, workers, business data, and external business actors that form the core of the business operation.

2. The *business environment* is defined by the vision statement describing the company strategies, goals, and market drivers. The core business niche is defined in terms of the services that are provided to customers. The business modeler should be careful to inquire early in the modeling effort into the business core customer base, the services offered, the general business structure created to provide those services, competitors, geographic location, regulatory laws, and primary problems for the business.

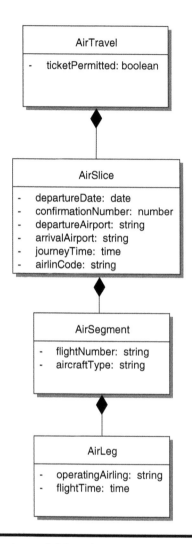

Figure 8-6   Data Domain Model for Air Travel

3. A *business workflow* is comprised of the actions performed by workers for different business functions. The workflow model will summarize and detail each activity performed as a result of an external business actor request for the company services. The recommended model form to capture this information is the UML activity diagram.

4. *Business workers* perform specific workflows by assuming a *role*. In addition, a worker may manipulate one or more business objects in each activity of the business workflow. Workers are organized by these roles they assume and roles are defined by the collection of workflows that are applicable to the specific tasks for which that role is responsible.

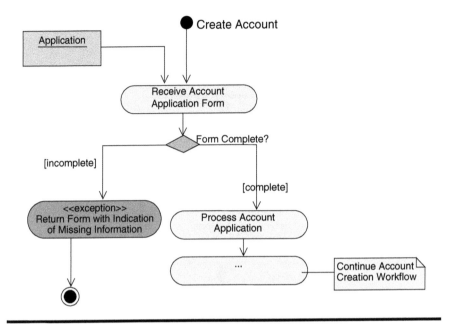

Figure 8-7 Indication of Business Form in Workflow Diagram

5. A *business actor* is any person or system that is external to the business requesting one or more business services. Business actors are also organized around roles that relate to the products or services provided by the business workflows.
6. The creation of a *business domain model* is a valuable exercise if a detailed understanding of the business control data is required (e.g., for the development of automated software systems). This type of model is based on the physical and logical business objects that comprise the business.

Tips and Traps

The level of detail incorporated into a business model will be directly dependent on the needs of the business. An organization that is intent on a security audit will need a model that is focused on the susceptibility of the business systems to attack or fraud. By contrast, a business interested in improving a highly manual process will want to measure the time each operation takes, as well as study the efficiency of worker motions (i.e., classic "motion studies"). The most important questions a modeler should ask are "why" and "who" when determining the purpose of the model.

Management often is loath to hear that there are problems with the way in which the business is conducted. This can lead to a situation in which suggestions for improvement will be ignored, delayed, or only given casual consideration. Although this is a natural response to change (e.g., avoiding the "trouble" associated with an alteration in business practices), in some cases these problems will be ones that may have severe safety or legal consequences. It is best to communicate these findings directly to senior management as soon as they are discovered, as the modeler has an ethical (and possibly legal) duty to report such findings to those in authority. However, care should be exercised because "killing" the bearer of bad news is a time-honored tradition in many companies.

An organization experiencing rapid growth represents a unique challenge to the business modeler. Young, growing companies tend to have very flexible procedures as well as a tendency to experiment with new business practices. As a result, there are few if any stable business processes that can be directly modeled. In these cases, it is best to study the core business drivers (e.g., business themes) and data (e.g., business objects). This approach will provide the company with a solid foundation when processes stabilize and can be automated.

Questions and Exercises

- Question #1:
  What services or products are provided by your company? Are you aware of your company vision statement?

- Question #2:
  What other kinds of context questions might be appropriate for specific businesses? How important are transportation concerns to a resort hotel? Why?

- Question #3:
  Consider a simple bank check deposit. How many steps are involved in performing a banking transaction? Are you sure? What about the clearing of the check and the transport of the physical check? What kinds of automated systems are involved? Is a cash transaction the same workflow or different? Why?

- Question #4:
  All of the workflows described in this chapter are shown with a single entry point into the workflow activities. Can you imagine a situation in which there are multiple entry points into a workflow?

- Question #5:
  A telephone call center operates with customer service representatives (CSR) taking orders on the behalf of a customer. Who is the business actor? (Hint: The CSR is a company-provided proxy for the customer.)

- Question #6:
  In moderate- and large-sized business, one business unit usually requires the services of another to complete a full business operation (e.g., order entry requires order fulfillment and accounting/billing). In these situations, does one group act as an external "actor" to another? How might this situation be modeled?

- Question #7:
  Domain models offer a very powerful mechanism for the capture and communication of significant business information. How might a domain model be used in a workflow reorganization effort? What about for system automation projects?

Exercise #1: Identification of Business Actors and Workers

Produce a list of workers and roles for your organization. As a starting point, consider your own job description: What tasks do you perform? Are these tasks associated with a single role? Capture a list of all of the business workflows that are your responsibility and assign these workflows to worker roles. Next, identify the business actors that are involved in the initiation or performance of these workflows. Remember that an actor includes any person or external software system that is involved in a business workflow. Consider how these workflows interact with one another and other workflows in the organization to complete a full business transaction.

Exercise #2: Business Workflow Modeling

Continue the previous exercise by detailing one of the listed workflows. Remember that all workflows have a defined start and one or more endpoints. Also, each activity must have at least one entry and exit transition as well as a guard condition (or decision point) for multiple exits. Mark all exceptional paths (e.g., those that are not considered "normal") and show how these conditions are resolved.

Exercise #3: Domain Modeling

Complete the exercises by creating a domain model for elements relevant to the workflows conducted for the business. Identify the business objects by looking for the enduring business themes involved in one or more workflows (Chapter 4). Detail these elements by adding attributes and relationships, particularly containment relations. Try to limit your model to a maximum of 10 elements.

References

[1] Pande, P.S. and Lawrence Holpp, *What is Six Sigma?*, 2001, New York: McGraw-Hill.
[2] Harry, M., *The Vision of Six Sigma* (8 volume set), 5th ed., 1997, Phoenix, AZ: Sigma Publishing Co.
[3] Advani, Suresh G. and E. Murat Sozer, *Process Modeling in Composites Manufacturing*, 2002, New York: Marcel Dekker.

Notes

1. You may notice that this description is very similar to that for use in case-based software development. Business cases are described in much the same way, but the focus is on business operations rather than a specific software system.
2. The Business Use Case is an extension of the core UML that is implemented slightly differently by different tools and vendors. As noted earlier, the style depicted here was developed by IBM-Rational as part of the RUP business model.
3. An example of time-critical handling would be a customer service call; the customer is waiting for help while the representative works other calls.

Chapter 9

Requirements Archaeology[1]

As a second example of system modeling, I will explore the recovery of legacy system requirements.[2] Because system requirements are at the heart of every meaningful system, it is of great importance to understand and maintain a complete set of requirements for every system the business creates. These requirements explain not only the behavior of the system but also provide insight into the minds of the system users who will ultimately benefit. Oftentimes, however, these requirements are either (a) partially captured in an informal or locally developed mechanism or (b) captured in the heads of the developers and the mystery that is code. Unfortunately for most development organizations either of these approaches ultimately leads to mistakes and added costs.

Although there are many kinds of systems that utilize requirements as part of their creation, requirements are of particular importance to the development of software systems. Given a software requirement set that is missing, incomplete, or inaccurate, there is a very high likelihood that the software in question will be fragile and expensive to maintain. Moreover, because the behavior of the software is not well defined, it is difficult or impossible to verify that the final system was built as intended. The addition of new functionality or behavior to the existing system complicates this issue until the system degenerates to a nonmaintainable state and needs to be replaced, rebuilt, or heavily refactored.

What is needed at this point is a more complete understanding of the original driving forces of the system: the behavior, states, data elements, and business rules. However, by the time a system has been in use for some time, much of this information has left the company via personnel change, or is only available from least desirable artifact remaining to the investigator: The Code.[3] In other words, there is a need for rediscovery of "lost" requirement "artifacts." Discovery of the system

Table 9-1 Legacy System Requirements Analytical Framework

Tools	Modeling Software, Word Processing, Requirements Management, Document Configuration Control, Code Analysis
Patterns	Requirement Engineering Patterns
Model Forms	UML Use Case, UML Activity
Techniques	Interviewing, System Execution, Document/Code Analysis
Organization	Use Cases, System Functional Dependency Graph
Skills	A firm grounding in the theory and practice of both Structured Requirement and Use Case based requirement analysis

Experience with research and cataloging of information

Experience leading small teams of engineer-investigators

Practice with presenting to, and facilitating for, small groups of business subject matter experts

Strong familiarity with UML modeling

Experience with the system programming language (optional, but it's always useful to speak the language of the "locals") |

requirements in this context is akin to an archaeological expedition into the deep past. Areas of investigation must be discovered; information sources interviewed and studied; a careful catalog of the available artifacts undertaken; interpretation of cryptic comments performed; and, finally, a picture of the software's story presented to the system stakeholders.

Preparation and Discovery

The prudent Requirements Archaeologist recognizes the need to acquire a few skills and supplies before embarking on an expedition into the Software Wilderness—preparation and forethought are the hallmarks of a successful venture. To this end, a well-prepared investigator should be competent in the following skills, as is noted in the Analytical Framework for Requirements Re-Engineering (Table 9-1).

Although it is possible to conduct a successful investigation lacking one or more of these skills or tools, having all of them at the investigator's disposal will result in a much higher probability of recapturing a full requirement set.

Surprisingly enough, requirements that require discovery are seldom left just lying about waiting to be found. Typically, they are deeply buried in legacy systems, legacy documentation, and legacy personnel. Before any attempt can be made to recover these lost artifacts, the potential location of useful information must be determined.

I have found that there are four primary sources of information about an existing software system (in order of information value):

- People
- Documentation
- Software Code
- Software Issue Tracking Reports

Each of these sources requires a different technique to sift through and recover meaningful descriptions of the software system. If a company has a defined requirement management team, then this is clearly an excellent place to start the investigation. Typically, these people will be titled "Business Analyst" or "Requirement Engineer," but they also may be members of product or project management, marketing, or even sales. In fact, anyone in the organization with a hand in determining system functionality will serve as a good source of information to discover and document the driving forces behind the original software.

Written documentation is a useful but occasionally misleading source of information. This is because many documents are not maintained and therefore tend to become obsolete rather quickly. In addition, this resource will be the most difficult to locate because a company that doesn't organize its requirements is unlikely to organize its documentation; critical system documents may only exist on local hard drives or difficult to access shared drives. Once collected, however, these historical records can serve as a good starting point for discussions and further investigation of system requirements.

The most accurate source of information on the system behavior is, of course, the software code itself.[4] However, some special skills are required to make use of this resource. In particular, the investigator should be familiar with the specific programming language(s) in use by the development team. This can range from assembly machine language, to C++, Java, or Visual Basic, to more specialized languages such as Perl and Fortran. Although proficiency in the specific programming language is very helpful for discovery of embedded requirements,[5] running and observing the application behavior will provide nearly as much information about the system's functional characteristics.

A company's issue tracking system (automated or not) often becomes the *de facto* repository of system requirements as enhancements are logged as system "fixes." If the investigative team is fortunate, reports can be run on issues logged as "ENH" or "Enhancement" or some other identifier that the "fix" was actually a new piece of functionality. If unlucky, then an extended excavation may be in order to locate requirements that are masquerading as system trouble tickets.

In addition to identifying sources of information, the environmental conditions of a system requirement investigation are also important. A company environment will be favorable, neutral, or hostile. The organization culture, market pressures, financial needs, and so on, will determine which of these situations is most likely to occur. A favorable situation is where the organization recognizes the need to reform the requirement process, and welcomes the investigator and his/her team. A neutral reception is one in which the local requirements team is "too busy" to be bothered with what the investigator is doing, but offers to help "when they get the time." A neutral environment will require a heavy reliance on independent study, as defined later. The final situation is a hostile environment where the senior management (in a fit of clarity perhaps) has decided that the current state of the system is desperate, and has called in the investigation team in an attempt to prevent total disaster. Needless to say, the local heroes will not look kindly on the efforts of the investigator. In this case, it will be difficult to establish a good relationship, as the team members will cooperate only under duress. However, even a hostile environment can be made productive once the initial negative reaction is reduced. The investigative team should focus on providing support and relief from delivery pressures to the affected requirement team members so as to foster goodwill and trust.

Investigation

Oftentimes, the principal investigator will work alone, sifting through the available materials to locate information of interest. Although this style of investigation may be the only one available in neutral or hostile site environments, there is a high probability of making an incorrect inference—that is to say, capture a requirement that was never actually implemented, or was later modified. I recommend that the investigation team work as collaboratively as possible with the existing development team. Most of the techniques detailed in this section are based on the availability of system experts, but a great deal of groundbreaking work can be performed before meeting with the system stakeholders. Although these steps need not be undertaken in any particular order, the order presented has proven to be effective in my experience.

Independent Study

A good starting place for investigation is a thorough review of all available documentation. Most organizations will have some form of documentation, even if it is not very accurate or complete. The investigation should start by reading and reviewing as much of this information as possible. Candidate requirements should be called out and recorded, preferably in a requirement management tool. Particular note should be made of exceptional handling (i.e., errors), as this is usually the last area for development and consequently the least well considered.

After the investigator has become familiar with the existing documentation, the next area to investigate is the application itself. For this, UML Activity Diagrams represent an excellent mechanism for rapidly capturing the system functionality and flows [1]. These diagrams are essentially, as a colleague once described them, flow charts on steroids. This is to say, they can be used to quickly capture a great deal of the existing system functionality in a clear, flow-based way. These models are rapidly created by exercising the application, either by the investigator alone or in conjunction with a system expert (such as an end-user or member of the testing team). If a system expert is available, a good approach is to allow the expert to use the application while the modeler records and/or diagram the user activity steps.

As the organization of the system behavior begins to emerge, it is likely some functionality will not have a corresponding set of requirements in the available documentation. Thus, the next step should include a review of the issue tracking reports. If the investigator is lucky, these will be organized by functional area via an issue tracking tool. In such a case, a report can be run on issues matching a particular functional area. System enhancements often masquerade as "fixes" and are therefore not captured within the legacy requirement documentation. Correct identification of these requirements usually requires a cross-reference against the documented feature requirements; which is a good reason why the existing documentation should be reviewed first! Note that there will likely be a chain of issue reports that chronicle the changes to a piece of functionality when the development staff uses the "trial-and-error" approach to software creation.

Requirements are frequently defined in e-mail conversation trails between product and system development groups. This represents yet another source of information on system requirements. If the e-mail system of the company is available (and records of messages are maintained), then the investigator can use this as an additional resource. Unfortunately, in companies that have poor documentation habits, there is little incentive to maintain a well organized e-mail repository.

A final task that can be accomplished by the independent investigator is to review the current source code base. Even if the investigator is not familiar with the coding language, there are often programmer comments that can be deciphered with references to issues (e.g., "Fixed BUG1403—01/03/2001"). The investigator can then request a programmer to review that section of code and report on the expected behavior. It is worthwhile noting that this technique may be the only way to find error conditions that are difficult to simulate and reproduce during the functional activity-modeling task described earlier.

The resourceful investigator can gain a good understanding of the existing system by using all of these approaches. Even a poorly documented legacy system will begin to divulge its secrets when approached with this form of systematic investigative technique.

Interviewing

In most organizations, a few key individuals maintain a great deal of the understanding of the system expected behavior. It is highly beneficial to engage these individuals in the discovery and extraction process.

As was noted in Chapter 5, individual interviews are typically conducted one-on-one and are best supported by the existing system documentation. The subject matter expert can validate the documentation and indicate areas of gaps or outdated information. Use of the diagrams created for the system functional flows is highly recommended for this process because these diagrams will highlight areas of the system that are not well defined, particularly the exception handling aspects of the system. Alternatively, the expert can walk through the application and comment on how and when each section of the system was established. Multiple interviews with experts are usually required to cover a reasonably complex software system. I referred the reader to Leffingwell et al., and Gause and Weinberg and references contained therein [2, 3] for additional information on solicitation of requirements using interviews.

As was also noted in Chapter 5, group sessions are an extension of the individual interviews and are usually best utilized to review updated documentation and other findings. These sessions will require the investigator to present her work and facilitate constructive review of the information. The use of a projector attached to a laptop computer is a particularly useful approach for display and direct capture of comments into the final documentation (see Chapter 13 for tips on model presentation). Experience has shown that this approach should be saved until a sizable portion of the system requirements have been rediscovered and documented.

A separate approach for unearthing system behavior is to use a facilitated Use Case Rediscovery session. In this session, the investigator will assist the team to rediscover the system use cases based on small focused teams in a multiday workshop. This approach provides a dual purpose; first, the requirements are captured and documented into use cases directly from the people who are closest to the system behavior. Second, this approach begins the process of teaching the team a good technique for capture, presentation, and maintenance of system requirements as a set of well-formed specifications.

Deciphering and Translation

After the capture of requirements comes the difficult but necessary task of deciphering and translation, as requirements are often captured using some form of functional decomposition technique. Although this common technique is useful for breaking a problem domain into manageable sections, it is often misused to dictate implementation details. This is because it is very difficult to interpret these collections of statements because they don't form a cohesive "story" about the system functionality. Even more common is capturing requirements as highly abstract business statements (e.g., "the system shall be intuitive and user-friendly"). Needless to say, performing this task will require diligent attention to detail and some form of context (such as a business vision document) that will provide guidance in piecing together the elements of system history.

Functional requirements represent the bulk of requirements for a user-intensive system. I often encounter legacy requirements that are formed by a collection of formal statements—typified by the classic "the system shall … " When translating these kinds of requirements, I often prefer to convert these statements to a more readable flow-based description (e.g., use case). I generally prefer to organize requirements with flows for several reasons. First, I have found that flow-based descriptions are more natural for people to understand and follow. It is easier to understand and remember a connected "story" than a series of stand-alone statements [8]. Second, I find that organizing the functionality in this manner directly supports two key areas of development, implementation and testing. Implementers can use the descriptions to code the basic logic flow, whereas testers can see all of the possible activity paths.

Because the traditional structured decomposition approach remains popular, I use this form for my example (see Appendix B for a complete translation example from structured declarations to use case flows and supplemental specifications). To translate structured declarative statements, look for phrases "the system shall present" or "the system shall display" to indicate requirements for user interaction. When a requirement begins with "the system shall perform," this is a good indication that the requirement is for a system-processing step. Any requirements that contain restrictions, such as "the system must respond within 60 seconds," are good candidates for overall system supplemental specifications, or as "special" requirements associated to a particular flow. Because decomposition by its very nature is hierarchical, this innate structure can help to indicate a separation of functionality. For example, if a requirement hierarchy is called "Stock Purchase and Reconciliation," this may represent a set of use cases around "Purchase Stock" and "Reconcile Accounts." Thus, an initial use case survey can be constructed from a primary grouping of similar functionality, or the structure of the requirement hierarchy itself. This provides a framework for tracing statements into functional flows.

Data descriptions are often found scattered about the documentation and code, and may contain more implementation detail than is appropriate for a requirements document. Examples of this can be seen when data dictionaries generated from database tables are placed into requirement documentation. Recalling from Chapter 6, setting the appropriate level of detail is the key to the creation of a good model; the details of primary/foreign key implementation and data types do not belong in a requirements description. The requirements are expected to describe the relationships between data elements and the restrictions on values that these elements can contain. For example, consider user activity audit trails:

Audit Trail:

- Date of Change
- Change Event (Refund, Pre-Paid Minutes, Bill Payment)
- Original Information
- Altered Information

- User Identifier (Lastname + Firstname + UserID)
- Supervisor Approval Indicator (Yes/No)

This approach describes the data elements at a level of abstraction that is more readily apparent to a business subject matter expert. They can see data relationships without being confused by implementation details that are better suited to a design document.

System business rules are often thought of using the abbreviation FURPS (functionality, usability, reliability, performance, supportability). These types of requirements are also found scattered throughout the legacy requirements documentation and should be reorganized into a set of nonfunctional requirements (i.e., supplemental requirements). Examples of these types of requirements include:

- Data Validation Rules
- Processing and Performance Restrictions
- Exception Handling
- External Systems Interfaces
- Security

The most logical place for these requirements is in system supplemental specifications [4]. These can be either directly associated with a particular use case, or created as global requirements for the full system.

Public Display

Once the original requirement base has been discovered and recreated, it is pointless to allow it to fall back into disuse. Thus, some method must be found for preservation and presentation of that knowledge to those needing to understand the system. The role of the software archaeologist doesn't stop once a system has been unearthed; it is also her responsibility to teach the individuals involved how to care for the system artifacts. To remain valuable, the requirements must be accurate, current, and presentable.

A requirements base is best maintained with the use of a suitable organizational tool. There are a number of excellent candidates including some that are relatively inexpensive. At a minimum, the features that should be present in any requirement management tool are the ability to record requested features, requirements (including use case scenarios), and supplementary documentation (e.g., glossary). There are a number of good papers and books on the topic of requirements management [2, 3, 5]. All of the discovered and created artifacts, including use case models, activity diagrams, and data dictionary information, should be controlled and maintained through such a documentation management system.

To ensure the continued maintenance of the requirement artifacts, a process of continuous training and development should be instituted for the requirement management team. This could include periodic attendance at industry conferences, consultants/trainers brought in to instruct new and existing personnel, or rewards to employees who seek out additional training and experience. At the time this book was written, there were no universally accepted certifications for requirement engineers.[6] However, many in the industry are attempting to build a body of knowledge that can be used for such certifications [6].

One of the greatest dangers after a requirement base has been reconstructed is the possibility of backsliding into the same problems that necessitated the reconstruction effort. By making the benefits of a stable, accurate requirements base clear—quality releases, faster development times, increased customer satisfaction—there is a higher likelihood that the requirements base will be maintained. Things to watch out for include inappropriate schedule pressures, changes to experienced personnel, funding cuts, rapid expansion of the system ("it's already built, so why bother to document"), and a drop in visibility (e.g., "hey it's working, let's forget about it!"). Constant vigilance is the price to be paid to prevent these pitfalls from destroying the team's hard-won work.

Summary

1. System requirements are essential for a well-constructed and maintainable system. However, because of personnel loss, schedule pressures, continuous enhancement, and other forces, the requirements for a legacy software system will become corrupted or lost over time.

2. When preparing to perform requirements "archaeology," the analysis team should be properly trained and provisioned with tools as described by the Analytical Framework for this task.

3. Recovery of system requirements requires the identification of likely sources of information:
   - People
   - Documentation
   - Software Code
   - Software Issue Tracking Reports

4. Interviews with existing personnel will provide the greatest benefit but at the highest cost. Prior review of existing documentation will reduce the overhead associated with becoming familiar with the project.

5. Documentation associated with legacy systems are an excellent and efficient mechanism to learn about system requirements, but they tend to be incomplete or inaccurate. The investigation teams should focus on confirming the documented information with the original authors (if available), or other knowledgeable sources prior to including the information in the newly recreated requirement set.

6. Code represents the least accessible of all information sources describing requirements. The use of analysis tools and profilers will be of great benefit when attempting to mine this resource for requirements information.

Of special interest will be error or exception handling, as these pathways are difficult or impossible to simulate via a testing procedure.

7. The issue tracking system will provide a great deal of information on incremental enhancements that have been added to the system over time. Rarely, these alterations are captured back into the original requirements documents. However, when utilizing this resource it is best to start as far back as possible and work forward as some functionality will be revised several times.

8. Investigations will be formed of a combination of individual study (e.g., documentation or code resources) and group settings (interviews, group reviews). The investigation team should be comprised of individuals skilled in both forms of research.

9. Structured requirements or general stakeholder request documents can be translated into flow-based descriptions using a systematic approach (as was described in Chapter 2). These requirements will be more accessible to stakeholders as they will tell a story of the system rather than simply being a set of disparate statements.

10. Business data and business rules are also vital to the requirement reengineering process and are often captured as part of the actual user flows (e.g., data elements) or as non-functional requirements (e.g., security, performance, etc.).

11. Public display of the requirement engineering process is an excellent way to gather support and approval for the team's efforts. The use case/activity diagrams can be posted in a conspicuous location to promote the team's progress and to provide a catalyst for hallway conversations. A requirement description is as important to the operating system as the performing code, but is far more difficult to maintain because there are few automated tools to support requirement generation or upkeep.

Tips and Traps

Justification for a requirements reengineering effort may be a difficult sell to management. This is especially true for legacy systems where it may seem like throwing good money after bad. However, there are several situations in which the expense is more than justified by the benefit. The first is for a full system migration to a new platform. The typical management comment is "make it do what it does now and add all of this new functionality while you're at it … " Unfortunately, without complete requirements this is more a guessing game than anything else. Handling of exceptional conditions (which may have been introduced over a long period of time as odd situations were encountered) will likely miss full coverage without some form of requirements archeology. The second situation occurs when the legacy system will continue to be maintained as is. The only way to reduce expenses in this case is to fully understand the impact that a change will have on existing functionality. The typical response is to ignore currently working code and graft new code on top. This approach, however, will eventually lead to a system that is excessively expensive to maintain—leading in turn to the first situation of a full replacement! Clearly, placing the full costs of these changes into monetary terms will be very convincing to management.

Questions and Exercises

▪ Question #1:
  Reengineering of requirements is an expensive undertaking; what are some reasons why a business would want to perform this task?

▪ Question #2:
  Four sources of information about software requirements are provided in the chapter. Are there others? What are they?

▪ Question #3:
  Which of the suggested approaches will have a greater chance of locating and documenting exceptional system behavior: test team interviews or code inspection? Why? When might this balance switch?

▪ Question #4:
  Team interviews are expensive in both time and money. Explain how a review of documentation reduces these costs.

▪ Question #5:
  Perl was suggested as a good code analysis tool because of this language's ability to be used for text searching based on repeated programming patterns (e.g., error handling). What other tools would be useful for this task?

▪ Question #6:
  How might you approach management with a proposal for creating or expanding a requirement engineering team? Would the following argument be of use?
  - Correct Requirements leads to a Correct System,
  - Correct System leads to Content Customers,
  - Content Customers leads to $$$,
  - therefore, Correct Requirements lead to $$$!

Exercise #1: Translation of Structured Requirements

Using the example provided in Appendix B as a guide, convert a set of your current system requirements into a use case form. If you already have use case-based requirements then review them for completeness. Be sure to note alternate and exceptional pathways through the requirement descriptions and highlight data element descriptions. Prepare a use case summary and present it to the development team/testing team for comments and critique.

References

[1] Lieberman, B., "UML Activity Diagrams: Versatile Roadmaps for Understanding System Behavior." *The Rational Edge,* 2001. April.

[2] Gause, D.C. and G.M. Weinberg, *Exploring Requirements: Quality before Design.* 1989, New York: Dorset House Publishing.

[3] Leffingwell, D. and D. Widrig, *Managing Software Requirements: A Unified Approach.* 2000, Boston, MA: Addison-Wesley.

[4] Kruchten, P., *The Rational Unified Process: An Introduction.* 2nd ed. 2000, Boston, MA: Addison-Wesley.

[5] Wilson, W.M., L.H. Rosenberg, and L.E. Hyatt, *Automated Analysis of Requirement Specifications.* ICSE 1997, pp. 161–170.

[6] Bourque, P., R. Dupuis, and A. Abran, *The Guide to the Software Engineering Body of Knowledge.* 1999, IEEE Transactions on Software Engineering.

[7] Eysenck, M., *Principles of Cognitive Psychology.* 2nd ed. Principles of Psychology, ed. M. Eysenck, S. Green, and N. Hays. 2001, Sussex, UK: Psychology Press.

[8] Lieberman, B., "Requirements Archaeology." *The Rational Edge,* 2002. November.

Notes

1. Much of the material in this chapter has been published previously in the IBM-Rational publication *The Rational Edge* [8].
2. Legacy systems are ones that are currently deployed into the business environment, as opposed to products under development. Although it is possible to consider the requirements analysis trailing the development effort for a new system, this is not a recommended best practice!
3. The code base I refer to here is the uncompiled source; on occasion, only the binary version is available, but reconstructing a system from disassembled code is not recommended because the symbols are usually obscured by the compiler.
4. One of my reviewers (Michael Chonoles) points out that even code is not always reliable—there are often areas of code that are no longer used, or represent outdated rules; consequently, the code base should be reviewed with the support of system experts.
5. I use the term "embedded" to refer to requirements that exist in no other location than the code base. This is often a result of direct communications between a specific developer and the client, where the functionality is included directly into the code base without review.
6. One of my reviewers, Tim Weilkiens, points out that there is a certification available in Europe (http://www.isqi.org/isqi/eng/cert/cre/).

Chapter 10

Modeling Software Architecture

For the final modeling example, I will review some critical aspects of software architecture modeling. There are few tasks more important to the success of a software development project than to ensure that the system architecture is well designed. This is for one simple reason—that which is well understood is more likely to be well done. For complex, highly involved systems, this can be a daunting task—especially for one person! For this reason, I recommend that the architecture modeling be broken out into sections and performed by different members of the development team. The system architect remains responsible for all system models but need not be the principal creator for every section of a software architecture model.

Modeling new or existing system architectures involves very similar content but utilizes slightly different approaches to access that information. For a new system, a top-down approach is often best starting with the Functional View and moving into the Static and Dynamic aspects of the system (see below). Alternatively, a middle-out approach is best for discovery of an existing system structure, which is quite similar to the approach described for requirements archaeology in the previous chapter; here the goal is discovery of "lost" system information.

In contrast to the previous two chapters, architecture modeling is focused on the technical solution to a problem rather than defining the problem itself. As such, the modeler is faced with the need to obtain and utilize a diverse set of tools (see Table 10-1). These tools are essential to efficiently investigate and synchronize model information with ongoing development efforts. Even for new systems, the formalization of the architecture into a model often lags behind code development. Thus, parts of the architectural model will need to be periodically synchronized with the development effort to stay current.[1] This can be a time-consuming task

Table 10-1   Software Architecture Modeling Analytical Framework

Tools	Modeling Software, Code Development IDE, Code Profiler, Software Architecture Document Template, Database Structure Investigation Tool
Patterns	System Design Patterns, Architecture Patterns, Data Storage Patterns, Software Deployment Patterns
Model Forms	Structural Models (e.g., UML Class, Function Call Map), Dynamic Models (e.g., Algorithm Charts, UML Sequence, UML State, UML Activity), Data Flow Charts, Database Entity Relationship Diagrams, Enterprise System Models
Skills	Programming Experience, Abstract Thinking, Critical Analysis, Organization/Categorization, Note-Taking
Techniques	Code Structure/Flow Analysis, System Behavior, Hardware Profiling
Organization	Functional Behavior, Component Dependency, Subsystem Dependency, Deployment Packaging

but has great benefits in reduced maintenance and training costs when the final system is delivered.

I tend to start my modeling effort by setting up a full development environment. At the very least, a complete copy of the most recent code base should be available for study. Some languages provide for automated generation of code documentation (such as JavaDoc and PerlDoc); a recent copy of such information should be obtained if available. Any and all development notes and records should also be gathered for inspection.

As noted in the Software Architecture Framework (Table 10-1), there are a number of tools available for code analysis. I have found that there are five tools that are indispensable to any development effort:

1. A Software Architecture Document template
2. UML modeling computer aided software engineering (CASE) tools
3. A Full-Featured Development IDE (integrated development environment), including pattern-based file search
4. Perl, Awk, Python, or other rapid scripting language for analysis of text files (i.e., code files).
5. Database structure and data schema viewer for systems using persisted data

The Software Architecture Document is the primary capture and presentation tool for software architecture. It is used to organize the many different aspects of a software system. These include the standard 4+1 views promoted by P. Kruchten [1], and other useful model views as suggested by Clements et al. [2].[2]

My architecture documents always begin with a discussion of Architectural Drivers and Constraints, which typically describe the nonfunctional requirements that the software system is expected to meet. This is done to set the context and goals for the architecture. Drivers are overall system goals, such as the ability to support any relational database, or operate at a certain level of concurrency. Constraints are imposed on the system, such as the need to deploy to a specific hardware platform. In short, Drivers describe what the system must do, whereas the Constraints are limitations on how the system may do it. The remaining sections of the document detail how the system resolves the Drivers and Constraints (e.g., Functional, Static, Dynamic, and Deployment Views).

Functional View (Requirements)

A software architecture document is primarily concerned with the system functionality that has the greatest impact on the overall software. This is functionality directly affecting the system design and technical risks. The modeler should be looking to find functional descriptions that require the most critical and/or highest number of architectural mechanisms be satisfied. *Architectural mechanisms* are part of the system infrastructure used to support specific system behavior. These include mechanisms such as Security, Transaction Management, Data Integrity, Performance, Scalability, Reliability, Error Recovery, Inter and Intra-System Communications, Persistence, Auditing/Logging, and overall System Usability. Such mechanisms may be indicated by interactions with external systems, security control, transaction integrity, or other such critical operations. Assuming an example system with use case scenarios describing a hypothetical Stock Trading system, a list of the required architectural mechanisms can be inferred (Table 10-2). Here it can be seen that the Manage Trade Order is an architecturally relevant use case, as it has interactions with external systems and utilizes complex mission critical processing (Figure 10-1). By contrast, the use cases for Manage User Account and Generate Trading Reports do not require these mechanisms and, thus, are not considered as architecturally relevant.

It is a useful exercise to create an UML activity diagram (or flowchart) showing the flow of each scenario contained in a particular architecturally relevant use case (Figure 10-2). This provides both the modeler and the reader with a detailed description of the expected system behavior described by the succeeding sections of the architecture document. As each system element's structure and behavior is described, a reference can be made to the specific use case scenario(s) being realized. In addition, the inclusion of this form of diagram rapidly illustrates the complexity of the use case and provides justification for inclusion in the architecture document.

Table 10-2 Architecturally Relevant Stock Trader Use Cases

Use Case	Architectural Mechanism
Manage Money Transaction	Transaction Management Automated Error Handling Auditing/Logging Communication Persistence Security
Manage Trade Order	Persistence Security Auditing/Logging
Maintain Trade Ticket	Persistence Security Auditing/Logging Communication Transaction Management
Manage Customer Account	Persistence
Generate Trading Reports	None

Static Structure View

The next model section is used to describe the logical and physical structure of the software. Logical structure usually includes a description of the components, subsystems, interfaces, design patterns, and frameworks that comprise the *static* aspect of the system. Typically, the static elements are diagrammed using a form of class or functional call diagram, package and subsystem dependency maps, network diagrams, data structure, and component descriptions. For system elements that have significant state, such as customer orders or inventory items, a state chart diagram may also be useful. However, as a state chart combines elements of dynamic and static behavior, such as events and object state, they often will be found in both the Static Structure View and the Dynamic View depending on the focus of the diagram. Figure 10-2 illustrates the dual nature of state charts by describing the changes in state for a mobile telephone headset.[3]

The static elements of the system that are appropriate for inclusion into the software architecture are somewhat subjective. Should the security mechanism be detailed even though it is provided as a service from the operating system? What about the logging mechanism? Which system components are relevant for description? These are nontrivial questions, as the choice of abstraction level is critical to a good architectural description.

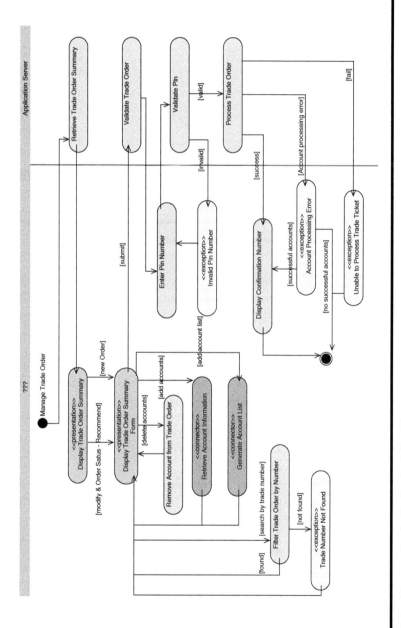

Figure 10-1   Manage Trade Order Activity Diagram

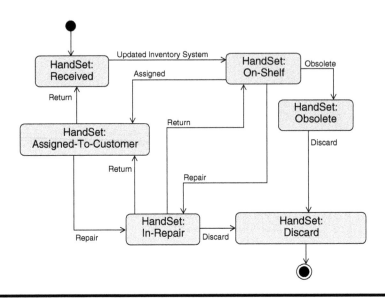

Figure 10-2 State Chart for Inventory Management

In general, the logical structure of the system can be described starting with the system layers. "Layering" represents the most common form of architecture, where the system is divided into separate areas of responsibility. A typical layered system will contain, at a minimum, the following four layers:

- Presentation Layer—responsible for the interaction with an external actor; this is usually in the form of a visual user interface for human users and a defined communication channel for automated systems.
- Business Logic Layer—contains the processing logic used by the system to provide functionality displayed by the presentation layer.
- Services Layer—provides the utility services and/or access to underlying operating system resources.
- Data Access Layer—primarily responsible for controlling access to data resources (e.g., database, network file share, Web services, etc.).

Each layer will provide functionality to other layer(s), usually in the form of dependencies between layers. For example, consider the layering structure in Figure 10-3. If a presentation layer element wishes to provide a lookup of a customer record then a call to the business layer will convert the external data view (say an HTTP post message) to the internal data view (data structure or object). The Business Layer components will then process the request using information acquired from the Data Access Layer and general utilities provided by the Services Layer. The modeler will need to determine which of the subsystems and components in each layer should be included in the software architecture document.

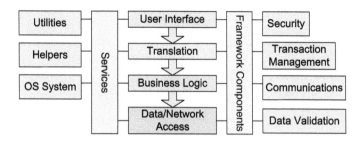

Figure 10-3   System Layer Structure

In addition to the primary system layers, there are often frameworks that are applied at each of the system levels. Such frameworks include logging, security, transaction management, inter-process communications, and so on. A summarized view of the prototypical system layer structure is shown in Figure 10-3. Framework elements often include:

- Transaction Management
- Security
- History Logging/Audit Trails
- Data Validation
- Data Access

Other frameworks may also be present for handling of events, interprocess messaging, common services registries (e.g., LDAP), or other such system services. The primary difference between a program layer and a framework is that frameworks are implementations of generic functionality, and may be employed on one or more system layers.

The next system description should be of all External Interfaces that are used by or presented to, third-party systems. These interfaces may take many forms ranging from Web services that are accessed via SOAP messages to highly specific, proprietary communication channels developed for legacy business systems.

The final static descriptions are based on the physical distribution of system functionality within each system layer. These are represented by the Subsystems and Components present in the system. Subsystems are differentiated from Components primarily in that a Subsystem provides a larger set of interfaces than does a component and will often contain components to provide implementation of the subsystem's services. For example, an Ordering subsystem may contain several components that handle inventory access, customer updates, billing access, and other order-related functions. Examples of a subsystem description and a typical class diagram for a specific system component are shown in Figure 10-4 and Figure 10-5.

Table 10-3 Example of System Communication Channels

Connector	Mechanism
RMI	Java Remote Method Invocation
SOAP/XML	Web-Service Registry
Socket/Byte Stream	Proprietary Data Transport
Socket/XML	Proprietary Data Transport
HTTP over TCP/IP	HTTP Web Access (ASP/JSP/CGI/etc.)
Java Applet	Java SDK
CORBA	IOR via Object Request Broker

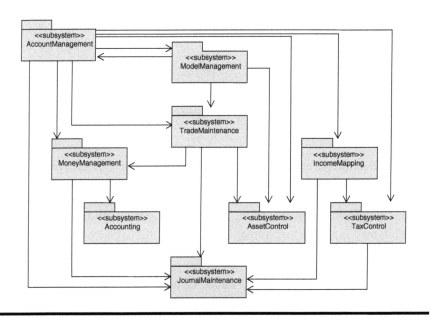

Figure 10-4 Trading Subsystem Dependency Map

Component View (Implementation View)

Logical code constructs (e.g., class, function, or other code structure) are realized into a physical system, most often using files. Dependencies between physical components are represented by build-time dependencies such as are found when a system requires linking with one or more pre-built libraries. These forms of physical dependency between files are often displayed using implementation diagrams such

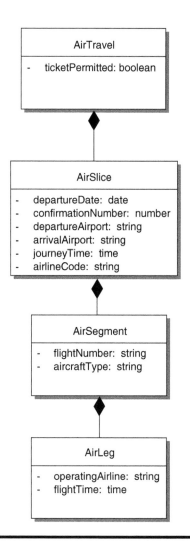

Figure 10-5   Core Air Travel Classes

as the one shown in Figure 10-6. This UML diagram view is based on the compile-time dependencies between physical system elements. In this figure, a C++ based component (where "header" files—.h—are used to define a class structure and "package bodies"—.cpp—describe the actual function calls) is described for the management of orders using two other classes to provide information about orders and customers that are stored in a data store (i.e., database). Dependencies stereotyped as "in-name-only" can be used to indicate where the compile-time dependency is only by-reference rather than by-value [4].

In addition to diagrams of the physical software realization, it is often useful to note the software configuration mechanisms. These may include property files, XML-based configuration settings, or database-driven system behavior. For example, many

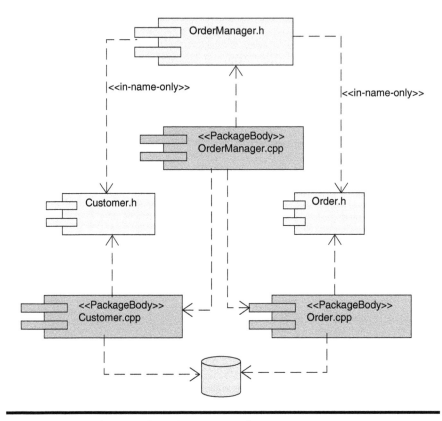

Figure 10-6 Implementation Diagram—Order Management Component

systems use configurable time-out settings on synchronous or asynchronous communication with external systems. These values may be provided to the application using one or more of the listed mechanisms. Each component of the system that uses configuration settings should be indicated in the software architecture document with a dependency listing for the particular setting name and location (e.g., a system properties file called "sys.config" with the property name of "channel_timeout").

Dynamic View

This section captures the *dynamic* interactions of the system; the interactions between key structural architectural elements to realize the architecturally relevant functionality. Most often, dynamic aspects are diagramed with some form of call sequence or object communication diagrams since the pivot of these model views is linear performance of tasks. Occasionally, flowcharts or activity diagrams may be used to describe system behavior, particularly when processing threads or other parallel processes exist [3]. As was noted earlier, state diagrams have a dual aspect that notes dynamic activity (events) and static information (state).

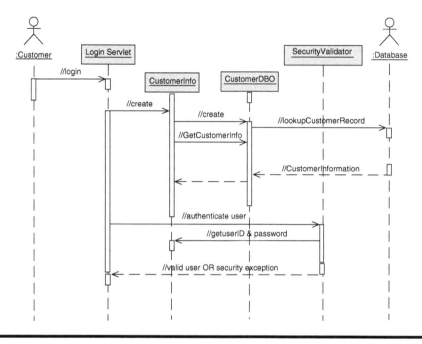

Figure 10-7 Sequence Diagram of a Standard Web-Based Authentication

For standard sequential processing, interaction diagrams are usually the best choice. Sequence diagrams (Figure 10-7) are best suited for illustrating the timing of interactions between system elements, whereas a communication diagram is useful for showing large numbers of interacting elements.

When a process is running multiple parallel threads, an Activity Diagram is currently the most useful UML model view.[4] Using the *swimlanes* provided by the model form to separate independent threads permits the modeler to show interactions between threads, such as messaging, synchronization, starting/stopping threads, and asynchronous operations. As shown in Figure 10-8, a Ticket Printing process controls one thread, PrintOutput to the physical printer. In this view, the process/thread idle state is indicated by the "idle" stereotype to show where the process/thread will stall waiting on a release event (arrival of a print request). Interactions between threads are shown by message objects being passed back and forth and error conditions, such as restarting a thread in the stopped state, are shown with the "exception" stereotype.

Deployment View

The deployment view is used to describe how the system will be installed in each of the key development environments:

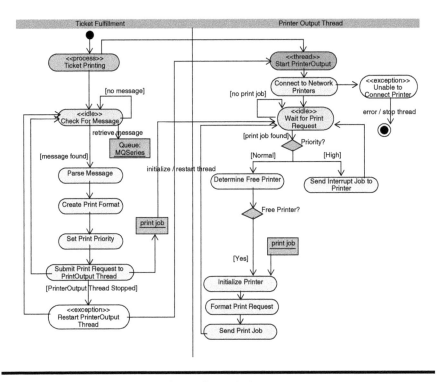

Figure 10-8   Process Diagram for Ticket Printing

- Production Environment—The final system that is provided to customers and end users
- User Acceptance—Used by system stakeholders to accept or reject a particular software release (i.e., before promotion to production)
- Testing Environment—Used by the Quality Assurance team to verify system compliance with defined requirements
- Development Environment—Software development environment for use by developers in system programming and unit testing

The description of each environment in the Deployment Plan will contain information on the servers, racks, power requirements, networking, gateways, data backup, failover support, monitoring, reporting, deployment scripts, and other production support information. In the Software Architecture Document, it is usually sufficient to illustrate the servers and networking connections because these are of most interest to those looking to gain an overview of the *software* system architecture.

Alternate Views

There are numerous other views that can be utilized in the construction of the Software Architecture Document, depending on the system under study. Clements et

Table 10-4   Alternate Architecture Views, from Clements et al. [2]

Module Views
Decomposition—Containment and Ownership
Generalization—Inheritance and Implements
Uses—Dependency between elements, interfaces, packages, etc.
Layered—Strict ordering of component usage
Component and Connector
Pipe & Filter—Data transformation
Shared Data—Multiple data accessors and persistence
Client/Server—Decoupled applications and services
Publish-Subscribe—Messaging between unknown recipients
Peer to Peer—Partition application by areas of collaboration
Communicating Process—Parallel system operations
Allocation Views
Deployment—Analysis of performance, reliability, security
Implementation—Indicates physical system components
Work Assignment—Allocation of system work loads

al. [2], suggest model-views for specialized system architectural components such as systems that are focused on data transformation (i.e., satellite transmission), interprocess communications, and parallel processing (see Table 10-1). These model-views have a more narrow focus than has been described in the other sections of this chapter. For example, the Publish-Subscribe view may be used to illustrate the transfer of messages based on message queues or topics. Alternatively, a Publish-Subscribe model-view can be used to describe the publication of code updates (e.g., Java Web Start).

The final view to consider is the application data repository. A large majority of business systems use some form of relational database system for data persistence. When documenting a database structure, the use of an entity-relationship diagram (ERD) is a very effective way to communicate database structure. Although this model-view form is not a formal part of the UML, it is well understood by many database administrators. The ERD diagram form illustrates tables, columns, data types, and primary/foreign key relationships between data elements. To support this architectural view, there are many tools that can "reverse-engineer" an existing database structure into a model so that the effort required to create these model-views are simplified. In some cases, it also may be useful to illustrate the creation of reports from multiple tables (e.g., data warehouse operations). Database dependent applications also may use some form of stored procedures or views to access the underlying database tables. For an architectural document, it is usually sufficient to note how this is being accomplished with a few examples. In my models, I usually show how the code performs a typical request mechanism (such as using system supported calls like ODBC), and how data is transferred and/or translated.

Clearly, the modeling of software architecture is a very complex task. It requires the architect to have a broad knowledge of the application and underlying system components, as well as understanding the needs of the system stakeholders. The system model I have described in this chapter would represent a very thorough investigation and documentation of a software system—which may be far more detail than is needed by the intended development audience! Remembering the Golden Rule of modeling from Chapter 1, "A model shall be as complex as necessary; no more or less," it may be that only a part of the described system model will be necessary to support the development of the system. Again, it is the modeler's responsibility to determine the appropriate level of model detail and content, based on the needs of the model's audience.

Summary

1. The job of documenting software system architecture is usually the responsibility of the Software Architect; the focus of this modeling effort is on the technical solution implemented to realize a set of software requirements.
2. The Software Architecture Analytical Framework describes the tools, techniques, and model forms available for investigation and creation of the Software Architecture Document.
3. A Software Architecture Document is composed of multiple sections (and views) that focus on the drivers, constraints, structural and dynamic aspects of the system. These sections also include a functional description of the *architecturally* relevant system requirements that are realized by the software architecture.
4. The Functional View is focused on a subset of system functionality to act as a guide to the architectural description. This functionality should focus on requirements that make heavy use of *architectural mechanisms*. These mechanisms include security, transaction management, communications, and other system-wide operations.
5. The Static View covers the *structural* aspects of the system. This is analogous to the interior support elements of a building and describes the functions, classes, components, subsystems, and interdependencies that are used to realize the architecturally relevant functionality.
6. The Dynamic View covers the *behavioral* view of the system. This is analogous to describing the moving parts of a machine, and describes the interactions between different system components during the execution of the system.
7. The Component View is used to describe the physical code constructs that implement the logical system design, which are frequently files on a file system. This view also can be used to describe the build environment including third-party libraries required for system function.

8. The Deployment View is focused on the assignment of system elements to servers that will host them. In addition, this view provides information on the physical environment used for the different system deployments (e.g., development, test, production, user acceptance).

9. Other views are available to describe specialized system architectural elements (such as client/server interactions or pipe/connector) used in addition to, or in place of other views. The Data Persistence mechanism is important for most systems and can be presented by using UML class diagrams, ERD diagrams, or other database-specific modeling forms.

Tips and Traps

Many of my system architecture documentation efforts have been done on legacy systems either to reduce maintenance costs or to determine if they are candidates for refactoring. This is because there are a larger number of existing systems compared to newly developed ones. In the case of a legacy system that is poorly documented, there are often additional system attributes that need to be discovered and noted in the model. Foremost of these are circular dependencies; circular dependencies arise when one component is dependent on another that is in turn dependent on the first (Component A → Component B → Component C → Component A). These code dependency chains are particularly bothersome with regards to maintenance because modifications have a "ripple-effect" across functionality that appears unrelated. It is valuable to document these situations where they arise and flag them for removal. Similarly, a proliferation of "long-distance" dependencies between unrelated components can lead to an application that is fragile for similar reasons—it is difficult to determine the impact of changes. Again, it is very valuable to note these kinds of dependencies where encountered as a first step toward refactoring the system.

Often during the modeling of a complex architecture, it is necessary to "walk" the code to determine system behavior and interactions. These behaviors can be very difficult to determine simply by reading the code, especially if object polymorphism is employed. In these cases it is helpful to have a tool that permits a stepwise execution of code (e.g., debugger) or a configurable tool that can capture calling-stacks (e.g., code profiler). As an inexpensive alternative the modeler can place trace log print statements at key points in the code (such as method invocations) to determine the actual calling paths during execution.

Questions and Exercises

■ Question #1:
Besides people, documentation, and system code what are some other sources of system design information?

■ Question #2:
The software architecture document is intended to capture requirements and designs that are "architecturally" relevant. By what criteria is this determined? What is the consequence of trying to describe the complete system rather than just a focus on the architecture? What is the difference?

■ Question #3:
When investigating system architecture design, of what importance is error handling? Logging? System performance audits?

■ Question #4:
Deployment has been included in this chapter. Is deployment really a part of the system architecture? Why?

■ Question #5:
Patterns are a very effective strategy for capture of design information; what kinds of patterns exist for the description of system architectures?

■ Question #6:
Name three groups in the development organization that would most likely need access to the software architecture description. How will they benefit from this information?

■ Question #7:
When, if ever, might test cases and scenarios be considered "architecturally relevant"?

Exercise #1: Framework Description

Frameworks are often found to be the foundation of robust systems. A reusable framework provides for an extensible system by establishing common well-tested mechanisms for recurring system problems. Examples of these benefits can be seen with regards to network communications, data store interactions, security, and transaction management. Examine a familiar system to identify all of the reusable frameworks that are in use. If you are unable to locate these frameworks, then consider when the system might benefit from the application of a reusable framework.

Exercise #2: Risk Analysis

Understanding risk is a critical skill for anyone modeling or designing software architecture. Consider all of the technical risks from a recent project—compile the list into risks that were addressed by design/technology decisions and those that were related to external influences. For the design risks, what trade-offs were made to mitigate those risks? Did these choices work? Create a pattern document to capture this information.

References

[1] Kruchten, P., *The 4+1 View Model of Architecture*. IEEE Software, 1995. 12(6): p. 42–50.
[2] Clements, P., et al., *Documenting Software Architectures*. 2003, Boston: Addison-Wesley.
[3] Lieberman, B., *Using* UML Activity Diagrams for the Process View. *The Rational Edge,* 2001. May.
[4] Lakos, J., *Large-Scale C++ Software Design*. 1996, Reading, MA: Addison-Wesley.

Notes

1. This is the so-called round-trip engineering, where a tool is used to "reverse-engineer" the code into a model, and/or generates code from a formal model.
2. Recall that a model view represents one part of the overall model, based on a central pivot (such as interactions between system components).
3. For those readers with a strong telecommunications background it should be noted that there are a number of additional states that have to do with activation and provisioning; these have been omitted for clarity.
4. UML 2.0 supports interaction diagrams with parallel processing and loops; see Appendix D for examples.

PRESENTATION

Chapter 11

Perception and Thinking

Perception refers to the ability for people to interpret the information that is provided by the five known senses of vision, hearing, touch, taste, and smell. Cognition is our ability to reason about the meaning of this information and apply previous experience to understand this sensory input. Together, these abilities allow us to recognize and apply information that is presented to us to move around our world, solve problems, and communicate with one another.

One of our primary sources of information is visual perception. It has been shown that humans are better able to reason about very complex problems when they are presented in an appropriate visual form [1]. However, finding that appropriate form is a challenge; it requires having an artist's eye and a teacher's wisdom. Psychologists have developed a theory of perception known as *Gestalt* (from the German word for "whole" or "pattern") that refers to our ability to perceive a pattern (*figure*) against a backdrop (*ground*) [2, 3]. These patterns must be either familiar to the viewer, or arranged in a manner that will evoke the intended response. Similarly, presenting familiar elements in an unfamiliar context, or in an unexpected way, will likely lead to confusion and misunderstanding. Consider the line elements in Figure 11-1; which of these two symmetrical arrangements of lines do you perceive as something familiar?[1]

Thus, the first consideration when modeling visually is whether your audience will *recognize* the symbols and their intended meaning. "Perceptual constancy"— that is, keeping each element's geometry constant—is key to ensuring understanding [2]. This is important because in our minds we map new shapes to previously learned ones. We also use *intuitive comprehension* to map model elements to real-life objects. Intuitive comprehension relies on the model viewers' common experience with the model creator to correctly infer the meaning of symbols. Road signs, for

Figure 11-1 Visual Recognition by Element Position, Adapted from [2]

Figure 11-2 "Intuitive" Traffic Signs

example, often use intuitive symbols to caution drivers about upcoming conditions or situations such as a picture of a mother and child indicating a pedestrian route (Figure 11-2); note how we assume the larger figure is female and not a kilt-wearing Scotsman. We use an image of a man digging to indicate construction ahead, or a leaping deer to warn that animals may dart across the road. Displays for computer operating systems rely heavily on metaphors for familiar objects to help control complex tasks. Diagramming software elements relies on an intuitive understanding of the symbology involved, especially when communicating between technical and nontechnical people (e.g., use case diagrams).

Gestalt Theory

Early in the 20th century, cognitive psychologists began to develop a theory of human perception known as Gestalt psychology. This approach was based on the ideas expressed by the early Gestaltist M. Wertheimer in his *Law of Prägnanz,* which states that psychological organization will always be as simple and as regular as conditions permit [4]. In other words, human perception is geared toward the simplest interpretation of a particular stimulus. Based on this principle, Koffka and his contemporaries developed a series of "laws" to describe human visual perception. Although other aspects of Gestalt theory have been discredited, the rules surrounding the description of perception and organization of objects has stood the test of time [5]. These principles will act as a guidepost for our later discussions on the visual presentation of model information.

Figure 11-3   Rubin's Vase/Profile Illusion [3]

The first principle, as was briefly noted earlier, concerns the importance of *Figure* and *Ground*. Here the idea is that people can only distinguish a figure based on the background on to which it is projected. The figure is considered "in front of" the ground, which is given lesser consideration. This principle has led to the development of a number of curious visual puzzles in which the figure and ground are interchanged.

In Figure 11-3 (first conceived by Rubin in 1915), the viewer is given the choice of seeing the black or white shapes as the figure against the opposing ground. This forms an image that can be interpreted as a vase (using the white as figure and black as ground) or as the silhouette of two faces looking at one another (using the black as figure and the white as ground). The image is identical, but our perception has changed. Strangely, it has been shown that an individual cannot see both images simultaneously; our perception moves back and forth between interpretations. Note also, as with to the first perception diagram (Figure 11-1), the removal of a few critical cues (such as altering the nose or mouth indent) will reduce the tendency to recognize the alternative silhouette. In system diagramming this effect can be seeing with the overcrowding of a diagram, especially if only outlines for elements are used (Figure 11-4).

In other cases, the perception of an image can be misinterpreted because of ambiguous visual clues. What do you see in the image depicted in Figure 11-5? Is this a picture of an old man with a large nose, or a young man looking over his left shoulder? Can you see both at the same time?

Again, our perception "mechanics" only permit one interpretation at a time depending on how we interpret the visual clues (such as the old man's nose becoming the young man's profile). When we "lock on" to a particular interpretation it becomes increasingly more difficult to reinterpret a particular image. When you first glanced at Figure 11-5, could you immediately see both interpretations, or did it take time to discover the "other" image? This observation has particular importance in diagramming because the use of icons will become associated with

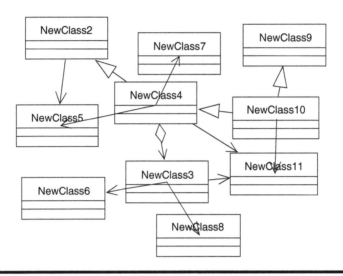

Figure 11-4   Overcrowding Confuses Figure and Ground

Figure 11-5   Is This a Picture of an Old Man or a Young One?

a particular interpretation (such as a code class represented as [class]), so that use of these icons in a different manner will lead to the potential for confusion and misinterpretation. As was noted earlier, people often associate the first interpretation of an icon with a particular mental model such that later occurrences of the icon are initially assumed to mean the same thing, even in an a completely different context; this is an example of the Gestalt Law of Past Experience.

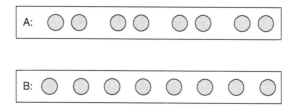

Figure 11-6   Principle of Proximity

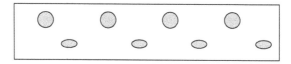

Figure 11-7   Principle of Similarity

There are seven Gestalt grouping principles but only four in addition to the ideas of *Figure and Ground* are of interest in most diagramming. These are the *Principle of Proximity*, the *Principle of Similarity*, the *Principle of Past Experience*, and the *Principle of Closure*. The Principle of Proximity states that elements that are close together (i.e., proximal) will be associated into groups. In Figure 11-6, the top section shows a series of dots that will be associated into four groups of two, whereas a very similar set in the bottom series loses this grouping with the slight movement of four of the elements.

In diagramming, this translates to the ability to infer element association in the model view simply by placing related elements closer together compared to other elements. This will be further discussed in Chapter 12 on diagram balance and composition. The point here is to be aware that simply by placing elements close to one another the viewer will draw a logical association between them, whether one exists or not!

The second Gestalt principle of interest is the Principle of Similarity, which states that "like bands together." Thus, elements of similar shape, size, color, and so on will be perceived as part of the same group. This is illustrated in Figure 11-7, in which the diagram has a well-defined "top" row and "bottom" row. For most diagrams, this principle is less important than the Principle of Proximity, but the combination of these two principles can be effectively used (or misused) to provide subtle emphasis.

We have already encountered the Principle of Past Experience in our discussion on icon recognition. This principle states that if a perceived combination of elements matches a previously encountered pattern then that pattern is preferred. This can be seen in Figure 11-8, in which recognition of letter form is affected by placement into familiar or unfamiliar arrangements.

In a model view, this principle applies to the constancy of shape, size, and color. Once a particular icon symbol has been defined, it is best to maintain that icon

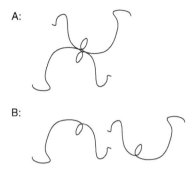

Figure 11-8 Principle of Past Experience (adapted from Wertheimer, [4]), Letter Recognition (M and W)

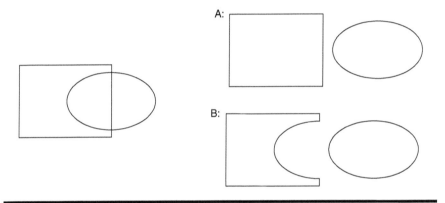

Figure 11-9 Principle of Closure—(A) Is Preferred Over (B)

position and shape throughout all views that utilize that element. This invariance is of great aid to the viewer because it reduces the need to "reacquire" the iconic meaning each time the element is countered.

The Principle of Closure (Figure 11-9) states that overlapping objects will be perceived as simple, complete objects rather than broken shapes. This is important in diagramming because perceived elements are preferred as uniform closed shapes rather than open, irregular shapes.

The Gestalt principles will be encountered frequently as we move into a detailed discussion of diagram balance, composition, and shading. Awareness of these effects will greatly improve the probability that the modeler's message will be accurately conveyed to the audience.

Diagrammatic Reasoning

The graphical display of model information is a strong aid to reasoning about complex problems. As far back as Plato the importance of a subject's ειδοσ (*eidos*), or

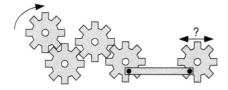

Figure 11-10   Mental Visualization—In Which Direction Will the Rightmost Gear Turn?

essential characteristics, was debated as a basis for reasoning about that subject [6]. In particular, categorization is based on the similarities and differences between subjects. Categories are frequently used in the analysis of complex topics as they allow for the segmentation of a problem domain into more manageable sections. In turn, categorization is aided by visualization as presented by model diagrams.

For many kinds of reasoning, written language is not required and may even disrupt the reasoning process. Such is the case when a baseball player moves to catch a ball in flight [7]. Instead of the player performing complex two-body gravitational calculations, she uses visual targeting cues to adjust speed and direction of approach to where the ball will land. Other areas of reasoning are also better served by visual display than by textual description. Consider the problem shown in Figure 11-10; how do you go about determining the answer? Most people will perform a visual scan of the diagram, and then mentally manipulate the diagram elements; here, by rotating the gears.[2] A textual description would make the problem much more difficult to solve.

Many mathematical proofs are also presented graphically, especially with geometric proofs. One of the most famous of these is the Euclid's proof of the Pythagorean Theorem, $c^2 = a^2 + b^2$ (Figure 11-11). Here, the elegance of showing that the sum of half the squares of the sides equals half the square of the hypotenuse is clearly shown by the visual diagram, and permits an almost intuitive grasp of this fundamental but complex principle of geometry.

The point here is not only to use diagrams to communicate information but that *well-formed* diagrams are far more effective in presenting that information. To paraphrase Tufte, a well-formed diagram is one that provides a maximum amount of information with a minimum of display [8]. In order to be of aid, the diagram should contain only enough information to provide guidance without adding any unnecessary clutter. One of the cardinal sins of diagramming is not including too little detail; it is including too much. So, for a diagram to be useful as a reasoning tool, it must be properly conceived and formed.

There are four principal ways that diagrams act to aid reasoning [9]:

■ Information Input
  Diagrams form an analogue for a physical problem and reduce the "cognitive" load required for solution by assigning data elements special dimensions (Figure 11-12)

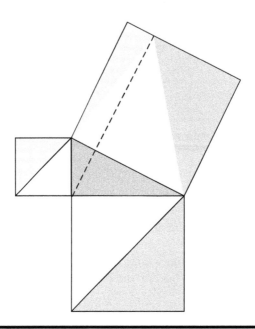

Figure 11-11   Euclid's Half-Area Proof for the Pythagorean Theorem[3]

- Mental Manipulation
  Envisioning a physical process permits using mental manipulation of the problem domain. This form of "animation" facilitates the discovery of critical interacting elements (consider Figure 11-10)

- Verbalization from Diagrams
  By performing a "gaze tour" of an image, aspects of problem domain relationships can be captured and processed using far less mental resources than textual descriptions. This may support either deductive or inductive reasoning

- Reasoning by Metaphor
  Analogical reasoning that is embodied in experience is aided by casting model elements into discrete diagram elements that mimic a previously encountered solution

It is of note that the three formal reasoning forms (deductive, inductive, and analogical) are all supported by visual representations. The last of the listed principal mechanisms, analogical (or reasoning by metaphor) is particularly useful as it enables our innate ability to infer relationships by analogy to previously encountered problems. The closer we can map an existing problem to a previously solved one, the better chance we can reuse the previous solution [1, 10]. This is because we rely heavily on our previous experiences to guide us in interpretation of newly encountered events.

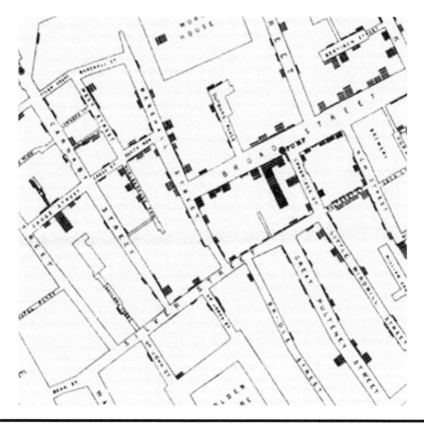

Figure 11-12   Dr. Snow's Map of London, Adapted from [13]

In addition to analogical reasoning, we also use *deductive* and *inductive* reasoning. Deductive reasoning is a powerful technique for evaluating the strength of an argument or hypothesis. A deductive argument takes the form of "if a is true, b is true, and if a and b support c then c is true." This is a form of *modus ponens,* in which the premise 'a' and 'b' are used to affirm the conclusion 'c' [11]. Diagrams are frequently useful in this form of analysis, as was shown in the formal geometric proof given earlier. An impressive example of the support diagrams play in deductive reasoning is shown with the example presented by E. Tufte of Dr. John Snow's research into the London cholera epidemic of 1854 [12] (Figure 11-12). Dr. Snow hypothesized that there was a relationship between the outbreak of disease and a physical location in the city. He proceeded to consider this multivariate problem by noting the location of sick individuals, the movement of people around the city at different times of day, and the sources of drinking water (cholera is a waterborne disease). By graphing this information against a map of the city, he was able to deduce that a particular water station was a focal point for the spread of disease. He ordered the replacement of a water pump handle (Broad Street) and noted the rapid drop in disease occurrence.

However, the power of visual deduction is so strongly influenced by the Gestalt principles that when Dr. Snow's data was replotted against a different geographical separation the apparent visual relationship between the Broad Street pump and disease incidence was lost [12]. Thus, although visual representation of model information is powerful for reasoning about complex topics, it is very easy to be misled into a false conclusion based on the apparent relationships between visualized data elements.

The final reasoning technique aided by visual representation of information is inductive reasoning. Inductive reasoning is the process by which a collection of specific observations is used to make a more general statement about a category. For example, consider the following statements: "Zebras like to eat cantaloupe; tigers like to eat zebras and cantaloupe; therefore, animals like to eat cantaloupe." Here, the two concrete statements about specific animals are expanded to the general category of all animals. Clearly, these two statements are insufficient to support the induction; a larger sampling size is required. However, the ability to generalize from the specific to the abstract is a critical skill for modeling. Diagrams are very useful in this regard, because model elements that share characteristics can be visualized together to show important areas of overlap.

In the chapters that follow, the principles of Gestalt psychology, as well as other elements of cognitive psychology involving perception, memory, and reasoning, will be reviewed as we discuss the construction and presentation of model diagrams and views.

Summary

1. Visual perception is a primary source of information for most people. It is often easier to reason about complex topics once they are cast into visual form.
2. Recognition of an image or icon is determined by the interplay of *figure* and *ground,* such that a familiar arrangement of elements will be preferred over an unfamiliar one. This is the basis for the intuitive comprehension of icons.
3. Perception of images (figures) is affected by the first interpretation reached by the observer such that additional reinterpretations are more difficult. This is an example of the idea that you only get one chance to make a first impression—so make the right one!
4. The core principle of Gestalt psychology, with regard to perception, is the Law of Prägnanz or that "simplest is best." This has led to the development of the Gestalt Factors of perception. In particular, the Laws of Proximity, Similarity, Past Experience, and Closure have a large impact on the recognition of groups of elements in diagrams.
5. There are three primary types of reasoning, *analogical, inductive,* and *deductive.* Analogical reasoning involves the ability to recognize a current problem is related to one previously encountered one. Inductive reasoning provides

the ability to infer a wider relationship based on a set of related observations. Deductive reasoning permits a narrowing of scope to determine the truth of a particular idea based on other supporting ideas.

6. Diagrams are particularly useful for analogical reasoning because visual metaphors have a very powerful ability to illustrate key relationships between problem elements.

7. Deductive reasoning is well supported by diagrams, as was shown by the careful analysis of cholera illness patterns to determine the likely cause.

Tips and Traps

A frequent problem encountered during the creation of diagrams is the tendency to either include too much information (leading to overcrowded diagrams) or too little information (leading to gaps). To combat these tendencies, try to ask the following questions when creating diagrams:

- Is the view based on a single organizing pivot?
- Are all of the elements related (i.e., cohesive)?
- Does the view tell an effective story without elaboration?
- What assumptions have been made with regard to the expected audience?
- Can the diagram be split to reduce complexity without destroying the overall message?

Questions and Exercises

- Question #1:
  Creating universally understood icons for public spaces has proven to be a difficult undertaking. Why are visual symbols for common activities so varied?

- Question #2:
  Wertheimer and other Gestaltists hold that the simplest explanation for a set of observations is preferred. How is this reconciled with the tendency for software systems to increase in complexity? Does this point have any bearing on design trade-offs?

- Question #3:
  Recognition of elements in a visual field is affected by cues that trigger image retention (recall the children's magazine *Highlights* from Chapter 1 where the common shapes are hidden within pictures). How might this point affect the layout of large diagrams?

■ Question #4:
The remaining Gestalt principles are the Factor of Uniform Destiny (common fate), the Factor of Objective Set (ambiguous arrangements focus into sets), and Factor of Direction (common directions are grouped). Are there areas in model or diagram construction where knowledge of these principles might be effective?

■ Question #5:
Visualization of complex problems, such as in mathematics or the sciences, is a powerful mechanism for reasoning. What other forms of problems are more easily solved by visualization?

■ Question #6:
Inductive reasoning is a less powerful technique for gaining knowledge because inductive conclusions cannot be "proven." Do you agree with this statement? If so, how useful are "hunches"? Can deduction be used in all cases? Why?

■ Question #7:
Other than Venn diagrams, can you think of diagram forms that will aid inductive thinking?

Exercise #1: Iconic Representations

Create a set of visual icons to represent the following areas:

■ Golf Course Crossing
■ Bird Nesting Area
■ Low Wake Zone (boating)
■ High Explosives

What metaphors did you use? Why? Now repeat the exercise, but now create auditory "icons" for the same representations. How was this different from the visual task?

References

[1] Eysenck, M., *Principles of Cognitive Psychology*. 2nd ed. Principles of Psychology, ed. M. Eysenck, S. Green, and N. Hays. 2001, Sussex, UK: Psychology Press.
[2] Massironi, M., *The psychology of graphic images*. 2002, London: Lawrence Erlbaum Associates.

[3] Rubin, E., *Figure and Ground,* in *Readings in Perception,* D. Beardslee and M. Wertheimer, Editors. (1915/1958), Princeton, NJ: Van Nostrand. p. 194–203.

[4] Wertheimer, M., *Laws of Organization in Perceptual Forms,* in *A Source Book of Gestalt Psychology,* W. Ellis, Editor. 1969, Routledge & Keegan Paul: London, UK. pp. 71–88.

[5] Rock, J. and S. Palmer, The Legacy of Gestalt Psychology. *Scientific American,* 1990. December: pp. 48–61.

[6] Grube, G., *Plato's Thought.* 1980, Indianapolis, IN: Hackett.

[7] McBeath, M., D. Shaffer, and M. Kaiser, *How baseball outfielders determine where to run to catch fly balls.* Science, 1995. 268(5210): pp. 569–573.

[8] Tufte, E.R., *Envisioning Information.* 1990, New York: Graphics Press.

[9] Blackwell, A., *Psychological perspectives on diagrams and their users,* in *Diagrammatic representation and reasoning,* M. Anderson, B. Myer, and P. Oliver, Editors. 2000, London: Springer.

[10] Kellog, R., *Cognitive Psychology.* 1995, Thousand Oaks, CA: Sage Publishing.

[11] Kelley, D., *The Art of Reasoning.* 1988, New York: W.W. Norton.

[12] Tufte, E.R., *Visual Explanations.* 1997, Cheshire, CT: Graphic Press.

[13] Snow, J., *On the Mode of Communication of Cholera.* 1854, London: C.F. Cheffins.

Notes

1. Readers with a background in electrical engineering may recognize the right-hand diagram as the wiring symbol for a battery!

2. As a side note, the gear will rotate counterclockwise.

3. Please see http://www.cut-the-knot.org/pythagoras/index.shtml for more visual proofs of this and other theorems.

Chapter 12

Composition[1]

A superior model is not only correct and complete, it should also be aesthetically pleasing to the audience, otherwise it risks being underutilized or ignored. Aesthetics in diagramming is more than creating a pretty picture; it is about creating effective views of a model. Unlike some abstract art forms, model diagramming is intended to provide a maximum level of clarity so that the modeler can accurately project his/her understanding to the intended audience. The more attention you pay to placement, size, color, balance, and the overall composition of diagram elements, the more likely your intended audience will retain the model information.

The construction of a useful, informative, and aesthetically pleasing diagram requires a great deal of attention to detail. It is not enough to simply "generate" a good diagram automatically from the underlying model, irrespective of the claims of tool makers. The presentation of model information must be carefully considered, with attention paid to the purpose of the model and the sophistication of the intended audience. Although there are a number of useful guidelines that will be detailed in this and the next chapter, there is no substitute for the considered judgment of the modeler. Thus, the art of model presentation is represented both as an intellectual endeavor and an exercise in aesthetic sensitivity.

Diagram creation begins, as was noted in Chapter 4, with the selection of a model form. The form of the model will dictate the model elements that will be included in the model view. For example, a UML model form will require specific semantics and notation. Other model forms, such as music notation, will require other notation and model elements (e.g., notes represented as dots with flags or connecting lines). Given a set of model view elements, the next consideration is the form of these elements; the contours of shapes and lines associating one with another, the balance of elements within the diagram, and the judicious use of emphasis to draw the attention of the model viewer.

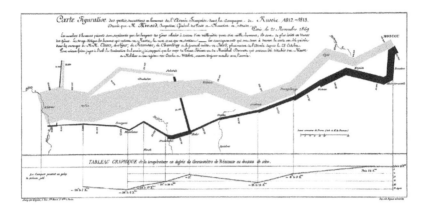

Figure 12-1   Napoleon's March to Moscow, by C. Minard (from [1, 2])

One of the finest examples of a model view is shown in Figure 12-1, which shows Charles Minard's famous graphic depicting Napoleon Bonaparte's march to Moscow in the 1812–1813 campaign. This amazing model view shows six critical pieces of information about the march itself: army size, geographic position (latitude and longitude), ambient temperature during the retreat, distance/direction traveled, and the effect of crossing points at rivers. Without knowing much else about Napoleon's disastrous campaign, it is clear from even a brief study of this model that attacking the Russian capital city in the middle of winter was a questionable strategic decision. Graphic models such as this illustrate the elegance and simplicity that are at the heart of all truly exceptional models.

Line and Contour

Lines are critical elements of many diagrams. In Minard's graphic, the width of the army's line is used to immediately convey critical information on troop size. This is also true for system models, such as UML-based diagrams, in which lines represent a variety of relationships between elements. For example, typical class diagrams have two primary line forms (solid — vs. dotted ---) and multiple line endings (open arrows for generalization ——▷, plain solid lines for associations ←, diamonds adorning one line-end to indicate aggregation ◇—— , etc.). Because each variation has a specific meaning, line forms must be chosen carefully. For example, *relationship lines* should be of equal weight and match the weight of the surrounding lines for solid objects. Relationship lines of unequal weight will confuse viewers and may incorrectly suggest greater importance for objects connected by heavier lines. In addition, if the element lines are too heavy, they will overwhelm the relationship lines and make the overall diagram much more difficult to understand, as in Figure 12-2.

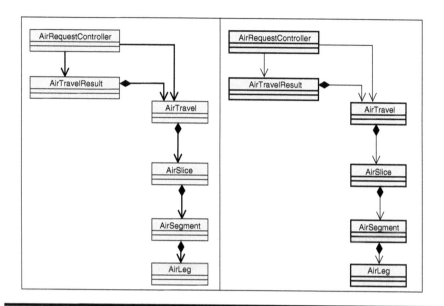

Figure 12-2 Mismatched Line Weights

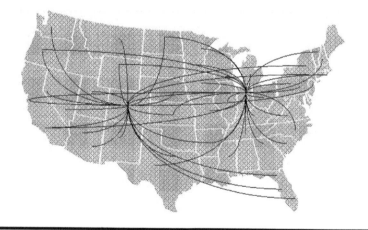

Figure 12-3 Flight Chart for a Fictitious Airline with Two Hub Airports

This leads to the first guideline regarding the creation of visual diagrams:

> Rule #1—Line widths should be only as wide as necessary for visual distinction

In addition to line weight, there are five other characteristics of lines that are of interest to our discussion. These are the characteristics of length, angle, color, style, and crossing points. The length of a line is a direct consequence of the distance between connected elements of the diagram—a fairly obvious point. Yet many diagrams are created where there is a proliferation of long crossing lines that resemble the strands of a spider web. Consequently, these long association lines cause confusion as the viewer attempts to trace the relationships from one element to another (recall from Chapter 11 that one of the primary values of a diagram is the ability to conduct a visual tour of the elements). Consider a typical diagram used to represent the flight routes for a large airline, as represented in Figure 12-3.

The visual "noise" caused by multiple overlapping lines obscures the ability to easily trace the flight paths. In fact, such a representation is only useful for emphasizing that the airline is focused around two hub cities, rather than providing the ability to trace any particular route. Thus, taking into account the need to limit these visual artifacts, and recalling the gestalt principle of proximity (place related or associated items near one another), suggests a second guideline:

> Rule #2—Line length should be minimized by placing linked elements in close proximity (where possible)

As will be seen with all of these rules, this one can be violated for good cause—such as showing that a particular element has many dependencies (Figure 12-4).

The next characteristic concerns the angles formed when two line segments meet in a diagram. This occurs when there is a need to route a line around an intervening element (it is *always* bad practice to cross an element with a line; the gestalt principle of closure states that an element crossed with a line may be perceived as two collocated elements—see later). When you have the option, it is preferred to use *rectilinear* lines—where the line ends meet in a 90-degree angle. This is opposed to an *oblique* line where the line ends may meet at any angle. The same holds for the intersection of a line and a diagram element. The meeting point should form a 90-degree angle whenever possible. This guideline is driven by the cognitive sensitivity to regularity of form and edges. Lines that are oblique tend to form a "web-like" appearance that can be distracting from the relationships being represented. Rectilinear lines also tend to seem neater and more regular, as illustrated in Figure 12-5.

This leads to:

> Rule #3—Rectilinear lines are preferred over oblique lines (wherever possible)

Again, a good reason to violate this rule is if the presentation is intended to show elements related to a specific central element (otherwise known as radial presentation, Figure 12-6).

When routing lines around other elements, always try to use a minimum of junction points, and avoid placing a line too close to a contour. This enhances the differentiation between an element's edge and the line, as well as ensuring a minimum of visual disruption. In the case of Figure 12-7, the simplification of

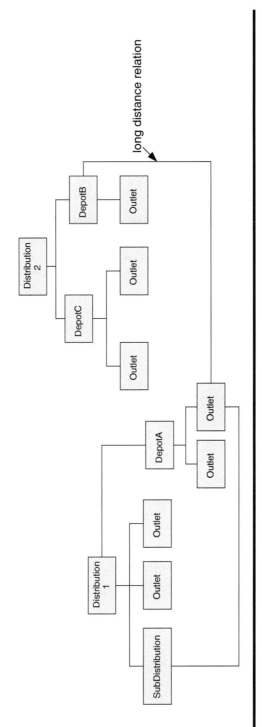

Figure 12-4 Illustrating Long Distance Dependencies

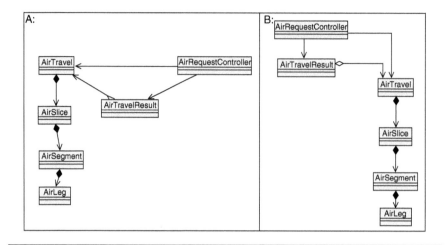

Figure 12-5 Oblique (A) vs. Rectilinear Lines (B)

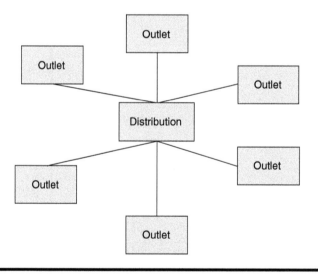

Figure 12-6 Radial Placement of Elements with Oblique Lines

the routing would be from the right side of the Depot to the bottom of the second Distribution object. Rearrangement or duplication of elements often will eliminate the need for long, twisting connection lines.

> Rule #4—Use a minimum of angles for rerouting; avoid tracing an element's edge closely

Line style is the next characteristic of interest. Line style is often dictated by the model form (as is the case for UML diagrams). However, when a choice is available,

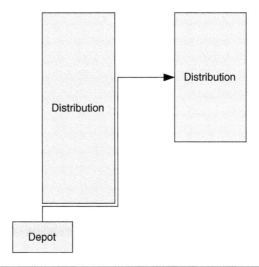

Figure 12-7   Avoid Close Tracing Around Diagram Elements

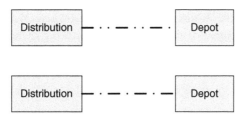

Figure 12-8   Use of Similar Line Styles Is to be Avoided

a solid line is preferred to a broken line (gestalt principle of closure). In particular, avoid using similar line styles to convey different information.

Line and contour color will be considered later, but a few key points can be made now; light colors and all shades of blue are to be avoided. It is difficult for the eye to distinguish blue edges, and light colors tend to blend with light backgrounds (most printed diagrams are on white paper). A black line on a white background will have the greatest contrast and is usually preferred. Regardless of the color selection, only use a limited number of color choices (or gray shades) for diagram lines to avoid a "pickup sticks" effect (Figure 12-9).

> Rule #6—Use black on white lines for maximum contrast; avoid multicolored (shaded) lines in diagrams

The final rule on lines concerns the inevitable times when lines must cross in a diagram. The rule here is quite simple:

> Rule #7—Avoid crossing lines

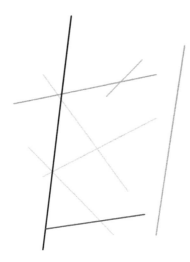

Figure 12-9   Avoid Multishaded Lines in Diagrams

Crossed lines are difficult or impossible to trace by eye. They frequently can be avoided by rearrangement of elements or by duplicating elements that lie at a distance from one another (consider Rule #1). In the rare case in which lines must cross, it is best that they cross at a right angle (Rule #3) and use a "jumper" if available (similar to electrical diagrams to indicate that a circuit is not connected to the crossing line).

Contour is where lines are used to create diagram shapes. The same rules apply to contour as to regular lines (e.g., weight, style, angle, crossings, etc.), with the exception that shapes have the additional property of an interior space that can be colored (shaded) independently of the contour. The actual shapes formed by contour lines are often dictated by the model form, but there is usually some latitude with regard to the size and proportion of diagram elements. This will be the concern of the next section on diagram *balance*.

Visual Balance

A model diagram often contains multiple objects in the same view. For example, in a UML class or communication diagram these objects are boxes; in an activity or state diagram the boxes have rounded corners; in a sequence diagram the boxes have lines emerging from the bottom, and so forth. Most UML tools allow you to resize each of these multiple objects, based on the text or other information displayed within the object box (e.g., class methods/attributes). *Scale* refers to the overall diagram size, and *proportion* refers to the relative size of each diagram element. Both the overall scale and the proportion of each element must be balanced in order to achieve a visually pleasing display.

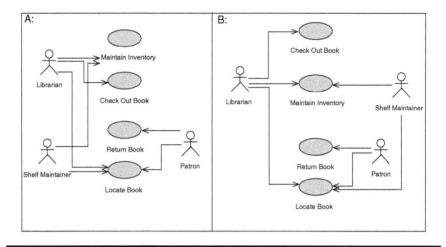

Figure 12-10 Crossed Lines Avoided by Rearrangement

Figure 12-11 Golden Mean Example—Nautilus Shell

The most important rule of proportion is the *golden mean,* which is a ratio of approximately 1:1.62.[2] The ancient Greeks discovered that many natural objects, such as pine cones, flowers, and animal shells, are constructed according to this proportion (for example consider the nautilus shell in Figure 12-11—the ratio between successive segments approximates the golden mean[3]); it is often what we have in mind when we say that something is "well balanced."

For diagramming, this value (1:1.62) is most useful when creating quadrilateral objects (e.g., rectangular or oblong), like those found in all UML diagrams. In Figure 12-12, the activity diagram on the left has elements of all different sizes, even though the tool maintains the same relative shape (a UML activity icon). In the diagram on the right, each element has been resized to a proportion roughly equivalent to the golden mean. The reader is encouraged to decide which approach is more aesthetically pleasing.

> Rule #8: Use the golden mean (1:1.62) when creating rectangular or oblong diagram elements

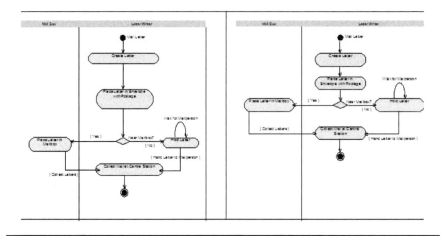

Figure 12-12   Activity Diagrams with Elements of Different Sizes (Left) and Uniformly Sized Elements Based on the Golden Mean (Right)

As noted in the previous chapter, the human eye is very sensitive to changes in shape and contour. As a result, differences in the size of elements tend to distract viewers from the content of a diagram. Uniform sizing of elements or groups of elements reduces this visual tension and allows viewers to concentrate on the model's content rather than on presentation details.

With respect to diagrams, the term *balance* refers to element layout. In most cases, it is desirable for the diagram to be symmetrically balanced vertically and horizontally (see Figure 12-13). This means that as many elements should be on the right side as on the left, and as many on the top half as the bottom. Most people find that symmetrically balanced images convey stability and calmness—a desirable effect if you are constructing a cathedral. In addition, symmetrical images mirror many living things, which tend to be either radial or bilaterally symmetric (e.g., starfish and people, respectively).

By contrast, asymmetrical diagrams can be useful for implying behavior or motion, or to emphasize specific groups of elements. Diagrams with a central focus on a few elements will draw the eye *toward* the center. Diagrams that cluster elements in the corners will draw the eye *from* the center. When used with care, such diagrams are particularly good at indicating the relative importance of diagram elements. On a UML communication diagram, asymmetry can be used to emphasize critical control elements. Keep in mind, however, that asymmetric diagrams can be disjointed and confusing if not carefully constructed.

Rule #9: Symmetrically balanced diagrams convey stability and harmony; asymmetrically arranged diagrams convey motion and can be used for emphasis

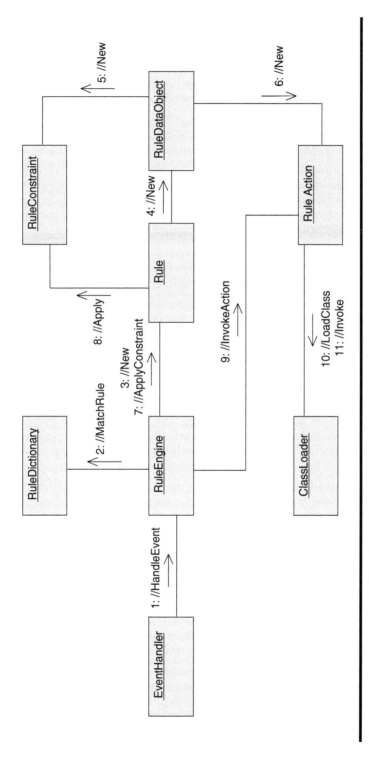

Figure 12-13 A Symmetrically Balanced Communication Diagram

Information Balance

Visual balance is only one half of the equation when creating model views. The other is to determine the quantity and quality of the information that is to be presented by each diagram. As discussed in Part I and Part II, each model is driven by a specific *purpose,* is created according to a specific *form,* organized around a *theme,* and presented in *views* defined by an information *pivot.* So, each diagram comprises a part of the whole and tells only a small faction of the full story.

Each diagram should focus on a particular aspect of the model (e.g., defined by the pivot), such that the information included in the view is cohesive with that aspect. The inclusion of information that is irrelevant to the current view will lead to confusion in the mind of the audience as they struggle to cope with incompatible information. Moreover, each diagram should have a single level of abstraction by avoiding the inclusion of generic and specific information in the same view.

The solution to balancing the presentation of information in a complex model is to use multiple cross-referencing model views that permit the audience to "travel" from one view to another. This visual tour must be done in such a way that the overall story contained in the model is not lost in the details of the presentation. Chapter 13 will discuss techniques of presentation including *progressive disclosure, detail hiding,* and *layering* that can be used to segment the model views. The key point with balancing information presentation derives from the findings of cognitive psychology that humans have a limited capability to store and process complex information. In particular, visual attention involves the ability to disengage from one view, shifting of focus and locking onto a new view. This is similar to a spotlight that shifts from one point to another; what is in the spotlight is available for processing, whereas information outside the spotlight is ignored [1]. Moreover, short-term memory is very limited (e.g., Miller's classic 7 ± 2 retained items [2]) and so must be assisted by "chunking" related elements. If diagrams are formed with these considerations, it will be much easier for the audience to retain and comprehend the model contents.

When relating one view to another, it is usually a good practice to use a special icon directly on the diagram to indicate a linking point. For example, classic flowchart diagrams use a pentagram shape (⬠) to indicate a link to another diagram. These linked diagrams may provide a greater level of detail, or a continuation of the current presentation (such as to another physical printed page). In UML diagramming there are no explicit links between views,[4] so it is necessary to introduce the idea of a linking stereotype, as illustrated in Figure 12-14. When linking views, caution must be observed to leave the current view cohesive so that even if the link is not followed, useful and accurate information can be obtained. If a complete view cannot be presented on the current physical medium, consider using a different medium (as will be discussed in Chapter 13).

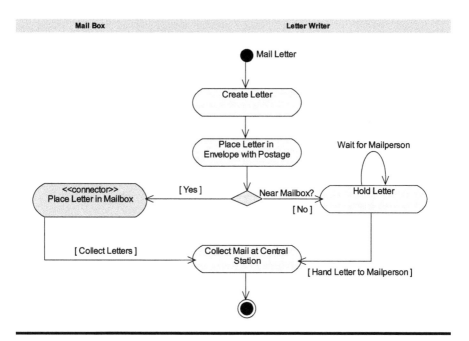

Figure 12-14   Use of UML «connector» stereotype in an Activity Diagram

Emphasis

Visual distinctions that provide emphasis in a diagram should be subtle but clear and effective [3]. The most subtle change is often to alter the relative alignment of elements; this follows the Gestalt principle of proximity. You also can emphasize an element by isolating it from other elements; the eye will be drawn to the isolated element and its unique aspects (Figure 12-15).

The next most subtle approach is to introduce variations in shape or proportion. For example, if you have one rectangular element but all the others are similar squares, the rectangle will garner more attention than the squares (according to the Gestalt principle of similarity).

Finally, you can add color or shading for emphasis; a judicious splash of color or differences in shading, in an otherwise plain diagram can direct viewers' attention to the most important elements.

Shade and Color

The application of color in diagrams is far from a trivial exercise. Color is very like a two-edged sword; used correctly, it can dramatically enhance a drawing's

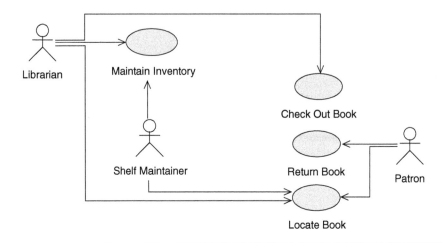

Figure 12-15 Emphasis by Isolation

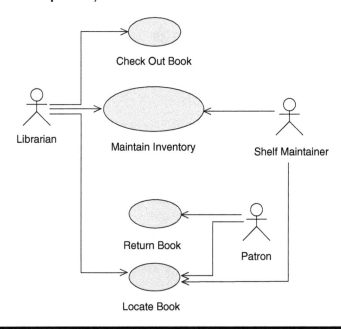

Figure 12-16 Emphasis by Size Variation

communicative power and information content. Used incorrectly, addition of color can destroy all aesthetic appeal, even to the point that a diagram will be rejected. Although there are specific empirical guidelines to follow, the final arbiter must always be the discerning eye. Thus, here is the primary color rule:

Rule #10: When using color—first do no harm

Never use color simply because it is available; always have a specific goal in mind.

There are many reasons to use color in diagrams, including to label, measure, or compare, to represent reality, to emphasize, or simply to decorate [3, 4]. For example, steadily darkening shades of blue are often used in bathysphere maps to indicate depth. This serves two purposes, first to indicate the point at which depth changes, and, second, to evoke an intuitive sense of how much change in depth is occurring. Thus, multiple shades of a single color are used to represent reality, measurement, labeling, and decoration all at the same time! By taking a more holistic approach to the use of color in all diagram views, a model can be presented in a clear and concise manner.

Visual aesthetics describes the overall emotional appeal that a diagram forms in the mind of the viewer. Although the technical information must be kept accurate, a poorly presented model view will result in a reduced comprehension of the diagram content. Thus, when creating color diagrams, it is important to consider the following [6]:

- Avoid the simultaneous display of highly saturated, spectrally extreme colors. This causes the lens in our eyes to rapidly change shape and so leads to fatigue. Instead, reduce the saturation of colors (e.g., use pastels), or else use colors that are close together in the spectrum.
- Avoid using pure blue for text, thin lines, and small shapes. Because there are no blue cones in the center of the retina, these elements are difficult to distinguish. However, light blue makes an excellent background color.
- Avoid using adjacent blues that differ only in intensity; because blue does not contribute to brightness, the edges will appear fuzzy.
- Be aware of the ambient light level; it affects how we perceive a color's hue. Avoid subtle variations in hue to distinguish elements.
- Use black lines to distinguish contour edges; it is difficult to perceive edges created by color alone.
- Because the rods/cones that detect red and green are located in the center of the retina, avoid red and green in the periphery of large displays.
- Opposing colors go well together; so do neighboring colors on the spectrum.
- For color-deficient observers, avoid relying on color distinctions between red and green or blue and green; this is important for the most common form of red-green or the less common blue-green color blindness.
- Printed colors rely on a subtractive method rather than an additive method to produce hue; colors on a monitor will not exactly match the more saturated colors on a printed page.

Personally, I have found that pastel colors (i.e., colors with lower saturations), combined with slightly more saturated colors to emphasize selective points work well in most diagrams. As noted in the color rules, heavily saturated or primary colors should be used sparingly because they command attention and draw the eye away from other elements (especially "arousing" colors such as reds). Overuse of strong colors also can lead to viewer fatigue and obscure text within or near the strongly-colored objects.

Shade/Color Emphasis

Edward Tufte likes to point out with regard to introducing emphasis into diagrams, that the modeler should only introduce "differences that make a difference" [5]. More often, modelers mistake difference for decoration—using color as an attempt to generate interest rather than to promote communication. In creating models, as with much of life, understated is usually best. The modeler should consider the value of drawing attention to a particular model feature; ask first if the feature is *really* all that important. If the answer is yes, then using color to emphasize that feature is justified.

Once again consider the Gestalt principle of figure-ground that was introduced in Chapter 12. Adding emphasis to one diagram element over others forces that element into the "figure" and the remainder of the diagram into the "ground" of the viewer's perception. Thus, if too many elements are emphasized, the distinction between them will be lost—if everything is important then nothing is given priority. Therefore, keep the total number of emphasized elements to less than ten percent of the total visual field.

Along with the limiting of emphasized elements, it is also important to avoid large swaths of bright field colors. This is for two reasons: the field of color will tend to reduce the visual recognition of differentiated elements, and large areas of color lead to a greatly increased cost of printing. A good alternative is to use shades of light gray as a neutral ground shade. This will provide much of the benefits of providing a visual differentiating field without adding greatly to the cost of printing (because black is usually much cheaper than process color).

As for the actual selection of emphasis color, strongly saturated colors will attract more attention than pastels. Any color may be selected as an emphasis color, but certain colors will be more effective than others. For example, "hot" colors (red, orange, yellow) will provide more interest and excitement than "cool" colors (blue, green, cyan). Again, the primary guide to emphasis color selection is the aesthetic sense of the viewer. If the color choice is pleasing to the eye, then it will likely be an effective choice. The only major concern is how color-blind individuals will perceive the intended differences. Because the majority of color-blind people are red-green deficient, avoid using these two colors to draw important distinctions.

The final concern is to establish consistency in color use. If purple is established as a emphasis color, it should be reserved for that purpose. By adopting a standard practice, the viewer will be prepared for reoccurrence of the chosen emphasis color, and correctly interpret the emphasized element as important. Similarly, a consistent use of neutral ground color will make the emphasis color all the more apparent and

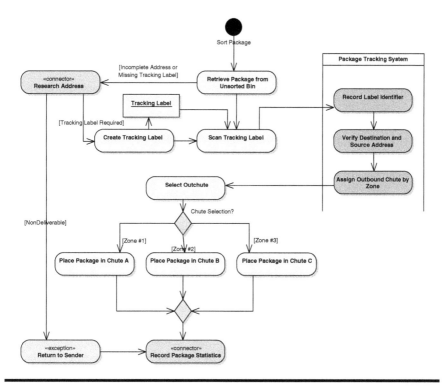

Figure 12-17   Use of Emphasis Shade on a Neutral Background

effective. Above all, it is important to remember that color is a potent, powerful tool for good or ill—it should be used with respect.

Summary

1. Aesthetics in diagramming involves the ability to form diagrams that are informative and pleasing to the eye. This involves attention to detail, awareness of the intended audience, and the purpose of the underlying model.
2. Diagrams are constructed of elements that are in turn created from lines and contours. The drawing of lines has the following guidelines:
   a. Line widths should only be as wide as necessary for visual distinction
   b. Line length should be minimized by placing linked elements in close proximity, where possible
   c. Rectilinear lines are preferred over oblique lines whenever a choice is possible
   d. Use a minimum of angles for rerouting lines; avoid tracing an element's edge too closely

   e. Use solid lines where possible; avoid using line styles that are visually similar in the same or related diagrams
   f. Use black on white lines for maximum contrast; avoid multicolored lines in diagrams
   g. Avoid crossing lines; reroute or manipulate elements (move/duplicate) to avoid crossed lines

3. Visual Balance in diagrams is based on the scale and proportion of elements as well as position in the visual field. The golden mean proportion (1:1.62) is a familiar and well understood technique for the creation of visually pleasing elements. The following guidelines affect visual balance:
   a. Use the golden mean proportion (1:1.62) when sizing rectangular or oblong diagram elements
   b. Symmetrically balanced diagrams convey stability and harmony; asymmetrically arranged diagrams convey action or motion, and are useful for emphasis

4. Information Balance in diagrams is based on the purpose of the model and the model form. Information on each model view should share a pivot and present a cohesive portion of the model story. Differing levels of abstraction should be avoided; use of linked model views provides a way to permit drill-down and view-up model navigation.

5. Emphasis in models can be provided by isolating particular elements, altering the element size, or by applying color.

6. There are a number of rules governing visual aesthetics, some of the most important are the avoidance of highly saturated, spectrally extreme colors, the use of blue for contour, borders or text, and to be aware of the difference between projected and printed colors.

Tips and Traps

Cultural norms sometimes come into play when creating diagrams. For example, in Western cultures, text is read from left-to-right and top to bottom. In many Middle Eastern cultures, text is read right-to-left. In Asia, many cultures read text top-down, then left to right. This is important in model view creation because the expectation for each culture is different. In Western cultures, the key elements of the view should be placed in the upper left versus the middle of the diagram, followed by a left-to-right placement of refining elements (such as the leaf elements of a composition).

Questions and Exercises

■ Question #1:
   The diagram rules presented in this chapter refer to straight lines. When would curved connector lines be useful in a diagram? When would they not be recommended?

- Question #2:

  When presenting a diagram to a large audience, what changes to the diagram rules, and in particular to Rule #1, should be considered?

- Question #3:

  Text is composed of curved and straight lines. Which of the diagram guidelines would apply to the display of text in a model view?

- Question #4:

  One of the recommendations for reducing line length is to duplicate diagram elements. When would you want to avoid this technique?

- Question #5:

  The golden mean is seen in many natural objects and as such seems familiar to most viewers. What other forms in nature would be useful as guides for diagrams?

- Question #6:

  Artists are very aware of the value of line and shadow to emphasize particular aspects of their paintings. How might these techniques be used in technical diagrams?

- Question #7:

  How would changes to model forms affect the principles of diagram balance? What about changes to model themes?

- Question #8:

  Are there other ways to emphasize particular diagram elements? What about variations in the contour line style (e.g., double lines)? When might this be a useful approach?

Exercise #1: Diagram Construction

Review diagrams that you have either created or seen on past projects. Rework these diagrams using the guidelines in this chapter. If you are a member of a team, have the other team members review your work and comment on the effectiveness of the reworked elements. Make note of diagrams that were effective versus those that were not effective—how aesthetically pleasing were the ineffective diagrams versus the effective ones?

References

[1] Eysenck, M., *Principles of Cognitive Psychology*. 2nd ed. Principles of Psychology, ed. M. Eysenck, S. Green, and N. Hays. 2001, Sussex, UK: Psychology Press.

[2] Miller, G., *The Magical Number Seven Plus or Minus Two: Some Limits on Our Capacity for Processing Information*. Psychological Review, 1956. **63**: p. 81–97.

[3] Tufte, E.R., *Visual Explanations*. 1997, Cheshire, CT: Graphic Press.

[4] Imhof, E., *Cartographic Relief Presentation*. 1982, Berlin: De Gruyter.

[5] Tufte, E.R., *Envisioning Information*. 1990, New York: Graphics Press.

[6] Murch, G. *Physiological Principles for the Effective Use of Color*, IEEE CG&A, November 1984, pp. 49–54.

Notes

1. Many of the examples in this and the following chapter are drawn from the UML; it is not necessary to understand UML semantics to follow the graphical principles presented here.

2. Mathematically, the golden mean is described by the Fibonacci sequence (0,1,1,2,5,8,13,21 . . .), which results in a ratio of approximately 1:1.62 between successive numbers.

3. For a full discussion, see: http://www.sacredarch.com/sacred_geo_exer.htm.

4. Some UML modeling tools permit the inclusion of a hyperlink attached to a specific diagram or element. This behavior, however, is not defined in the UML specification.

Chapter 13

Presentation

We have all seen different ways to present a model. A sculptor might create a small three-dimensional model out of clay for a larger piece she plans to chisel from marble. An architect might create a scale model of a new building with balsa wood, paper, and other materials to better understand the proportions and balance of the building and its surroundings. Software developers create visual models to tell specific stories about a system, with each diagram depicting one aspect of that story. UML models are a very effective way to tell the story of developing a software system, starting with use cases, moving through analysis and design, and finally implementation and deployment. Each part of the story should trace to each other part so that the viewer can follow from one model to the next without becoming lost. These model links are almost as important as the content of the model itself, because you can get the full story only through this progression. Think of the plot in a novel; each new incident typically relates in some way to an earlier incident, which moves the story along and gives it consistency and cohesiveness.

The successful presentation of a model requires the careful consideration of the level of sophistication of the audience, the complexity of the model, and the available techniques for display of the model views. Just as a good novel has a certain rhythm and flow, so should a good model presentation. This can be accomplished by using techniques for managing the presentation flow, and appropriate use of model display mechanics.

Presentation Flow

Several powerful techniques are available to control the flow of information to viewers, including *progressive disclosure, linked views, detail hiding,* and *layering* [1].

189

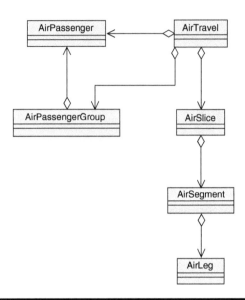

Figure 13-1 Air Travel Domain Model: Essential Air Travel Objects

As Massironi notes in his treatment of graphic images, "useful drawings are not exhaustive; they are selective" [2].

The first and perhaps most generally useful technique is *progressive disclosure.* This approach provides the viewer with successively more detailed information on a specific collection of elements. This incremental revelation of information permits the viewer to maintain a continuous connection between increasingly complex model views. The key to this technique is to avoid presenting unrelated information while maintaining a clear connection between one view and the next.

Figure 13-1, Figure 13-2, and Figure 13-3 show an example of progressive disclosure through a series of three UML class diagrams detailing an air travel domain model. Figure 13-1 shows the core travel objects and containment relationships. The successive diagrams add the search and result object and show relationships relative to the core travel objects. This allows viewers to "track" the constant core elements as new elements are added.

Figure 13-4 shows another form of progressive disclosure; here the core element associations are expanded with multiplicity and constraints. This form of disclosure is similar to a "drill-down" view, in which more detail is provided for a selected part of the overall model.

Detail hiding is a technique that is exactly what its name implies. The UML provides for extensive capture of information about software systems, most particularly for structural elements (e.g., classes and associations). However, a model may contain a great deal more information than is necessary for most views. The primary goal of these diagrams is to allow system designers to intelligently discuss elements of the emerging system, rather than as detailed construction blueprints

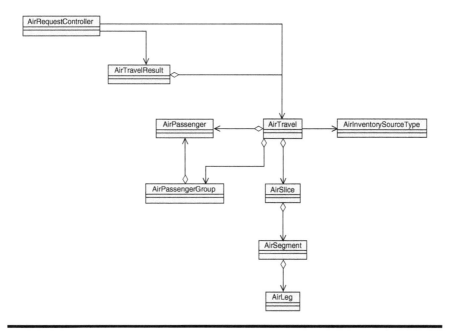

Figure 13-2   Air Travel Domain Model: Essential Air Travel Objects with Controller and Search Request

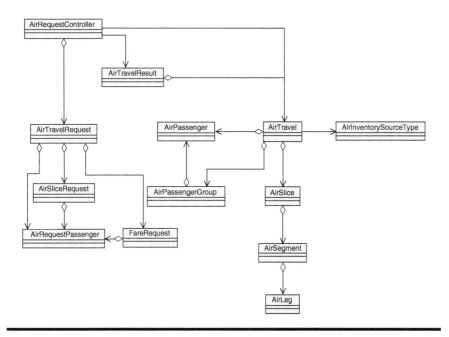

Figure 13-3   Air Travel Domain Model: Essential Air Travel Objects with Controller, Search Request, and Search Result

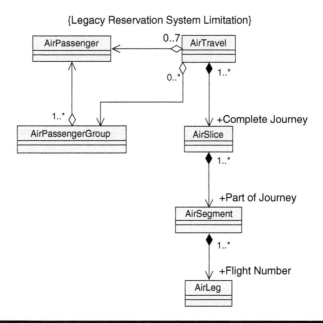

Figure 13-4   Core Air Travel with Multiplicity, Roles, and Constraints

such as those used for civil engineering projects. Although *model driven development* (MDD) is gaining popularity (in which the model represents the full software control structure) the complete disclosure of every method, attribute, role, multiplicity, and so forth, for every system class would result in a diagram that is cluttered, incomprehensible, and ultimately useless.

Layering is similar to progressive disclosure, but this technique is more effective for displaying disparate but related information. For example, the human body contains multiple interconnected systems. Two of these, the central nervous system and the muscular system, are essential for movement. If you were to display one of these systems in isolation, you would not get a full picture of how nervous signals cause muscles to contract during movement. However, if you were to display both systems simultaneously, the result would be visually confusing. An alternate approach is to separate the two views: first provide a picture of the muscles, and then add a separate, progressive overlay of the nervous system. That way, viewers can see one system in isolation and then come to a gradual understanding of the interconnections between the first and second systems.[1] For software development, there is similar approach: first, show a communication diagram without method calls to indicate connectivity; then overlay that diagram with details about the method calls (method name, calling order, etc.). In this way, a complex system behavior can be understood in stages rather than all at once.

Linked views are used when a particular model is too large to be displayed in a single model view, or the view needs to be segmented (such as is the case in both the layering and progressive disclosure technique). In this case, the model view is created with indicators showing where a model view is linked to another view, possibly an embedded view (such as with UML state diagrams and substates). While some tools support the direct embedding of an active hyperlink, the addition of an annotation with the name of the model view is usually sufficient to lead the viewer to the correct diagram.

Presentation Techniques

There are two principal ways that visual models may be presented, either by projection onto a screen or by paper printout on a suitable printer. These two methods, however, can be employed in several different ways depending on the purpose of the presentation and the available technology. In particular, a model view can be shown to an audience directly on a monitor, by projection onto a screen (either as a static view, such as a slide show, or directly from the modeling tool), by printing into a standard-sized document with descriptive text, or by printing using large-scale plotters. Each of these techniques has different advantages and benefits.

- Screen projection
  Because computer monitors have limited screen space and viewing angles, if you are working with a group, you can use a specialized projector to project the model onto a screen or wall. This technique is particularly valuable when moving through a sequence of diagrams when the presenter can use a pointer to highlight various elements.

  When using projection remember to keep the projected model view as simple as possible. This is mostly because of the limitations in resolution available by current projectors. If too many model elements are displayed at the same time, it will force the image to become crowded and confusing. Instead, focus on using the technique of progressive disclosure and linked views to provide for a smooth presentation.

  Sometimes the projection of the live modeling tool is a useful technique during a review session. This permits the live review and editing of the model directly into the tool, thus by-passing the intermediate step of recording the changes to paper. As an added benefit, the live model can be projected onto one whiteboard, whereas design points are recorded onto a second co-located board. This combination of techniques gains a synergistic benefit for discussing, reviewing, and recording design level decisions.

- Hard-copy printouts
  If you print a model view with a plotter, you can produce a hard-copy printout. The primary advantage of a printout is that you can directly edit on the diagram and record comments during reviews and discussions. A large printout also allows the viewer to see a substantial portion of the model at a time. Because most model views do not translate well to an 8½" × 11" format, it is

a good idea to purchase a wide-carriage printer, many of which sell for under $5,000. Typically, 24" × 36" printouts are good for small team discussions, but these printers can create prints as large as 36" × 60" to place on a wall during a model review.

If the modeling team is absolutely constrained to 8½" × 11" model views, either by cost of the plotter or by an unenlightened management decision, then the techniques described in the previous section for segmenting the model become even more critical. To maintain a legible size (e.g., a minimum of 10 pt. text) it will be necessary to divide the model views across multiple pages. The challenge will be to connect the views in such a way to maintain continuity. This can be accomplished by looking for natural "fault" lines in which a view pivot detail changes or the view's subject matter is altered. Consider reserving a particular color to indicate the connection of one model view to another (as described in Chapter 12). Finally, use descriptive names rather than letters or numbers to indicate the connecting view, as this will make it easier for the viewer to recognize a linked view of interest.

■ System architecture wall
Printouts also allow you to publicly display the development team's work. I have found that displaying model views on a "system architecture wall" helps "advertise" the progress of the development team and also elicits hallway discussions on specific points of the architecture. Fortunately, most offices have areas that are off the primary traffic flow (e.g., through which clients may be moving) where the company executive management may be willing to permit the nonstandard wall decorations represented by the printed model views. For this form of display, it is recommended to use poster-size printouts that are either a uniform 24" × 24" or 36" × 36". Larger sizes can be used (such as 36" × 60"), but continuity in printout size will provide a nice symmetry to the display; similar to the way that an art museum might display a collection of paintings. Be sure to update these printouts regularly as they tend to change over time.

■ Portable portfolio
If you have to take your diagrams off site to present to a small client audience, you can safely organize and carry your printouts in an art portfolio with protective plastic sleeves. These portfolios come in a variety of sizes, but I find the 14" × 17" size easiest to manage. The model views can be printed on paper sizes that will fit inside the sleeves (or cut to size), and then organized for a progressive disclosure style presentation.

Alternatively, larger model printouts can be bound together along one edge with fasteners (avoid using staples since these have a tendency to snag) to create a model view "book." The collection of diagrams can then be rolled up and placed into large poster mailing tubes for transport or long-term storage. For display, the model view collection can be unrolled on to a suitable conference table.

Summary

1. Presenting a model requires a careful consideration of the audience experience, model complexity, and presentation mechanics (printed vs. projected).
2. The *progressive disclosure* technique uses a stable base view that is built on with increasing complexity. The incremental revelation of data permits the audience to maintain context as new information is shown. The disclosure may be of information at the same level of detail as the stable base (e.g., horizontal expansion) or at a different detail level (e.g., drill-down).
3. *Detail hiding* prevents visual overload by deliberately omitting elements of a model view that are not necessary for the current discussion. When used in conjunction with progressive disclosure, this technique is a powerful way to reduce information overload.
4. *Layering* is similar to progressive disclosure but involves the overlay of information onto the stable base rather than the expansion outward (or downward).
5. *Linked views* permits the segmentation of a complex model while maintaining continuity between related views.
6. Projected models are very useful for review sessions and other direct interaction sessions with the audience. Projected models suffer from the same limitation as a monitor-based display—limited image resolution. Therefore, keep the views as simple as possible. Be sure to use an appropriate font size and style for text.
7. Printed models are a very versatile approach to model display. Printed models can be posted on walls around the development area to provide a basis for discussions. Printed models can be used as an aid for review and editing, and they also can be combined into formal presentations to clients.

Tips and Traps

In one company for which I consulted, I had to argue with the executive management to convince them to relax the "post-no-bills" policy of the company to allow the display of architectural models on the walls in the development area. After protracted negotiations, I was given a small interior hallway to display the system models. Two months later, these same executives were proudly showing "our" system architecture and design models to visiting customers. To paraphrase the old saying, "pictures sell better than words."

When using large-scale model plots, the diagrams frequently accumulate as a collection of tightly rolled "scrolls," making easy recognition of each sheet difficult. To help with the identification I like to include a second title on the edge of the sheet, as shown in Figure 13-5. Thus, when the sheet is rolled the printed title block on the edge will be exposed. Because most plotters use either 24" or 36" rolls, this technique is very handy for organization of printouts.

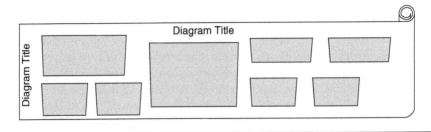

Figure 13-5   Double Titles for Rolled Printouts

Questions and Exercises

■ Question #1:
What strategies can be used to present a model to a diverse audience? What concerns are there for both the quantity and abstraction level of the information?

■ Question #2:
The text discusses the use of projected models during a design review as an aid to edits; when else might this technique be useful?

■ Question #3:
What other techniques can you imagine that would be useful in controlling the flow of information to the audience?

■ Question #4:
How might a printed model presentation be combined with a projected model presentation? When might this be a useful technique?

■ Question #5:
Consider how you might arrange the diagrams on an "architecture wall" to take advantage of traffic flow and visibility. At what height should the diagrams be displayed and how closely together?

■ Question #6:
Considering the Gestalt principles, how should the overall presentation be arranged to maximize the retention of information in the mind of the audience? How would you gain feedback that the audience has understood the model?

■ Question #7:
Given a series of wire-frame models that describe a graphical user interface (e.g., static Web pages), what form of presentation would be most effective for a technical audience? What about for an audience of end users?

Exercise #1: Observing Presentation Techniques

The next time you are attending a presentation or viewing a news story, take a moment to focus on the *form* of the presentation rather than the content. What kinds of images were used? How well did the pictures/diagrams integrate with the flow of information? Did the images add significantly to the understanding of the topic or were they just for decoration (in other words if you closed your eyes would you understand the same level of information)? How might you arrange the presentation differently? Make a note of the number of different images shown and how long the speaker spent describing each one.

References

[1] Tufte, E.R., *Envisioning Information*. 1990, New York: Graphics Press.
[2] Massironi, M., *The Psychology of Graphic Images*. 2002, London: Lawrence Erlbaum Associates.

Note

1. For a particularly fascinating use of this kind of display, see work from the Visible Human project, at: http://www.nlm.nih.gov/research/visible/visible_human.html. A video can be seen at: http://collab.nlm.nih.gov/webcastsandvideos/visiblehumanvideos/visiblehumanvideos.html.

APPENDICES

Appendix A

Example Business Workflow: Execute Trade

Brief Description

Mutual fund trades are performed by Securities Traders at the request of an Investor primarily via a Customer Trade Order (CTO). For trade execution, multiple CTOs are gathered into a single Trade Ticket. CTOs are manually generated (see **Business Workflow: Build Trade**), or automatically entered into the system via a instruction file download.

Purpose

This workflow provides a Securities Trader the ability to execute orders on a properly formed trade transaction (e.g., a "good" ticket).

Definitions and Acronyms

Term	Definition
CTO	Customer Trade Order—used to indicate a trade in a specific financial product (e.g., mutual fund) for client(s).
Trade Ticket	A collection of one or more CTO(s) "rolled" together for execution.
T+1 Trade	Trade +1 day settlement, the trade receives are settled, (paid for) the next day.
T+0 Trade	Settlement occurs on the Trade Date.
Terminating CTO	This form of a CTO is generated when all holdings for a client are to be sold (e.g., in the event of a transfer of Custodian).

Dependent Workflows:

Business Workflow: Build Trade
Business Workflow: Maintain Trade

Included Workflows:

Business Workflow: Maintain Trade

Extending Workflows:

Business Workflow: Validate Trade Ticket

Business Actors

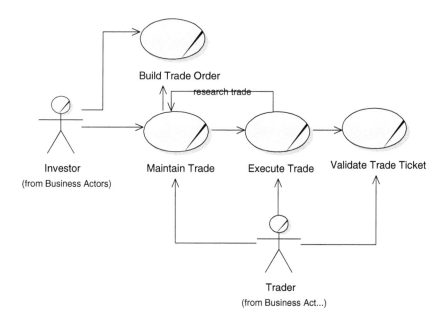

Actors	Description
Investment Advisor	Acts on the behalf of Investors to recommend mutual fund trades
Fund Representative	Mutual Fund customer service representative tasked with taking trades and answering client questions.
Calendar	Time-based initiation of trades (i.e., Terminating CTO)

Business Workers

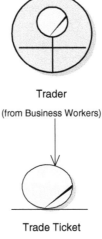

Trader

(from Business Workers)

Trade Ticket

(from Business Entities)

Worker	Description
Securities Trader	Responsible for ordering mutual fund transactions on behalf of clients. Also, maintaining, tracking, and entering trade information into the Host system.

Preconditions

■ A Trade Ticket (containing one or more CTO(s)) in the Approved state

Workflow

Basic Workflow: Execute Trade Ticket

1. Retrieve a ticket from the **Ticket Queue**
   a) Sort all tickets to view a specific Trade Ticket or set of Trade Tickets
   b) Select for Printing one or more Trade Tickets
   c) Sort and assign Trade Tickets to available Securities Traders
2. Ticket Maintenance
   a) Use the Trade Ticket number to display the current Trade Ticket
   b) Insure that the Trade is in the Approved state (upper right corner)

NOTE: If the Trade is not in the Approved state, it may be necessary to perform Business Workflow: Maintain Trades, Scenario: Research Trade Ticket

3. Review all Ticket information for accuracy against the system display; CTO changes may occur after the printing of tickets if the tickets are reinitialized for printing.
   a) For a late arriving CTO, the Securities Trader can add it by "rolling" it into the current Ticket using **Trade Order Maintenance**
   b) Reset original ticket and late arriving ticket—type "reset"
   c) Downgrade ticket status for both tickets to "intent"
   d) CTO Queue
   e) Select and "approve" all CTOs from the altered tickets
   f) The system will automatically "roll" the tickets together
   g) Reprint the newly combined ticket
      a. On all ticket transactions in excess of $1 million, higher level review is required. The Reviewer will verify the transaction to ensure that all is in order:
         i. Compare the desired trade size to the bimonthly "Trade Size report" (see **Business Workflow: Generate Reports**).
         ii. Review the indicated model(s) size with the desired trade using a comparison of trade size compared to the bimonthly "Trade Size report"
         Trade Size Report
            a. From = six months ago
            b. To = last Friday's date
            c. Report Type = "Trade Size"
         Print three copies; one set for the counter with average trade size highlighted for both dollars and shares, one set to the Trading VP, one set to the Trading Manager and the last goes to the Senior Trader.

         Note: The Trade Size report will provide the average and high dollar trade for each advisor covering the previous 6 months.

         Review of the model(s) size in comparison with the trade.
         For Buys, verify the trade is funded by checking the customer account for available cash.
         iii. Orders over $3,000,000 must be reviewed by at least the Supervisor. Orders over $6,000,000 must be reviewed by at least the Director of Trading. Further review can include both of the following:
            Repeat of review, by a person of higher authority.
            Discussion with the Investor to confirm the validity of the order.

iv. Once all reviews are completed, the Ticket is logged into the "Large Order Log" for tracking, a "Large Order checklist" is attached and then distributed for execution (see Appendix B).

(see **Exceptional Workflow: Supervisor Denial of Trade**).

2. Change the Ticket status to "Execute"
   a. Place a memo on the ticket indicating the Trader Name, Time and Date of trade.
3. Call the Security Market and speak to a Broker to conduct the trade (or a Representative for Mutual Fund Trades). The phone number will usually have a "T" code for Sell and "Y" code for Buy.[1]
   a. The Representative/Broker may ask for the following information
      Account Number
      Verification of Tax ID and Client Address
      Amount of Trade/Shares
   b. For a Sell transaction the proceeds will need to be transferred to THE COMPANY
      i. Wire transfer (with or without a fee).
         A Confirm Wire is for transactions on the next business day
         A Direct Wire is for transactions on the current business day
         Accounting Department reviews all wires
         (see **Business Workflow: (Accounting) Wires In**)

         NOTE: Trade wires DO NOT go through Accounting if in "approved" status

      ii. Check-based transfer

         NOTE: Automatic Clearing House transactions (electronic transfers) are not currently supported by trading.

   c. The confirmation number may be given as the Broker/Representative name, Execution time, and phone extension. This information is input into the **Trade Maintenance** view into the comment line for a Sell, and in the confirmation field for a Buy (to ensure correct money transfer for the transaction).
4. Change the Ticket state to "Settled"
5. The Trade System will run a nightly batch process to Post all "Settled" tickets (see **Scenario: Post/UnPost Ticket**).

   NOTE: Some trades are left in the "Executed" state if transaction fees need to be pulled prior to posting or if the trade is an electronic trade and must be manually posted.

6. After a ticket has been "Settled" and posted the Validate Trade workflow is performed (see **Business Workflow: Verify Trade Ticket**).

Alternative Workflows

Scenario: Overnight Trade Instruction Letter (Mutual Funds)

ABA # XXXXXXX

Acct # XXXXXXX

Company Name

FFC: Trading

Close: If you have any questions or need additional clarification, please contact me at (###) ###-####. Thank you for your immediate response to this Letter of Instruction.

Sincerely,

(your name)

(SIG GUARANTEE)

Trader

Company Name

   a. Include a SEALED, current version of the Corporate Resolution and photocopy the letter.
2. Package Preparation and Delivery
   a. Shipment method:
      i. Package Delivery Service "NEXT DAY EARLY AM" option
      ii. Select "Letter"
      iii. Confirmation: Verify and finalize the information pertaining to the shipment, (company name, contact person, address, and the method of delivery)
   a. After verification, select "Ship the Package"–this generates a barcode screen
   b. Print two copies of the barcode screen
   c. Attach one copy of the barcode to the outside of the Delivery Service packet and hand-deliver to the mailroom
   d. The second copy needs to be signed as received by a mailroom worker.
   e. Staple the signed copy to the ticket as confirmation that the package was shipped

3. Delivery Confirmation, (Next morning)
   a. Call Fund to verify receipt and confirm Trade Date
      i. before 10:30 MST
      ii. Note on copy to whom you spoke and the time
   b. If Fund claims NOT received
      i. Notify Trading Manager or Senior Trader IMMEDIATELY
      ii. Call Package Delivery Service
      iii. Get the time of delivery and who signed for it at the Fund
      iv. Call Fund back, have them find the package

Scenario: Generate and Execute Terminating CTO

1. When an Investor has elected to move one or more accounts to a new Custodian, all of the existing holdings must be sold. This is referred to as a Terminating CTO.
2. Terminating CTOs are indicated by a special code and are automatically generated as Sell CTOS by the Trading System.
3. Terminating CTOs are manually "Approved" on an "as soon as possible basis."
4. The workflow is otherwise identical to the **Basic Flow: Execute Trade Ticket** for executing a trade.

Scenario: Trade Settlement

After the execution of a trade (**Basic Workflow: Execute Trade Ticket**), a wire of money into or out of the company needs to occur. The creation of a pending Cash Transaction Event (CTE) is used to indicate the expectation of funds (e.g., Wire-in or Check), or the generation of outgoing funds (e.g., Wire-Out or Check).

1. **Ticket Maintenance**
   a. After the execution of the trade, the ticket will be in the "Executed" status.
      i. A manual Cash Transaction Event can be created for the Ticket in the "Executed" state.
      ii. If the transaction is for a Direct Wire to be sent on the current day (e.g., Money Market purchase) then the CTE will be created with the ticket in the "Executed" state.
   b. Change the state to "Settled"
      i. if no CTE is currently associated with the trade then the **Cash Transaction Event** display is shown.
      ii. Otherwise, if a CTE already is associated with the ticket, the current CTE transactions are not displayed.

2. Cash Transaction Event
   a. On a sell transaction
      i. Comment: Ticket Number associated with the sale
      ii. All other information will default from the associated ticket
      iii. Ensure the Wire In information is valid for THE COMPANY.
   b. On a buy transaction
      i. Enter the buy confirmation #.
      ii. Ensure the default Wire Out instructions are correct

The settled ticket will be verified the following day (see **Business Workflow: Validate Trade Ticket**) and then the incoming wire(s) can be reconciled to the current account (see **Business Workflow: Reconcile Trade Payments**).

Scenario: Post/Unpost Trade Ticket

Tickets are Posted automatically every evening by the Trade System once moved to "Settled" status (see **Scenario: Trade Settlement**). Once posted, tickets are normally reconciled against fund wires (see **Business Workflow: Reconcile Trade Payments**), although there are occasionally imbalances with the received funds (e.g., fee assessment).

1. Ticket Maintenance
   a. Enter the Ticket number of the trade to unpost
   b. Change the status to "Settled"
   c. Add or correct the fee amount listed on the ticket
   d. Spread the fees to the Ticket CTOs and repost the ticket

Scenario: Execute Electronic Trade

1. At step 5 of the Basic Flow, a Trade is executed electronically via Electronic Trading.
2. The Trade is created as normally (see **Business Workflow: Build Trade**), but the security(s) of that trade must be enabled for Electronic trading (see **Business Workflow: Establish Trading Account**).
3. Electronic trades will be automatically sent to the participating Broker/Fund for processing; the system will automatically POST the trade and generate the necessary CTE transactions for settlement (see **Business Workflow: Reconcile Trade Payments**).
4. The Trade Tickets will be printed overnight and placed into the validation workflow for next day validation of the trade (see **Business Workflow: Validate Trade Ticket**).
5. If an Electronic Trade is rejected for any reason the Trade Ticket will remain in the 'Executed' state and must be manually settled, as detailed in this workflow document (see **Scenario: Execute Trade Ticket,** above).

See **Electronic Trading** (references below)

Exceptional Workflows

Exception: Investor Oversold Shares or Other Trade Correction

As a result of the time it takes for a buy transaction to complete, it is possible for an Investor to issue a sell for shares that are not yet available, which results in an oversell condition. To correct this situation, the Company must purchase the excess shares and then generate compensating CTEs to cover the difference. The Company will then sell the shares the next day to the fund for whatever profit/loss may have occurred over the course of the trading day.

1. There will be four tickets total that must be created to correct the oversale.
   a. The original sell ticket for the fund, corrected to the actual shares sold to the fund
   b. An Investor sell ticket for the overage shares
   c. A Company buy ticket for the overage shares
   d. The Company residual sell for the overage shares

   NOTE: The original ticket source is altered to the Company so that the Company will "buy" the shares at the day's trading price. Tracking code 509 is used to indicate the linkage between accounts.

2. Determine the shares that the COMPANY will need to buy to make the Investor whole at the fund.
   a. **Customer Trade Order**
      i. Money Manager = the COMPANY
      ii. Product Number
      iii. Omnibus Account
      iv. Trade Basis = Shares
      v. Trade Date = date trade should have occurred
      vi. Set the source code to 509
      vii. Ref Account = Account 1, number of shares THE COMPANY oversold
      viii. Set the status to "Approve"
   b. **Ticket Maintenance**
      i. Retrieve the ticket produced containing the CTO
      ii. Execute the ticket using the price on the day the trade should have occurred.
      iii. Create a COMPANY CTE for the buy transaction.

    c. Cash Transaction Event records for the source code 509 (overage) tickets will be off-setting and are balanced to avoid the creation of an unnecessary wire for the purchase.
      i. Cash Transaction Event
        1. Retrieve the Original Trade CTE
        2. Merge this CTE with the newly created COMPANY trade CTE to avoid the generation of a wire for the COMPANY purchase of the overage shares.
    d. The following business day, create and execute the COMPANY residual sell ticket (see **Business Workflow: Build Trade**) at the fund. The difference in price will be reflected as a gain or loss to COMPANY account 1.
    e. Complete an error account document and report the incident to the Trading Director.

    NOTE: this is performed immediately after the error is detected.

Exception: A Trade Ticket Does Not Post Correctly

If ticket that does not post exactly as printed and priced, use **Scenario: Post/Unpost Trade Ticket** to move the ticket to the "Settled" state. The ticket can now be corrected to ensure that the values match the executed trade and reposted. This exception is often a result of incorrectly applied transfer or wire fees but also may result from an incorrectly placed trade.

Exception: Trade Not Conducted before Market Closure

1. In the rare instance when all Trades cannot be conducted before the market closure, the COMPANY be responsible for handling the trading price difference.
2. These are coded as COMPANY trades and handled with House Funds
3. If there is a Price Decrease:
    a. Place a Buy trade for the amount specified by the Investor
    b. Go to Cash Transaction Event and place in 'Hold' status
    c. Day 2: Place the purchase order at the fund for the dollar amount specified and post the ticket using the previous day NAV.
    d. Day 3: Send the money to the fund for the T + 1 purchase. The share amount will not reflect the shares posted due to the decrease in price
    e. Day 4: Determine the extra shares that were gained by placing the purchase one day later. The transaction will result in a gain for House Account 1. Redeem the extra shares at the fund.

   f. Day 5: Trading will receive a wire for the amount of the sell that was placed on Day 4. When the wire is received, trading will deposit the wire into House Account 1

  g. IRA Transactions

     i. New to create a new journal entry

     ii. Account = 1

     iii. Account Code = Cash Deposit

     iv. Cash = dollar amount of the wire

     v. Wire = Yes

     vi. Description: Reason for receiving the wire (e.g., "missed trading date")

     vii. Cash Transaction Event Selection, the CTE number of the wire

4. If there is a Price Increase:

  a. Place the Buy ticket for the shares the Investor was entitled to.

  b. Execute the ticket as if the trade occurred on the trade date, Day 1.

  c. Go to the Cash Transaction Event, and place the CTE into the 'Hold' status

  d. Day 2: Place the purchase order with the fund. If share buys are not allowed by the Fund, place for 105–108 percent of the original order. Post the Ticket with the Day 1 NAV.

  e. Day 3: Send the money to the fund for the T + 1 purchase, remove the hold status on the CTE

  f. Day 4: Determine if enough shares were bought in part (a) above.

     i. If short, place a purchase order for the difference at the Fund. The transaction will result in a loss in House Account 1.

  g. Day 5: Send the proceeds for the purchase order in Day 4; **IRA Transactions**

     i. New to create a new journal entry

     ii. Account = 1

     iii. Account Code = Pay From Account

     iv. Cash = dollar amount of the wire out

     v. Wire = Yes

     vi. Description: error correction IA #

     vii. Cash Transaction Event Selection, create a new CTE for the purchase wire (record the number)

     viii. A blank ticket is necessary for this transaction because the Trading Department needs to send money to the fund; **Print Ticket Forms**

       1. Product Type = (M) Mutual Fund, (MM) Money Market

       2. Product

       3. Money Manager

       4. Omnibus Account

       5. Firm of Fund Family

       6. Instruction = Buy, Sell

       7. Number of Copies = 1

Exception: Supervisor Denial of Trade

1. At step 2(c)(iii) of the Basic Flow, if a Buy Trade is in excess of $1 million and the account does not have the cash on hand (i.e., the Investor is attempting to sell current assets to purchase additional assets), then all buys for the account are placed into the "Hold" status (not "Approved") and the Investor is informed that the buy trades will not be performed until the following day when the Sell Trade proceeds are available.

Improvement Possibilities

None Identified

Special Requirements

All trades must be completed before the close of the Securities Market.

Extension Points

Automated Trades can be expanded to include multiple market trades as part of a single trade ticket.

Post-Conditions

All Trade Tickets are executed; All Buys or Sells are conducted.

Activity Diagram

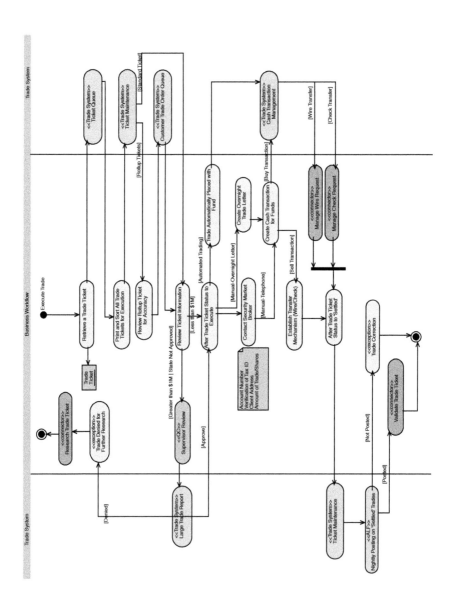

Issues

None.

Notes

None.

Questions and Answers

Question	Answer	Respondent	Date of Reply
How does a Company House Trade work?	Account 1 (house account) is used to make clients "whole."	Fred E.	6/23/2004
What happens when a Ticket does not post correctly?	Any ticket that does not post may do so as a result of an overdrawn account. This must be researched and then the Ticket manually posted or corrected.	Fred E.	7/13/2004
What is done if the trade size as shown on the Large Order Report is smaller than the current trade?	The trade error must be researched and corrected as soon as possible.	Fred E.	6/23/2004

Note

1. Occasionally, a contact number needs to be updated for a specific Mutual Fund or Security Market. Please refer to **Business Workflow: Maintain Trade**.

Appendix B

Structured Requirement to Use Case

Brief Description

The following statements are excerpts from a larger requirements definition for a customer care and automated service-provisioning system requested by a fictitious telecommunications firm. These requirements can be used to identify actors, initial use cases, and to extract the beginnings of a data dictionary for the system.

System Requirements—Customer Care System

Service Provisioning

1. Customer shall be able to call a specific 888 number to automatically provision the telephony service after headset purchase via the PHONEMaster provisioning system.
2. The customer shall be able to call a specific 888 number or a Web site to suspend telephony service for a period up to six months. The Web interface will be easy to use and intuitive to the user.
3. The customer shall be able to have service disconnected by calling a specific 888 number or a Web site.

Customer Service

1. The system shall support Internet capabilities for the customer to access and check their account(s), service status, and remaining prepaid minutes.
2. The system will permit the Call Center to accept payments into the system via check, cash, credit card or electronic fund transfer. Payments that are overdue will be noted and charged a 2 percent late fee; however, this fee will be waived in the event the customer has premier service account status.
3. Call center personnel will be limited to a $50 refund without supervisor approval.
4. All call center or customer actions will be logged and tracked for audit purposes.
5. The Web interface will be easy to use and intuitive to the user.
6. Call center personnel shall be able to access the same information as well as issue refunds and add additional prepaid minutes (within specified limits unless approved by the supervisor).

Translating into Use Cases:

The "requirements" presented earlier are a collection of statements intended to describe the desired system. However, there is no clear theme or story. At first glance, there seem to be two clearly defined systems: one for Service Provisioning and a second for Customer Care. Reading the Service Provisioning section, it is clear that the term "customer" is used frequently to describe the functionality. This suggests that this functionality can actually be considered part of Customer Care. So I begin by defining a system boundary:

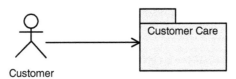

Next, I look for actors to the system. A "customer" is noted in line 1, 2, 3, and 4. Call Center personnel are noted in line 5, 6, 7, and 9. A system called "PHONE-Master" is noted in line 1. So I amend the diagram:

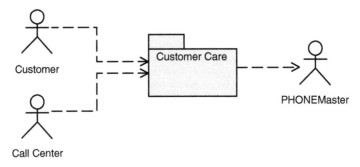

Now I look for use cases and assign an actor for each. Line 1 suggests some form of ability for the Customer to activate phone service, whereas line 2 suggests the ability to suspend said service, and line 3 provides for disconnection of service. Additionally, there is some interaction with a separate system ("PHONEMaster"), although it is unclear whether this interaction is only for "activation," or also for the "suspend" and "disconnect." The implied supplemental requirement is that we will be developing a system that can be accessed via a regular telephone (see line 1, 2, 3). I usually capture these kinds of information directly into the documentation for a use case diagram element using a UML note or the documentation section of the element.

I now capture the following use cases:

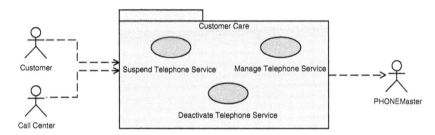

Line 4 is a combined requirement statement providing for account management services and something called "pre-paid minutes." Note that this line also contains a nonfunctional requirement for Internet-based access. Line 5 is another compound requirement that combines information on acceptable payment types (check, cash, credit card, and EFT) with requirements about handling overdue payments. The astute investigator will note that line 5 mentions something about "premier service account status." This suggests that the account management functionality noted in line 4 will have some kind of information about the customer's role with the company (I can also capture this information into the use case documentation section of the diagram). Our use case model is now:

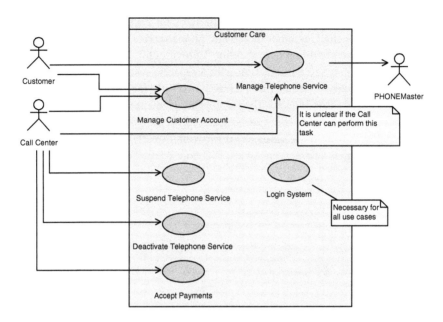

Line 6 suggests that the Accept Payments use case will also have a scenario for refunding customer accounts, with value limitations on the amount and approval requirements.

Line 7 introduces a new functionality, logging. Also implied is some form of security (it would be hard to log a Call Center individual without unique identification). So we have an additional use case:

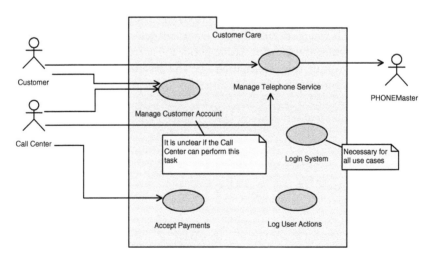

Line 8 is not a requirement. This is a generic statement about usability that cannot be measured or tested.

Line 9 suggests that Call Center personnel can "access the same information," but is unclear on what information is referenced (Customer Account?). Also, a reiteration of refund capability is noted, as is the ability to add "prepaid" minutes to a customer account (with supervisor approval, and undefined limitations).

We can now trace all of the provided statements to the use case model, with capture of nonfunctional requirements that are directly associated with specific use cases. We also can rework the Telephone Service use cases to take advantage of the similarities among activation, suspension, and deactivation:

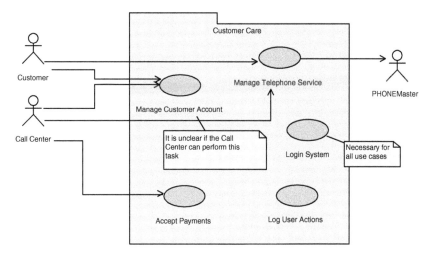

Clearly, this analysis has lead to more questions than answers. Some additional follow-up activities can include definition of the "prepaid" minute functionality; clarification of the 888 number interface; a definition of "headset" (line 1); Inquiry on the logging needs and data elements:

- Audit Trail
- Date of Change
- Change Event (Refund, Prepaid Minutes, Customer Data, Payment)
- Original Information
- Altered Information
- User Identifier
- Approval Indicator

The next steps also include the creation of user flows to describe each of these system interactions (e.g., activity diagrams), and a further description of alternate and exceptional scenarios for each use case.

As shown in this example, even starting with a minimal description of the system it is possible to create a reasonable model to capture and organize requirement information. I often use a UML modeling tool to assist my analysis; I have found this permits me to capture and organize my models in one step. Alternatively, the investigator could use a less complex approach with a simple drawing tool and skeleton use case documents. The key is to take an analytical approach and maintain traceability to the original requirement statements.

Appendix C

Answer Key and Discussion

The following answers are to the questions posed in each chapter. Please note that these are my own opinions as to what is a "correct" answer—there is usually more than one correct response to each question. The questions are intended to encourage you and your teammates to consider other possibilities that I have either overlooked, or did not have sufficient time and space to explore.

Chapter 1

Answers

1. Attention, in the Cognitive Psychology sense, is about focusing our mental processing power onto a restricted number of areas or problems. This allows for efficient use of our limited resources for memory and reasoning. The alternative is to have every perception causing an interruption (consider trying to read this book while a two-year-old is yelling in your ear and pulling your sleeve). Our attention "wanders" when we are fatigued or when a (relatively) more important event is called to our attention, such as a child crying. In some cases, the intent is to divert our attention, as is the case with roadside advertising.

2. This is a timeless question—what exactly defines "beauty." If the great philosophers were unable to decide this question, I will certainly not attempt to here. However, I will state that I believe that a balanced model, one that is well designed in both information content and presentation, will be more effective and useful than one that is not.

3. If art forms can be considered models of reality (and what else is a painting or sculpture?), then I can add emotional response to the list of model purposes.

223

Exercise Discussion

Although this may seem like a silly exercise, it serves to highlight the difficulties in communication between unrelated cultures. These types of communication breakdowns have resulted in some of the worst conflicts in human history. Although the creation of models doesn't compare to, say, the Holy Crusades, it is important to highlight that everyone has a different view of the world, and what works well for one set of people will fail miserably with another.

Chapter 2

Answers

1. Although all of the listed approaches are useful for investigating systems software automation, I have found the Systems Analysis approach to be the most generally applicable. Because most software systems are based on automation of existing business practices (i.e., tasks that are currently performed manually), the Systems Analysis approach of establishing boundaries, interdependent components, data, and controller entities allows the best "fit" for modeling business problems. Controllers are abstractions of the actual workers and their workflows; data elements are the information, often in the form of paper, that is manipulated; interfaces are external contact points with customers, clients, and other business divisions; boundaries are found between business divisions (although these are sometimes artificial and unnecessary); components are groups of workers performing complementary tasks.

2. Analysis is often the consideration of many possible explanations for the observed behavior. When an experiment (or software development project) doesn't work as expected, it can still provide a great deal of information by study of what went wrong. Perhaps the error wasn't with the design, but with the execution. Perhaps the initial assumptions about the problem were incomplete or incorrect. Perhaps the choice of tools was inappropriate for the need. By performing what engineers refer to as a *failure analysis,* it is possible to avoid similar mistakes in the future.

3. The cheat answer is to say "both." A software system is closed when it is performing the functions of a closed system, such as one that is embedded in a toaster to control temperature and time (but isn't monitoring the condition of the final product—which may lead to burned bread vs. toast!). The software system is open when it responds to external cues, such as the autopilot in an airplane monitoring position via a compass, or satellite signals. A software system will rarely switch from closed to open but may switch from open to closed. This can be a result of sensor failure where the same autopilot disregards external signals and instead relies on internal inertial guidance for navigation.

4. As suggested by the hint, all of these are natural processes. Some are very simple and static (rock); some are quite dynamic and constantly changing form (cloud); some are flexibly constrained (river), and some represent a combination of composite behavior (forests are composed of individual trees). All of the listed systems may coexist and interact (the rain from the clouds falls on the rock, which is eroded to form soil that is carried and deposited by the river, so that trees can grow). These examples are intended to illustrate that systems are all around us, and that we participate in many systems simultaneously.

Exercise Discussion

Living things are excellent examples of a complex system. They are composed of multiple interacting parts (system analysis), have observable and alterable traits (scientific analysis), have distinct hierarchical dependencies with other organisms (functional decomposition), and significant behavior (process analysis). This exercise encourages the utilization of all of the presented techniques to describe one such class of living organisms—a tree. Trees exist in a variety of ecological niches; they have multiple forms evolved to exploit those environments, such as pine needles to reduce loss of moisture by evaporation in dry mountain environments. Trees have internal structure, and are part of a larger biome—a forest. They can be grown under controlled conditions to study changes due to environment and genetics. Finally, each type of tree will respond differently to changes in environmental conditions (such as disease, drought, fire, etc.). The groups should be encouraged to consider all kinds of different conditions and situations that affect tree growth and development. Some of the groups should focus on the internal structure and behavior of trees, such as water transport. Others can focus on the interaction of many trees to form a forest (such as shading undergrowth or providing a home for small furry creatures). Each group should present their models to the others for comment and consideration.

Chapter 3

Answers

1. In small organizations, say from 2 to 50 people, there is usually one pervasive culture. This is often established by the founders of the organization and can range through any of the four primary types described. However, in larger organizations, there are often multiple cultures present—including hidden ones! The hidden culture forms when the members of the organization are acting in a manner different from the one promoted by the organization leaders. This can happen, for example, in a corporation where the leadership is publicly promoting the idea of teamwork and cooperation, all the while infighting and power plays are ripping relationships apart. When looking at

your own organization culture, be aware of the differences between the outward presentation and the true behavior. If they don't match then it is very likely that a hidden incongruent culture has formed. It is rarely healthy for such an organization to exist in this manner for any length of time.

2. One of the greatest challenges to an investigator is gaining access to the company "guru." These individuals wield a disproportionate amount of power based on some facet of the business which only they know. It is rarely written down or otherwise accessible except through one or two individuals. As a business, this is a very risky behavior for two reasons. First, the guru may leave the organization for a variety of reasons (more pay, illness, injury, family emergencies, etc.), taking with them critical knowledge. Second, by wielding their knowledge power, they prevent the company from expanding beyond them. In essence they become bottlenecks to further development in their area of expertise. Although subject experts are critical to the function of a business, their knowledge should also be accessible in some other form, such as written documentation or models.

3. With flexibility often comes complexity. As system behavior (as evidenced through the user interface), becomes more flexible and powerful, it often exacts a price of increased complexity of use. UNIX systems have been developed for decades, and as such have developed a suite of very powerful applications. However, the learning process for such systems is equally high. The command line interface permits direct access to this power, such that one who is familiar with the command structures can perform tasks quite rapidly. I liken this to controlling a fighter jet by manually adjusting the electrical signals sent to the control motors. By contrast, a graphical interface may require navigation through multiple views to accomplish the same task but has the advantage of using the human visual processing system and iconic recognition to assist in the discovery of system behavior. Thus, for system users of less experience, the graphical display is preferred.

4. Each type of stove serves the same purpose—to heat food. But each uses a different mechanism. The electric stove uses resistance to electrical current to generate heat. The gas stove uses combustion of propane, methane, or other flammable gas to generate heat. The first type of stove is dependent on a consistent supply of electricity; failure of the electrical grid will result in system failure—the inability to perform its purpose. By contrast, the gas stove is independent of power supplies, but can fail in far more dramatic fashion—say by causing an explosion. Finally, both stoves may exceed their designs by igniting uncontrollable fires. The model for these systems should take into account the failure modes and likely consequences of these failures by noting the conditions that may cause failure (e.g., power outages, gas regulator failure, kid with a hammer), and the expected behavior of the system in these instances.

Exercise Discussion

Business Modeling:

Here is my list of desirable skills:

- Interviewing
- Observation and Note-Taking
- Business Writing
- Independent Document Analysis
- UML Modeling (or other appropriate model form)
- Specific Business Experience
- Group Leadership

Here is my list of useful tools:

- Modeling Software
- Word Processing
- Document Configuration Control
- Code Analysis Tools (for automated business processes)
- Wide Carriage Plotter (for presentation of workflows)

Organizational Mapping:

The purpose of this exercise is to gain awareness of each group's organization and structure. This permits each group to gain an understanding of the interdependent nature of most organizations, and practices the critical thinking and observational skills that are most important to a system modeler. Each group should present their findings to the other groups and look for gaps, assumptions, and omissions in each other's models.

Team Behavior:

The primary purpose of this exercise is to gain awareness of the behavior of development teams. The best way to perform this task is to assign one member as the "observer" who will take notes on the behavior of the team. The observers can then present their findings back to the group at the end of the exercise. This kind of "self-observation" is valuable for a modeler, because we all bring our own assumptions about the relative importance of what we are studying. By observing others, we can gain an understanding of ourselves, and thus become more accurate modelers of the behavior of different systems (including those consisting of people).

Chapter 4

Answers

1. The obvious answer is a public library. The less obvious repositories are found in private collections, including most business information. Even less obvious are the repositories that exist in someone's head in the form of experience. Each of these sources is increasingly more difficult to access because of the nature of the information. Public information is freely accessible, but may not be very specific. Business information is more difficult to access (since it is often proprietary), but will be much more likely to be directly applicable to the current business problem. Finally, human experience is very difficult to access, but is most relevant to the problem at hand. Each of these sources is of value to spend time investigating and utilizing when faced with a new investigation effort. Remember, there is very little new under the sun; most problems have been solved at one time or another. The tricky part is finding these preexisting solutions.

2. You could consider shopping for groceries to be an analysis pattern. You begin with a general set of element descriptions (milk, eggs, cheese, cereal) and end with a specific set of items (Royal-Crest milk, Ascott eggs, Tillamook cheddar, Post cereal). The prototypes could have been satisfied by multiple concrete items; the decision as to which to choose is the basis of marketing and taste rather than part of the initial pattern.

3. It is more usual to find a group that performs too little early analysis, rather than one that attempts to go too far. Both situations have unpleasant consequences. In the first case, the likelihood is that the team will build the right solution to the wrong problem, whereas in the latter case the risk is that the team will not build a solution at all! The best defense against both types is the "analyze a little, build a little" approach. This is the underpinning of iterative development and serves to provide guidance as the team moves down the development path.

4. Retrospectives (sometimes known as Post-Mortems—a term I detest because it brings up displeasing images of cut up corpses) are an excellent way to learn what worked well, and what didn't, in a just completed (or canceled) project. Learning from our mistakes is how we gain experience; if we ignore the mistakes of the past we are condemned to relive them.[1] One of the reasons I have heard for not holding a retrospective is that these meetings take up valuable time from the next project, and so they aren't conducted. This has always seemed a "penny-wise, pound-foolish" approach to me, but then again, I think rain is wet, so who am I to judge.

Exercise Discussion

Finding Enduring Themes

The main commonality between these different environments is the storage of automobiles in one form or another. At the most abstract, all four can be considered

Auto Storage Locations. Beyond that, they differ significantly in their functions. A home garage and long-term storage garage will share many similar features, such as a building to house the vehicle, locks for security, and some way to remove the vehicle periodically (e.g., driveway or ramp). The auto repair shop will also store vehicles but may use outside locations as well as inside. Also, storage of vehicles is actually a side effect of the business, which is to repair broken autos. Finally, the harbor ferry is used to transport autos from one side of a body of water (river, lake, bay) to another. Again, the storage of vehicles is secondary to its primary purpose.

When constructing a model of each of these locations, the common theme of auto-storage should become apparent as the attributes of each type of location are compared. This is one of the primary techniques used to determine an enduring theme; the theme should be universal.

Creating an Analytical Framework

The expectation of this exercise is not to have a fully formed framework suitable for publication. The intent is to begin to consider all of the tools and techniques available to each member of the group. By starting to create a catalog of these successful approaches, each team will be able to use what has been discovered in the past to assist them sometime in the future. Furthermore, thinking more deeply about all of the skills required for a successful project will better prepare them when forming a team to address the next project.

Chapter 5

Answers

1. As was noted in the text, written notes have several advantages over electronic ones. Portability is certainly high, as is durability in adverse environments. I like to use several notebooks for different purposes. I maintain a daily activity journal, where I track my consulting time, my task lists, project notes, and activities. I also use it as a way to record ideas or thoughts that occur to me during the day that I want to remember. Finally, it serves the basic purpose of keeping a record of each day's accomplishments. I use a second book as a kind of book report journal. When reading a book or article, I write the title and author at the top of a clean page and then write notes on points that I wish to remember or look up later. This makes my writing much easier as well as helping me to retain the information in a summarized fashion. Finally, I wrote many of the chapter ideas of this book into a third journal, so that I had a way to record ideas as they came to me.
2. Most software developers work in cubicles rather than offices. Thus, they are prey to the noise level of the surrounding office. In very large offices, this noise factor can become a major impediment for the interview, as well

as inconveniencing surrounding workers. If an interview is conducted in an office, then the questions of noise are eliminated but others remain, such as phone calls, pagers, random visits from other workers, and so on. The best way to conduct interviews is in a semiprivate location (such as a conference room) or in a separate location altogether. Unless it is critical, ask that the interviewee turn off cell phones to avoid interruption (the same goes for the interviewer).

3. Public or private libraries are seldom used by software development teams. I am not sure why this is, but I suppose that one factor is access. A truly useful library is often located at a university campus, which may be inaccessible to the team. Another reason may be lack of familiarity with the usefulness of library resources. A third may be that teams see library research time the same way they see a root canal; it is to be avoided at all costs. I have found that my job is made significantly easier when I take a day or two early in a project to see if there is any information available a the local university library or via the Internet. I have seldom been disappointed in locating something useful.

Exercise Discussion

By interviewing one another, the members of the group will gain experience in dealing with one-on-one situations. Because this is likely to be a primary source of information for the model and the project, it is good to practice these skills in a simulated environment before trying them out for real. The time limit is especially critical. By limiting the interview time, each team member is forced to stay on topic with directed questions. It will rarely, if ever, be the case that an investigator will have unlimited time with a subject matter expert. More often, you will need to use your time wisely. After the exercise, the group should be encouraged to share what worked well and what went badly with the interviews.

Chapter 6

Answers

1. I hope that I have made clear this point: I believe that modeling is inherent in our understanding of the world. We create and use models unconsciously all the time. By taking active notice of these models, it becomes possible to learn how to better communicate with one another. Reading is a form of model use; if you don't understand cuneiform it will be rather difficult to read ancient Sumerian text. Etiquette are simply rules for interacting with other people in social situations; a model of personal behavior. There are many such examples; just look around.

2. A model form is simply a way to capture and organize model information. It may be complex or simple. It may have specific rules to determine how

and where information will be stored, or it may be no more rigorous than a diagram on the back of napkin. The nature of a model form is dictated by the information to be stored, and the audience that is intended to use it. Thus, as long as the form matches the expectation, it can be effectively used.

3. Almost any common attribute of the model information can be used as a pivot. If the idea of customer interaction is central to a model view, then this becomes the pivot. As such, information on system administration would not be appropriate in that view (although this may act as the pivot to another view). As long as the information within the view is cohesive with the selected pivot, the model view will likely be understandable.

4. Context for a model is represented by the environment in which the model is placed. A business transaction would be in a monetary context (the trading of one commodity for another or its equivalent in money), whereas a screenplay would be in the context of entertainment (or possibly education). The context is important because it will influence the kinds of information that is captured in the model, such as the amount of a business transaction and the plot of a screenplay.

5. A sports team would have public entertainment as *one* of the possible key abstractions. Another is competition for a prize. The business side of a sports franchise has many of the same key abstractions as any other business, for example, the making of a profit.

6. I have given several relationships that I feel are important to understanding interactions between elements. The ability to "own" another element, such that its existence depends on the owning element, is one additional possibility as a core relationship. I encourage you to explore these basic concepts as a way to better understand the dependency of system elements upon one another.

Exercise Discussion

This exercise is directed toward cataloging and organizing information. The bicycle is used as an example system because it is constrained and has only a few basic functions (propulsion, steering, and transport). Others, such as entertainment or exercise, can be thought of as incidental to the basic functions of a bicycle—or not, depending on the context of the model. In this exercise, the goal is simply to enumerate the parts of the system and define them in relation to one another. In this way the group will gain experience in studying the parts of a problem, and will note how each part participates in a basic system function.

Chapter 7

Answers

1. I have presented all of the verification techniques with which I am experienced. Experimentation, simulation, testing, independent review, and direct

application are all very powerful model validation techniques. Time is usually the only true way to know that a model was built correctly. Over time, a model will either be found useful and corrected as errors are found or it will be discarded.

2. I will use the typical dodge for a tough question, it depends. I have found that well-organized and lead formal reviews can be immensely valuable in correcting mistakes in a model. I also have seen them as a terrific waste of time. The same goes for informal reviews. My advice is that formal reviews are usually a more effective way to verify a model because informal reviews often take a long time and involve people with only marginal interest in the end result.

3. Questionnaires can reach a large audience and provide valuable feedback on a focused topic (such as user interface design). They are also time-consuming, resource-intensive, and prone to many sampling errors. It is best to reserve the questionnaire approach for times when the questions are very clear and concise, and to take as many precautions as possible to avoid biasing the results from sampling too small a population.

4. No simulation can ever be completely accurate to the real world. However, they can be very, very close. The best way to perfect a simulation is to use it over a long period of time and refine the simulation to better match real-world events. For example, flight simulators started out as simple boxes on pivots; they are now so sophisticated that virtually every possible flight condition can be simulated and practiced. Of course, the existence of plane crashes indicates that even these simulations are still lacking in some critical areas.

5. My personal belief is that experimental validation is stronger than direct application because the theory must explain *all* experimental results, there can be *no* contradictions that are not accounted for in the model. Direct application of a model may never encounter certain conditions that would show the model as lacking (such as very rare error conditions). Others may take the more pragmatic approach that says that direct application is the only way to show a model is useful rather than simply correct. I encourage you to see for yourself which approach is most effective.

Exercise Discussion

I am a big fan of critical reviews. Although as an author and modeler these review sessions can be brutal to the ego, they often result in a much improved final product. No matter if that product is a software model or an article for a trade journal. The only rule is to avoid personal attacks; the review is of the work, not the worker. For a critical review to be successful, the moderator must ensure that all participants follow this rule.

Chapter 8

Answers

1. This question is intended to explore how well a company has communicated its core business functions to those tasked with performing them. I have often found that people have no knowledge of the company vision statement, or even if one exists.

2. In previous chapters, the idea of a model's context was considered critical to its construction. Businesses also exist in environments that affect how they conduct business. A hotel that does not provide transport to and from a nearby airport will suffer losses compared to a hotel that does provide these services. Similarly, when modeling a business it is important to understand these external effects.

3. This question is intended to explore the complexity of what on the surface seems a simple transaction, the cashing of a check at a bank. The hidden complexity is all of the processes that must be performed (manual and automated) to complete the transaction with the issuing institution. When modeling a business flow, it is important to trace *all* of the steps from beginning to end, and to be aware that simple can turn into complex when all of these possible steps are considered.

4. There are often multiple entry points into a workers workflow. Examples include manual delivery, automated delivery, batch delivery, returns, and so on. Each of these multiple entry points should be captured in the model along with the kinds of information included (such as reason for return).

5. The hint gives this one away; in this case, it is the CSR that is the system actor. In some forms of modeling, the customer would be shown to have a dependency on the CSR, but for most applications I have found this to be confusing and unnecessary. Remember, even someone from within the company can take on an external *role* if they are acting on behalf of an external service requestor.

6. As with the previous answer, I prefer to look at each business part independently and model the other business divisions as consuming or providing services (e.g., external to the current business unit), and the workers as performing roles for these units. This approach has the advantage of avoiding questions like, "Mary is in accounting, but sometimes does the billing—is she external to billing or internal?" In this approach, Mary would be performing two roles, one that is internal to billing and another that is internal to accounting.

7. Domain models of manual operations, usually involving information transmitted by paper forms, can be used to form the underpinning of an automated system. Because the information is the same, just provided in a different form, the business domain model may have parts coopted by the software

development group for use in the programming effort. Domain models also have the advantage of showing where information is flowing to and from, and how many people are touching the information as it flows by. In some cases, there are so many workers required to contribute to a particular information flow that the business grinds to a virtual stop. Reorganizing the flow of information is a major technique used by business to increase efficiency (and profits).

Exercise Discussion

Identification of Business Actors and Workers

The key to this exercise is to remember that people in a business are performing roles. They may perform multiple roles for several business units, but it is the role that matters. Watch for any model that contains names of particular people, or roles that are too fine-grained (such as "Copier" and "Filer" as separate roles for someone responsible for document archiving).

Business Workflow Modeling

This exercise extends the previous one by exploring the workflows performed by the identified workers. It is common to find that a particular role was either too broad (performing too many tasks) or too narrow (performing too few). In this case, the worker and actors should be refined to provide a more uniform level of abstraction so that one role is not doing all the work of the business for a single external actor.

Domain Modeling

This final part of the exercise focuses on the "things" manipulated by the business workers. Again, look for categories that are too broad to be useful, and others that are so narrow that only one or two items fit. Any domain element that is identified, but is not used in one or more workflows is suspect; perhaps it should be combined with another, eliminated from the model, or a workflow step was missed in the previous exercise. The domain elements should NOT have detailed descriptions, such as "Form 3b, box 7, Name," it is sufficient to simply use Customer Information and Customer Name to describe the form (element), and box (attribute).

Chapter 9

Answers

1. Often the most difficult part of a requirements archaeology expedition is to obtain the necessary funding and support. The usual response from manage-

ment is "why should I pay to document a system that already exists?" Business owners often prefer to look toward the next revenue-generating opportunity. However, the following arguments are a powerful persuasion:

a) Maintenance costs are directly tied to the complexity of an application— if the development staff doesn't know how something works it is very risky to change it. Thus, costs will rise as more and more logic is grafted on to the system (what G. Weinberg refers to as "design debt").

b) System replacement is impossible without a detailed understanding of the system functionality—especially the exceptional cases. Over time, a system will accumulate business logic squirreled away in the code, increasing the risk that business critical logic will be missed in the new system.

c) Decreased strategic flexibility is a direct consequence of the lack of system knowledge. It is all but impossible to rapidly change business goals when the underlying business systems are fragile and poorly understood.

d) Dependence on key heroes results over time because fewer people will be able to maintain the systems due to staff turnovers. Only well-documented systems can be rapidly taught to new employees without impacting current maintenance efforts (e.g., via hands-on mentoring).

2. In addition to the sources described in the chapter, consider e-mail trails, marketing specifications, meeting notes, and other semipermanent sources of information. A key to unearthing system information is to look under every rock for anything that may aid the investigation; the most unlikely places can contain useful information.

3. Usually, code analysis will have a higher chance for discovery of exceptional system behavior. This is because the code is the ultimate arbiter of system behavior, and is usually changed only in a controlled manner (e.g., configuration management). By contrast, the development team is often unaware of subtle nuances of the system, such as failure condition handling, in unfamiliar areas. However, the team can provide critical guidance in situations in which the error handling mechanisms are not uniform, making direct analysis of the code a time-consuming process.

4. There is much to be said for doing one's homework before a test. In this case, interviews are costly because the people of greatest help are the same ones that are critical for the system support (see Answer 1d). All existing system documentation should be reviewed before holding interview sessions to provide the researcher with context and background information. Moreover, if time has been spent on reviewing the overall structure of the system, this will be an aid in formulating useful questions and understanding the expert answers.

5. There are quite a number of text manipulation languages/tools, such as awk, grep, PERL, and Python. Basically, any tool that permits the search and reporting of repeated code structures will be of value in the analysis of text-based programming languages. In cases in which automated tools have been

developed for analysis of a specific language (e.g., C++, C, Java, C#), these tools will be of value in locating particular code elements. Finally, integrated development environments (IDE) contain tools for tracking code dependencies and locating specific components.

6. This argument is the classic "do it right the first time." Expenses for incorrect development increase geometrically as the project proceeds (e.g., if it costs $1 to fix a problem during project inception, it costs $1,000 after production deployment). The earlier a risk or issue is discovered the cheaper and faster the fix. To this end, creating and integrating a requirements analysis team into the development environment is a very cost-effective approach, because they will be able to uncover trouble early in project development.

Exercise Discussion

Appendix B provides a detailed example on how to convert structured requirements into a more story-based form (e.g., flow based). Often the requirements will have already been grouped in some hierarchal format; look for these structures when performing this exercise. These can form the basis of the initial functional breakdown. Next would be to identify potential actors and system boundaries, followed by the functional flows (basic, alternate, and exceptional). Requirements that do not fit the flow-based form should be maintained in their original format, but moved to a separate section (if local to the current flows) or separate document (if global to the project).

The best way to conduct a group session with existing requirements is to segment the teams into groups of three to four people, to simulate the difficulties of finding consensus. Assign a part of the requirements base to each group (e.g., two to three major sections) and allow 30–45 minutes for the teams to establish the initial groupings (use cases), actors and scenarios (flows). Have each team create a preliminary diagram to show dependencies between each of the functional areas. As part of a full-day exercise, each team could further develop the specific functional flows in diagram form and present their work to the other groups for review.

Chapter 10

Answers

1. Other locations for information could be the issue tracking system, e-mail trails, WIKI electronic discussion boards, and training materials. Creativity and imagination is required to identify all possible sources of information.
2. It is always difficult to know where to stop when constructing a model. In this case, the model is intended to convey the structure and reasoning used to create the core structure of the system—its architecture. When determining what to include in a software architecture document, the level of detail should

be enough to convey the outlines of the system, the critical components, the interfaces, and other key system elements. Inclusion of database access details is usually too fine-grained, as is enumeration of every code class in the system. By analogy, if you are modeling the structural core of a building, you would include the load-bearing walls but exclude the office partitions.

3. When considering an architectural description of a system, the details of error-handling and logging are usually reduced to descriptions of the common mechanisms utilized to perform these tasks. Thus, if Java exceptions are used to handle the majority of system errors and log4j is used to log system events, then only one example of each would suffice. Typically, system details such as performance metrics are located in the requirements, and the software architecture document only addresses areas of the system where critical performance-driven design decisions have been made.

4. In my opinion, yes, the deployment is part of the overall architecture. This is because a system is quite useless unless it is deployed into an appropriate production environment. The deployment view ensures that all relevant structures are included in the architectural description.

5. Interestingly enough, I have found very few such patterns. Clements et al. provides some basic descriptive structures and guidelines for inclusion of information into these structures, but I have yet to find patterns specifically formed to address questions of system architecture documentation. This may be because of the inherent flexibility required to determine what is critical and what is not to an architectural model, complicating the capture into a pattern form.

6. Developers, Production Support, and Testers: Each group will need the information for different reasons. Developers need a broad overview of the system before delving into details; Production Support need to maintain the system over time; Testers need a broad view of all of the system components to see how the full system provides for functionality.

7. I can only think of one situation in which a test case would be considered "architecturally relevant"—verification of simulations. Here, the test case is critical because it describes the real event that the simulation is meant to represent. In this case, mention of test cases in the architecture document would be appropriate.

Exercise Discussion

Framework Description

Reusable frameworks are to a software architect what prefabricated fittings are to a plumber. They represent the ability to solve a common problem (such as database access), and reuse that solution in multiple other systems. There are many such frameworks (as described in the exercise). This exercise is intended to encourage the teams to look for areas of their systems that could be abstracted and placed into a reusable framework library. The framework elements are usually abstract and require concrete implementation, but sometimes there are specific framework features that are useful in many settings. Most modern languages such as C#, Java, and Perl have extensive associated frameworks.

Risk Analysis

This exercise is focused on determining how design decisions affect project risk, and vice versa. When a design decision is made, if there is a way of retiring one or more technical risks (such as an interface that is not sufficiently stable), then it is a good idea to document those decisions. Risk analysis is a very deep topic, and beyond the discussion in this book, but it is important to understand how a system implementation (or model thereof) can be used to show reduction in the riskiest technical elements of a project.

Chapter 11

Answers

1. Icons rely on commonly understood metaphors that are shared by all viewers. Symbology must trigger the same response based on these metaphors for it to have the intended effect. The existence of many cultures around the globe that do not share common metaphors is what makes international symbology so difficult. Consider the old half-moon symbol to represent a public toilet—will this work well in a Moslem country such as Turkey (where the national flag contains the same symbol)? How about the swastika (originally a Greek good luck symbol)?

2. The term "elegant" is reserved for simple solutions to complex problems. Most people find that these solutions are actually very difficult to discover, and so paradoxically more complex solutions are frequently chosen. Schedule constraints (such as timed tests or product delivery dates) only compound this situation by increasing the likelihood that a suboptimal solution will be chosen over a superior one.

3. In large complex figures, key elements may become obscured by the surrounding detail (refer to Chapter 1, Figure 1-7). This forces the observer to hunt for the diagram core message, which is more likely to be misunderstood if he/she is rushed. In this case, simplification of the image is preferred to emphasize the most important elements of the model view.

4. Of these three, the Factor of Objective Set, where random arrangements are taken to be ordered, may come into play with large database diagrams. Many times, I have seen data maps that show all of a large database schema. Thus, unrelated tables are very likely to be randomly placed together, which can

lead to them being perceived as having some formal relationship that does not otherwise exist.

5. Engineering and architecture employ visualization to aid construction. In particular, consider a highway project that uses a 3-D simulation to understand and predict traffic patterns. Architects often build similar 3-D simulations to show key building features to clients and construction personnel.

6. Inductive reasoning—or generalizing from limited information—is often the only way to proceed with incomplete information. Scientists operate this way all the time; if everything could be deduced then there would be little need for experimentation. So, from a *logical* standpoint, induction is a weaker form of reasoning than deduction. But, from a *practical* standpoint, induction is often the only way to move forward based on limited information.

7. Diagrams that highlight relationships between model elements are all useful for inductive thinking. I have found that Busan's mind-mapping techniques are particularly interesting for their power to show categories and relationships in an intuitive, visual manner (see http://www.mind-map.com for more information).

Exercise Discussion

This exercise explores the idea of common experience, and the difficulty in creating a universally understood set of symbols. The auditory element is meant to show how understanding based on hearing is particularly difficult to capture. As a side note, auditory "symbols" are in everyday use with emergency sirens, crosswalk alerts, and car alarms.

Chapter 12

Answers

1. Curved lines are often useful for showing particular routings in construction diagrams. For example in an architectural rendering for a building, the lights are connected to switches using curves to distinguish them from other diagram elements (such as walls or windows). Thus, anytime there is a need to distinguish connections between model elements based on linear versus nonlinear, curved lines should be used.

2. Large groups usually require some form of projection to make the model visible to all participants. This means that each element, including connection lines, should be made larger to permit easy identification at a distance. Typically, line widths should be 1 to 1.5 points in thickness, but the best way to determine this amount is to project the model and view it from the farthest audience position.

3. Text should almost always be shown horizontally (with exceptions for languages that are more often displayed vertically). On rare occasions, text can

be angled, such as for the titles on graphs. Even more rarely (or better yet, never) should text be shown vertically as this is very difficult to read.

4. When a diagram is created to highlight dependencies, duplication of elements will confuse the viewer who is expecting to see only one of each element in the diagram. Duplicate elements may also confuse viewers who expect a one-to-one mapping between model elements and real-world objects, such as a building architecture model.

5. Many regular sided objects (such as hexagon, octagon, pentagon, etc.) are found in crystalline structures. Branching structures are very common in trees and bushes. Radial plots (aka webs) are found wherever there are spiders.

6. Although I personally avoid drop shadows (except where the modeling tool won't let me turn them off), they can be effectively used for subtle emphasis of specific model objects. Line styles, such as double lines, can be used to highlight connections if permitted by the model form.

7. Some model forms are inherently asymmetric, or are only symmetric around a single axis. Chart contents are frequently asymmetric with the placement of data points. Time lines are only symmetric around the horizontal axis.

8. As noted in the answer to question 6, if the model form permits, lines can be doubled or even tripled to draw attention. Shading of background around selected elements can have the same effect as directly adding shading to the interior of those elements.

Exercise Discussion

This exercise is intended to develop a sense of aesthetics for model diagrams. As with any skill, creating visually pleasing diagrams takes time and effort. By reviewing previous models and diagrams in a new light, the modeler can improve their "eye," as well as more readily recognize what parts of a model are not contributing to its effective communication.

Chapter 13

Answers

1. When presenting to a diverse audience, there are two problems to avoid—playing to the lowest common denominator ("dumbing down") and alienating a segment of the audience ("overwhelming"). In this case, I recommend using a progressive disclosure technique from simple to complex to provide a path for the less technical audience members as well as a providing a review for the more advanced members. This compromise permits everyone in the audience to participate, without catering to a specific group.

2. I have found projection is also very useful during a design or capture session. I can project the growing model onto a screen/wall while I simultaneously take notes in my notebook or onto a whiteboard. This more efficient style of modeling requires the modeler to be very familiar with both the model form and model tool to avoid slowing down the process.

3. Session breaks are a great way to build in transition points in a lengthy presentation. I usually try to break every one to two hours, when I can "shift gears" between topics, or move to a different level of detail. This is also a good time to move to the review of examples before moving onto a different area of the model.

4. Reviews seem to work best with a printed set of overview/summary diagrams, and using the projector for more detailed views. This allows the review team to move back and forth between abstraction levels whenever they choose. The main value seems to be the ability to place the detail diagrams in the context of the summary, and to maintain concentration when the model focus shifts between functional areas.

5. As with paintings, wall diagrams should be placed at eye level, or about five to six feet from the floor. As for arrangements, I recommend the same style as an art gallery, where work from a particular artist or style is often arranged chronologically. Model views can be likewise grouped by area and shown in progressive detail along the wall. Remember also that lighting is important; make sure the diagrams receive adequate light for easy viewing.

Exercise Discussion

News stories often blend multiple channels of communication, particularly auditory and visual. Study of the techniques used to present news stories in a concise fashion is a great way to learn how to organize a complex model. The combination of text and pictures is far more powerful than either alone, as has been discovered by news programs and infomercials.

Note

1. "Those who cannot remember the past are condemned to repeat it." George Santayana, *The Life of Reason,* Prometheus Books, Amherst, NY, 1998.

Appendix D

UML 2.0 Overview

Visual Software Modeling—UML (version 2.0)

There are many ways to represent a system, everything from simple sketches consisting of boxes and arrows, to sophisticated representational 3-D models. For very complex systems, a number of detailed schematic approaches have been developed. Blueprints have been used for many years to represent complex building projects. Electrical engineering schematics are used to represent the massive complexity involved in silicon chip manufacture. Plumbing, lighting, decorating, and landscaping all use detailed diagrams to represent an abstract view of the finished product.

In software development, a common notational system has only existed for about ten years, when the Unified Modeling Language (UML) was published. Before that, software developers made do with a collection of mismatched diagram techniques, notation, and semantic approaches. The introduction of UML was a breakthrough because it allowed software engineers and architects to share the same diagrammatic approach using a unified notation and semantic model. Analysts, project managers, configuration managers, and production support personnel also were able to benefit from the introduction of a unified software modeling language.

The latest release of UML, version 2.0, dramatically enhances the representational power of the model language (albeit at the cost of increased model complexity). There are now 13 core models, which are all designed to work together to visualize the key software elements of Dynamic Behavior and Structure. Structure is shown with structure diagrams, deployment diagrams, component diagrams, and package diagrams. Behavior is illustrated by communication, activity, state, interaction, and timing diagrams.

In addition to the core set of modeling diagrams, the UML meta-model[1] provides support for the creation of UML "Profiles," which are extensions to the core UML. Profiles exist for Business Modeling, Data Modeling, and other valuable areas. Using the UML extension mechanisms (stereotype, constraint, and profile), a system modeler can create a model form that is appropriate for virtually any development effort.

Package Diagram

The package diagram is used to illustrate system structure and key system groupings. For example, packages may be used in a logical model to indicate a core system framework, or indicate a collection of library routines. All UML structural diagrams have packages available for grouping and partitioning.

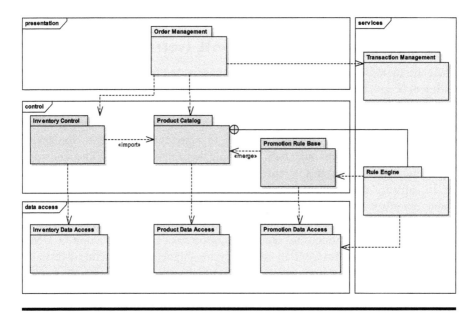

Figure D-1   Package Diagram

Useful for:

- Indicating system groupings
- Illustrating component containment
- Showing high-level system dependencies
- Abstracting key system and subsystem elements

Use Case Diagram

All software systems are created to provide value to some key system stakeholder. Use Case Diagrams are used to indicate system functional boundaries, external interactions with system "Actors," and core system functionality as a set of flow-based requirements. Use Case diagrams are central to the requirement definition process.

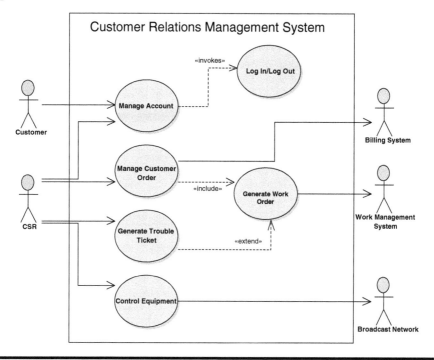

Figure D-2   Use Case Diagram

Useful for:

- Indicating system boundaries
- Detailing communication paths between system elements and external Actors
- Summarizing system functionality as a set of Use Cases
- Illustrating dependencies and interactions between system functional areas

Structure Diagram

The UML was designed with object-oriented programming as a core concept. Structure diagrams illustrate this approach by using the "class" as the core modeling elements. Classes are used to encapsulate system behavior and relevant data into a single operational unit. Structure diagrams are central to the UML representational scheme.

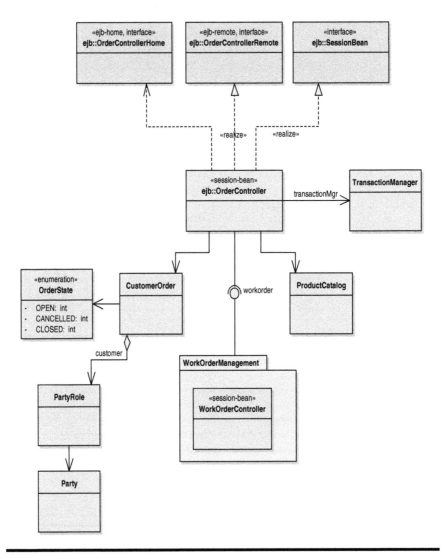

Figure D-3   Class Diagram

Useful for:

- Illustrating system class details and dependencies
- Showing interfaces and required system interactions
- Detailing generalization hierarchies
- Representing class containment
- Representing implementation details and constraints

Object Diagram

Object diagrams are used to show structural relationships between instantiated class instances (e.g., objects). These diagrams are very similar to class diagrams but are more concrete in that every object represents a true in-memory software element, rather than a definition of those elements (e.g., class).

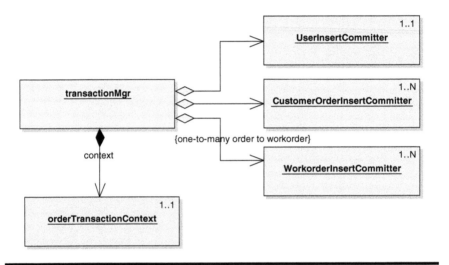

Figure D-4   Object Diagram

Useful for:

- Showing object dependencies
- Illustrating run-time object structure
- Reasoning about complex containment hierarchy structures
- Illustrating constraints on object interactions

Composite Diagram

A composite diagram combines elements of other structural diagrams to illustrate "collaborations" between system components. Collaborations occur when a group of classes interact to provide a defined system functional behavior.

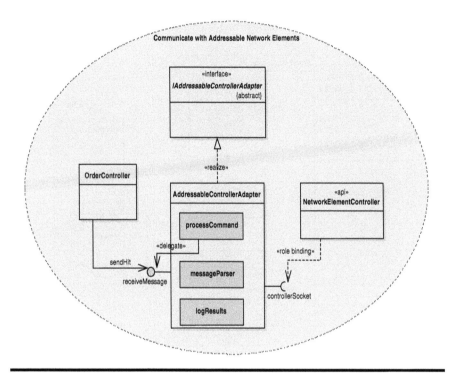

Figure D-5   Composite Diagram

Useful for:

- Showing collaborations between system elements
- Abstracting the system structure into a series of collaborating components
- Drawing attention to core system functional behavior
- Diagram component internal structure and interfaces

Component Diagram

Components represent the physical realization of the system elements. Components are typically constructed from one or more classes that provide a set of defined behavior. Collaborations may be used to indicate component internal structure, whereas Component diagrams are used to show dependencies between components and other external systems via defined interfaces or other dependencies.

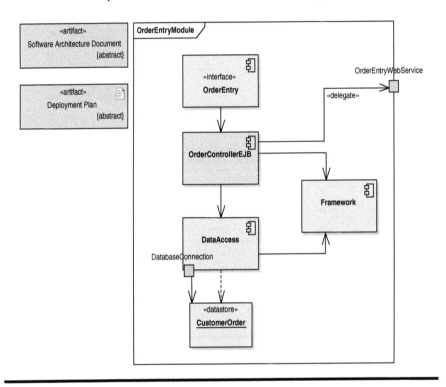

Figure D-6   Component Diagram

Useful for:

■ Showing system physical structure
■ Detailing system architecture and module
■ Illustrating dependencies between internal and external system elements

Deployment Diagram

All software systems must be deployed to a physical computer system to be functional; typically under the control of operating systems and networked to other computer elements. Deployment diagrams take the system components, show how they are packaged for delivery to target computers, and the key networking elements that exist between devices.

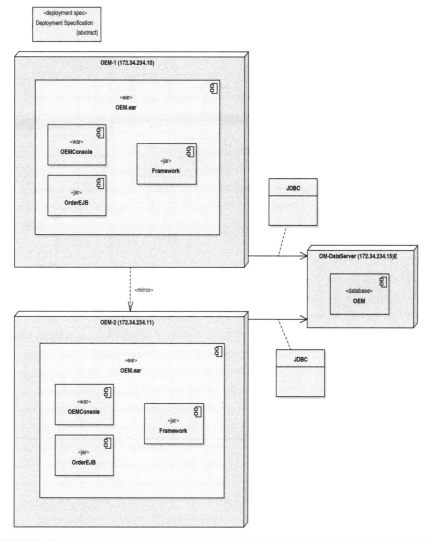

Figure D-7   Deployment Diagram

Useful for:

■ Detailing software packaging
■ Illustrating system deployment onto various computer devices

Activity Diagrams

Activity diagrams are very similar to the old concept of flowcharts but contain much more expressive power. Activity diagrams are useful for illustrating use case behavioral flows, interactions between different system components, algorithm details for processing, and other flow-based system behavior.

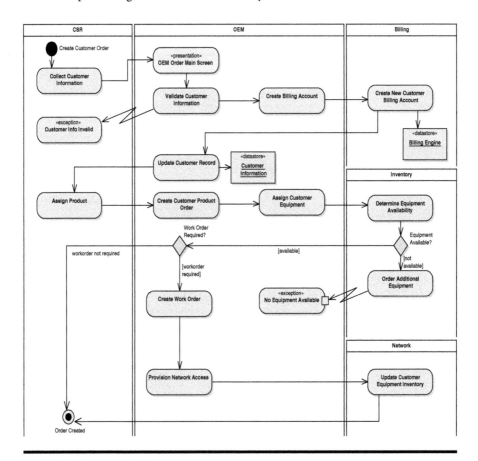

Figure D-8   Activity Diagram

Useful for:

- Use Case Flow modeling
- Process view dynamic system activities
- User interface flow modeling
- Algorithm processing
- Business activities (processes and worker actions)

State Diagrams

State diagrams capture key system states, events, guards, and actions. The state diagram summarizes system behavior as a series of state-transitions as a result of one or more events. States can be subdivided to show internal substate transitions (such as within a solid-state device).

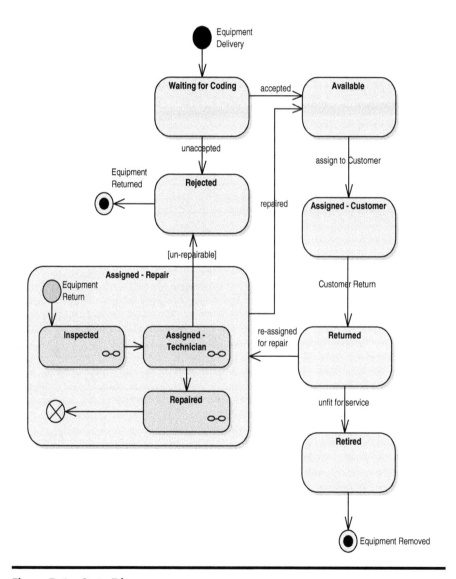

Figure D-9   State Diagram

Useful for:

■ Describing system state
■ Dynamic aspects of system behavior
■ Entry and Exit actions for a state change
■ System trigger conditions
■ Internal state behavior (substates)
■ Application of historical state information

Communication Diagrams

Communication diagrams illustrate messages passed between system objects. These messages are usually method invocations of the object's interface but also may represent more abstract communications (such as a customer ordering products). This diagram is very similar to Sequence diagrams but is focused on the objects and the number of messages between them, rather than on a sequence of events.

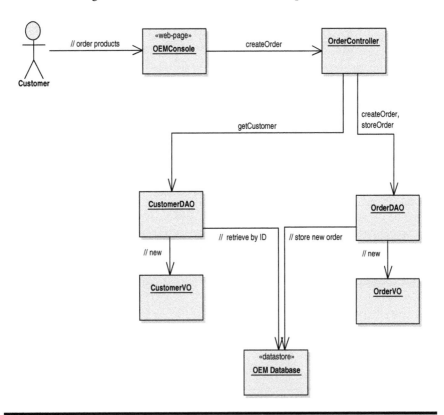

Figure D-10   Communication Diagram

Useful for:

- Illustrating object interactions and dependencies
- Object messaging pathways
- Showing overall number and type of object messaging

Sequence Diagram

Sequence diagrams focus on the series of messages passed between different system components and objects. Sequence diagrams typically have a single flow, but it is possible to have sequence "fragments" that show looping, branching, or other kinds of procedural processing events.

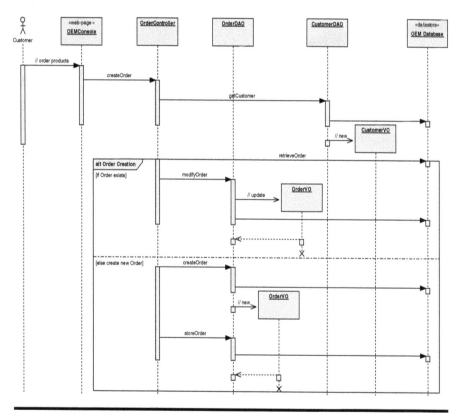

Figure D-11   Sequence Diagram

Useful for:

- Describing relationships between model elements (system components)
- Describing sequence-based dependencies
- Showing extent of physical dependencies between systems and system components
- Indicating the nature of system messaging (message signatures)

Timing Diagram

Timing is a key feature of all real-time systems, whether for an oven timer or a flight surface control element for a jet-fighter. To diagram these time/event dependencies, UML 2.0 introduces the Timing diagram. These diagrams can be shown as either object state transitions or as value changes over time. Additionally, it is possible to show the duration and event for a particular state change.

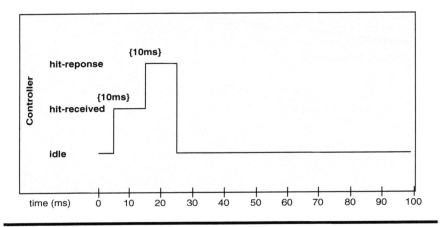

Figure D-12   Timing Diagram

Useful for:

- Showing timing constraints on system components
- Illustrating state changes as a result of time-based messages or events
- Detailing the system time requirements

Interaction Overview

The Interaction Overview diagram is intended to provide the ability to show an abstract view (collapsed) of a set of complex system operations. The diagrams show activity and interaction diagram elements, as well as collapsed regions where additional diagram detail is hidden.

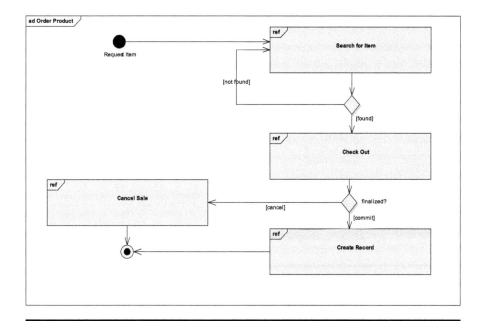

Figure D-13   Interaction Overview Diagram

Useful for:

- Abstracting complex flows and interactions
- Showing high-level system interactions
- Focusing attention on key system behavior while collapsing detail

Variations (UML Profile)

As noted earlier, the UML provides for extension in the form of Profiles. These are UML models that represent additional modeling areas apart from the core UML diagrams. Profiles are a very powerful way to apply the UML to areas of development that can benefit from a common modeling approach but do not directly fit into any of the UML core meta-model concepts. Examples include Business Modeling, System Analysis Modeling, and Database Entity Modeling.

Business Process Model

Business processes are the inputs, work steps, and outputs to a particular business operation. For example, a bank may process a deposit by accepting a deposit slip and cash from a customer, which is then reviewed by a teller, who inputs the deposit into the customer's bank account and prints a receipt.

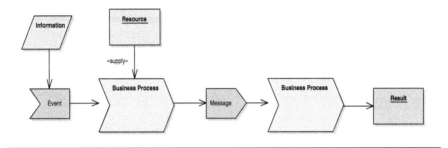

Figure D-14   Business Process Diagram

System Analysis Model

Classic system analysis uses three elements to describe critical system operations, the Interface, the Controller, and the Entity. By showing the dependencies and interactions between these diagram elements, a complex system can be initially abstracted to a few key Interfaces (input/output) that use Controllers (processor) to modify system Entities (data).

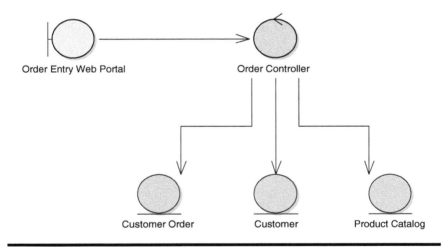

Figure D-15   System Analysis Diagram

Database Entity Diagrams

Entity Diagrams are an application of UML Class diagrams to perform domain modeling. The intent is to capture the system entities that are manipulated during system processing or otherwise hold some state. The database details, such as primary key, multiplicity, and column descriptions are also captured using this diagram.

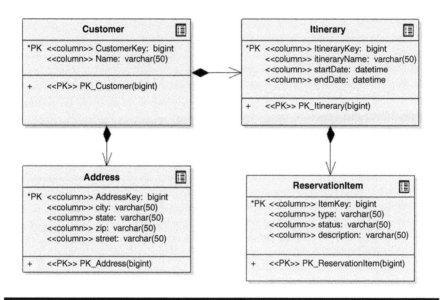

Figure D-16   Data Model Diagram

Useful for:

- Describing relationships between system entities
- Describing ownership and containment multiplicity
- Showing entity attributes
- Indicating system entity complexity

Note

1. A meta-model is a "model of a model," in which the elements of the meta-model describe the meaning (semantics) of concrete diagrams generated from the meta-model structure.

Index

A

Abbreviations, importance of defining, 90
Abstraction, 7, 12, 59, 231
    choice of levels and architectural
        description, 138
    pivot as example of, 83
    and recognition of symbols, 6
    role in modeling, 3
Accuracy
    with audio/video recording, 67
    sacrificing in favor of understanding, 8
    validating, 95
Acronyms
    in Execute Trade business workflow, 202
    importance of defining, 90
Active listening, 67
Activity diagrams. *See also* UML activity
        diagrams
    basing on golden mean, 178
    Execute Trade business workflow, 214
    UML connector stereotype in, 181
Adaptability of goals, and process approach, 25
Adaptation, of analysis patterns/frameworks,
        56–57
Adjacent blues, avoiding in shading, 183
Aesthetics in diagramming, 169, 185, 240
Air transportation business, domain model
        example, 116, 117
Allocation views, 147
Alternate views, in software architecture
        modeling, 146–148
Alternative paths, 113
    in Execute Trade business workflow, 207
Ambiguity, 157
    sources in interviews, 68
American Automobile Association, 84

Analogical reasoning, 162, 164, 165
Analysis models, 51
Analysis paralysis, 57, 58, 59
Analysis pattern catalog, 53, 228
Analysis patterns, 50, 59
    pattern structure, 50–54
    predominance of design patterns over, 54
Analytical frameworks, 50, 54–55, 57, 229
    for business workflow analysis, 110
    creating, 59–60
    framework elements, 141
    for legacy software systems, 124
    modifying, 58
    for services registries, 141
    software architecture modeling, 136, 148
Analytical patterns, 51
Analytical thinking, 49
    adaptation and application in, 56–57
    analysis patterns in, 50–54
    analytical frameworks for, 54–55
Angles, minimizing, 185
Antilock brake control unit
    model example, 87–90
    sequence diagram, 89
Application data repository view, 147
Archetype patterns, 51, 52
    variables in, 52
Archetype variation, 52
Architectural drivers and constraints, 137
Architectural mechanisms, 137
Art of modeling, 3–5
Asymmetrical diagrams, 240
    motion in, 178
Attention, 223
Audience sophistication, and presentation
        choices, 189
Audio recordings, 66

Audit trails, of user activity, 129–130
Automated code documentation, 136
Automated systems description, 114

B

Banking regulations, 107
Baseline verification, 100
Beauty, 13, 223
    and Gestalt theory, 10–12
Bias, modeler, 81, 96
Binary branch points, 113
Black on white, 183, 186
    maximizing contrast with, 175
Blue, 186
    avoiding in lines, 175, 183
Blueprint drafting, 91
Bottom-up approach, 17, 28
    positive/negative aspects, 18
Bound notebooks, 76
    for recording research information, 66–67
Brainstorming, 72
Branch points, 113, 240
Broken lines, 175
Bug fixes, 127
Building patterns, 53
Business actors, 108, 118
    in Execute Trade business workflow, 203
    identifying, 234
Business analysis framework, 54
Business analysts, 34
Business case diagram, 108
    package delivery service example, 111
Business domain archetype patterns, 51, 53
Business entities, 115–116
Business environment, 116
    evaluating for workflow analysis, 106–107
Business logic layer, 140
Business marketing models, validating through
    execution, 99
Business models, 237
    components of, 108
    defining scope of, 35
    developing in workflow analysis, 107–109
    icons and relationships, 108
    visual models in, 83
    why and who questions for, 118
Business objects
    identifying, 113
    mechanisms of control, 116
Business problems, questioning, 107
Business process model, UML 2.0, 258

Business process stability
    measuring with Six Sigma, 107
    problems in rapidly growing companies, 119
Business processes
    defined, 34
    mapping, 46
Business rules
    behind legacy software, 123
    challenges in investigating exception
        handling, 42–43
    for legacy software, 130
    vs. business domains, 53
Business stakeholder, 108
Business systems, modeling of, 33
Business use case, 111, 113
    use in discovery phase, 110
Business workers/actors, 108, 115, 117
    in Execute Trade business workflow, 204
    handling of multiple roles by, 115
    identifying, 120, 234
    vs. roles, 115
    workflow entry points, 233
Business workflow analysis, 105
    business entities in, 115–116
    business environment evaluation for,
        106–107
    business model development, 107–109
    business workers and actors in, 115
    business workflows in, 109–115
Business workflow modeling, 105, 120, 234
Business workflows, 117
    analytical framework, 110
    business form indication in, 118
    Execute Trade example, 201–215
    identifying unique, 110
    models of, 98
    package delivery service example, 109
    swimlanes in, 114

C

Call sequences, 144
Candidate architecture, 99
Cataloging information, 231
Categorization, and visualization, 161
Cellular telephony product, interaction of
    multiple sub-systems in, 23, 24
Central themes, in model creation, 83
Chemical representations
    glucose, 6
    visual models in, 83
Chronological organization, 77

Civil construction blueprints, visual models
    in, 83
Clarity, 169
Class diagrams, for system components, 141
Click-through models, 98
Closure, in Gestalt theory, 11
Code dependency chains, 149
Code reviews, 41
Cognition, 4, 155–156
Cognitive dissonance, 5
Cognitive Psychology, 10, 12, 13, 180
Cognitive psychology, benefits of active
    listening per, 67
Cognitive resonance, 5–7, 12
Cohesive behavior, 86
Color, 181–184
    consistency in use, 184
    for emphasis, 182
    emphasis in, 184–185
    reserving for model view transitions, 194
Command-line interfaces, 46
Communal cultures, 39, 45
Communication breakdowns, 224
Communication diagrams, UML 2.0,
    254–255
Communication models, 9
Company guru, 226
Company size, 107
Company structure, 106
Competitor review, 106
Compile-time dependencies, 143
Complexity, 225, 233
    and flexibility, 226
    and progressive disclosure, 190
    reducing through models, 13
Component, 19, 20
Component diagrams, UML 2.0, 250
Component view, 147, 148
    in software architecture modeling, 142–144
Composite diagrams, UML 2.0, 249
Composition, 169–170
    emphasis, 181
    information balance, 180
    line and contour, 170–176
    shade and color, 181–184
    shade/color emphasis, 184–185
    visual balance, 176–179
Computer aided design (CAD), 91
Computer aided software engineering (CASE),
    56, 136
Computer systems, purpose of modeling, 33
Conceptual patterns, 53

Configuration settings, 43
    in software architecture modeling, 143
Connector views, 147
Constraints, 137, 190, 192, 238
Content selection, 86–91
Context
    effect on perception, 10
    role in model presentation, 91
Context-free questions, 69
    for interviews, 68
Contour, 170–176
Contrast, maximizing with black on white,
    175
Controlled operations environments, 44
Controller, 19, 20
Cooperative interactions, 65
Core business niche, 106, 233
Corporate anthropology, 34
Corporate culture, 38–40, 45
Cost issues
    and concerns about unemployment, 40
    in mercenary cultures, 39
Creative process, mind-mapping of, 53
Creativity, systems models for, 37–38
Critical review, 102, 232
Crossing points, 186
    avoiding by rearrangement, 177
    avoiding in visual maps, 171, 172, 175
Cultural norms, and visual presentation, 186
Customer base, 106
Customer service, example system
    requirements, 218
Cybernetic systems, 25, 27, 29

D

Dance movements chart, visual models in, 83
Data access layer, 140
Data descriptions, 129
Data dictionaries, 129, 217
Data persistence mechanism, 149
Data processing/storage, 40, 41, 45
Data recovery, 43
Data validation, 95, 100, 130
    direct application for, 99
    review questions for, 97
    simulations for, 98
    team review for, 95–97
    test-based verification for, 100
Database design, ERD in, 81
Database entity diagrams, 259
Database structure viewer, 136

Deciphering and translation, in requirements
    archaeology, 128–130
Deductive reasoning, 162, 164
    visual aids to, 163, 165
Definitions
    in Execute Trade business workflow, 202
    in model content, 86
Dependencies, 91, 92, 172, 231, 233, 240
    compile-time, 143
    between logical layers, 140
    long distance, 173
    in model content, 86
    between physical components, 142
    trading subsystems, 142
Dependency-based organization, 77
Dependent workflows, 202
Deployment diagrams, UML 2.0, 251
Deployment view, 149, 237
    in software architecture modeling, 145–146
Design patterns, 50
    predominance over analysis patterns, 54
Detail hiding, 180, 189, 190, 192, 195
Development environments, 43, 146
    vs. production environments, 46
Development expenses, 236
Diagram construction exercise, 187
Diagrammatic reasoning, 160–164, 165
Diagrams, verbalization from, 162
Direct application, 95, 100, 101
    for data validation, 99
Direction, in Gestalt theory, 11
Discovery
    business use case in, 110
    questions for core business niche, 106
    in requirements archaeology, 124–126
    of system components, 105
Discussion, in analysis patterns, 50
Distributed review format, 96
Document storage, 35
Documentation
    independent-study review of legacy, 126
    as key information source, 74
    of legacy software requirements, 125, 131
Domain data model, 118
    for air travel, 117
    air travel example, 189
    business entities in, 115–116
    of manual operations, 233–234
Domain entity, 108
Domain modeling, 234
    exercise, 93
Dotted lines, 170

Drivers, 136
Dumbing down, avoidance of, 240
Dynamic behavior, 86, 91, 144–145, 887
    antilock brake control unit example, 88, 90
    in model content, 88, 90
Dynamic systems, 25, 26, 29, 33
Dynamic view, 148
    in software architecture modeling, 144–145

E

E-mail trails, 236
Efficiency, in networked cultures, 39
Electronic-based recordings, 66
Element position, and emphasis, 181
Embedded views, 193
Emphasis, 181, 186
    on neutral background, 185
    by size variation, 182
Emphasis colors, 184
Enduring business themes (EBT), 51, 228–229
Enterprise modeling, use of Zachman
    Framework for, 81
Entity, 19, 20
Entity-Relationship Diagrams (ERD), 81, 147
Environmental conditions
    of legacy software requirements, 126
    simulating, 98
Environmental impact, and process approach,
    25
Environments, 45. *See also* Business
    environment
    considering in modeling, 43–44
Error management, 237. *See also* Exception
    handling
Exception handling, 41–42, 45, 126, 130
    in Execute Trade business workflow,
    210–213
Exceptional paths, 113
Excluding information, 65
    from model content, 86
Execute Trade business workflow, 201
    activity diagram, 214
    alternative workflows, 208–210
    brief description, 201
    business actors, 203
    business workers, 204
    definitions and acronyms, 202
    dependent workflows, 202
    exceptional workflows, 210–213
    Execute Electronic Trade scenario, 209
    extending workflows, 202

extension points, 213
Generate and Execute Terminating CEO
    scenario, 208
improvement possibilities, 213
included workflows, 202
issues, 214
notes section, 214
Overnight Trade Instruction Letter
    scenario, 207–208
post-conditions, 213
Post/Unpost Trade Ticket scenario, 209
preconditions, 204
purpose, 201
special requirements, 213
Supervisor Denial of Trade exception, 213
Trade Correction exception, 210–211
Trade Not Conducted before Market
    Closure exception, 211–212
Trade Settlement scenario, 208–209
Trade Ticket Does Not Post Correctly
    exception, 211
workflow description, 204–206
Exercises
    business process mapping, 46
    business worker/actor identification, 120
    business workflow modeling, 120
    creating analytical frameworks, 59–60
    critical review, 102
    diagram construction, 187
    domain modeling, 93, 120
    finding abstract themes, 59
    framework description, 150–151
    iconic representations, 166
    interviewing, 79
    observing presentation techniques, 197
    organizational mapping, 47
    problems with communication, 14
    risk analysis, 150–151
    system analysis, 30–31
    team construction, 47
    translation of structured requirements,
        133–134
Expected system behavior, process approach
    to, 28
Experimental validation, 100, 101, 232. *See also*
    Test-based verification
Experimentation, 78
    in research phase, 74–75
Extended interviews, 72
Extending workflows, 202
External business actor, 107, 115
    at presentation layer, 140

External consultants, 35
External systems interfaces, 130

F

Facilitator responsibilities, 71
    in review sessions, 96
    separating from scribe responsibilities, 71
Factor of Objective Set, 238
Failure, reasons for modeling project, 45–46
Failure analysis, 224
Field deployment environments, 44
Figure and ground, 157, 164, 184
    confusion by overcrowding, 158
Flow-based descriptions, of software
    requirements, 129
Flow charts
    establishing workflow boundaries with, 11
    for hidden processing steps, 41
    in legacy software requirements project, 127
    vs. UML activity diagrams, 112
    worker interactions, 36
Focus groups, 65, 73, 99
    audio/video recording in, 66–67
Fragmented cultures, 39, 45
Framework description exercise, 150, 237–238
Free-form conceptual association, 53
Full-featured development IDE, 136
Function Flow Block Diagram (FFBD), 18
Functional decomposition, 17, 20–24, 28, 29,
    85
    positive/negative aspects, 22
    use in legacy software rediscovery, 128
    vs. flow-based descriptions, 129
Functional elements, distinguishing from
    physical elements, 51
Functional view, 148
    in software architecture modeling, 137–138
FURPS, 130

G

Generation phase, in brainstorming, 72
Geographic distribution, 107
Geographic models, pivots in, 83
Geographical organization, 77
Gestalt theory, 11–12, 13, 155, 156–160, 184
    Law of Past Experience, 158, 160
    Principle of Proximity, 159
    Principle of Similarity, 159
    visual deduction and, 164
Glossary, defining jargon/acronyms in, 90

Golden mean proportion, 177, 186
Golden Rule of Modeling, 8
Graphical user interface (GUI), 40
    validation of, 98
Ground, 164
    figure and, 157
Group agreement, and Law of Group
        Interactions, 37
Group dependencies, 38
Group facilitation, 70–73, 78
    responsibilities of group members in, 71
Group membership, 70
Group sessions, 65
    in legacy software rediscovery, 128

H

Hard-copy printouts, 193–194
Harmonic resonance, 5
Hazardous environments, 44
Hidden processing steps, 41
Hierarchical organization, 77
Hierarchical requirements, 70
High availability/reliability environments, 44
Homeostatic systems, 25, 26–27, 27, 29
Hypothesis, 29
    in scientific method, 24

I

Icons, 6, 12, 238
    exercise, 166
Image resolution, for screen projection, 195
Implementation diagrams, 142–143
Implementation phase, scientific method in,
    24
Implementation view, in software architecture
        modeling, 142–144
Impressionist painting, modeling and
        perception in, 4
Included workflows, 202
Independent investigation, 73–74, 78
    in requirements archaeology, 126–127
Independent observation, 34
Index-based organization, 77
Indirect observation, 44
Indirect study, with scientific method, 24
Individualism, in fragmented cultures, 39
Individuals, observing, 34–37
Inductive reasoning, 162, 164
    visual aids to, 163, 164
Informal patterns, 49, 57, 59

Information balance, 180, 186
Information input, 161
Information recording, 66–67
Information repositories, 59, 228
    for legacy software details, 125
Information sources, 65
    identifying potential, 73
    for legacy software requirements, 125,
        131
    visual perception, 155, 164
    workflow documentation, 113
Integrated Definition models, 18
Intended audience, 87
Intended system behavior, 44
Interaction overview diagrams, UML 2.0,
        256–257
Interactive discovery, 34
Interdependency, 86, 87
    in model content, 90
Interfaces, 19, 20, 40, 45
Intergroup interactions, 35, 44
Internal control, and process approach, 25
Internal goals, in cybernetic systems, 27
Internal processing steps, hidden, 41
Interpretation, 164
    of visual clues, 157–158
Interviews, 65, 67–70, 76, 235
    context-free questions, 68
    group, 230
    noise factor, 229–230
    for requirements archaeology, 127–128
Intragroup dependency, 38
Intragroup interactions, 35
Intuitive comprehension, 155, 156
Inventory management, state chart for, 140
Investigation
    independent study, 126–127
    for requirements archaeology, 126
Isolation, visual emphasis by, 182
Issue tracking systems, 127, 236
    use in legacy system discovery, 125
Iterative development, 228

J

Jargon
    defining in model glossary, 92
    translating/defining, 90
JavaDoc, 136
Joint Application Development (JAD), 65,
    73
Junction points, minimizing in diagrams, 172

K

Key abstractions, 86, 238
Key individuals
    dangers of dependence on, 46
    dependence on, 38
Known implementations, in analysis patterns, 50

L

Law of Group Interactions, 37, 38, 45
Law of Prägnanz, 11, 13, 156, 164
Layering, 192, 195
    in presentation, 189
Layering architecture, 140
Learning
    models as central to, 9–10
    role in model construction, 85
Legacy computer systems, 44
    analytical framework for, 124
    continued maintenance of artifacts, 130–131
    design rediscovery for, 56
    exception handling in, 42
    investigating, 40–43
    middle-out approach to, 135
    recovery of software requirements, 123–124
Legal and regulatory requirements, 107
Library resources, 230
Light colors, avoiding in lines, 175
Line, 170–176
    element relationships and, 170
Line endings, 170
Line length, 185
    minimizing, 172
Line styles, 174–175, 230
Line weights, 239
    for emphasis, 240
    mismatched, 171
Line width, 185
Linked diagrams, 180
Linked systems, 225
Linked views, 189, 192, 193, 195
    in screen projection presentations, 193
Linux, 41
Listening skills
    active listening, 67
    notetaking and, 66
Logical elements, 138
    difficulty of identifying, 116

M

Mac OS X, 41
Maintenance costs, and application complexity, 235
Manage Trade Order activity diagram, 139
Mathematical symbology, 6
    visual representation of, 161
Mechanisms of control, 116
Mental manipulation, 162
Mental visualization, 161
Mercenary cultures, 39, 45
Message generation, 9
Message interpretation, 9
Meta-modeling, 82
Meta-questions, for interviews, 68
Metadata-based organization, 77
Metaphorical reasoning, 162
Middle-out approach, 17, 28
    to legacy system modeling, 135
    positive/negative aspects, 18
Military operations, 43
Minard, Charles, 170
Mind-mapping, 53
Miscommunication, risk with jargon and acronyms, 90
Mission-critical systems, 43, 44
Mobile environments, 44
Model complexity, and presentation choices, 189
Model construction, xv, 85–86
    review questions on, 97
    speed of creation, 85
Model content selection, 86
    review questions on, 97
    translating into model format, 86–90
Model context, 83–84, 231, 233
Model-driven development, 192
Model forms, 81–82, 91, 169, 230–231
    choosing, 85
    construction of, 85–86
    content selection for, 86–91
    dynamic behavior in, 88, 90
    examples, 82
    interdependency in, 90
    purpose and form, 82–84
    static structure in, 88
    tool support for, 91
    translating information into, 86–90
    translating jargon in, 90
Model presentation, 189. *See also* Presentation
Model sections, 86–87

Model validation, 231–232. *See also* Data
    validation
Model views, 83, 91
    identifying with double titles, 195, 196
    Minard's Bonaparte march to Moscow, 170
    reserving colors for transitions between, 194
Modeler bias, 81
Modeling, 230
    Golden Rule of, 8
    systematic approach, 17–18
    theoretical considerations, xv
Models
    aesthetics of, 169
    emotional response to, 223
    visual presentation of, 156
Module views, 147
Modus ponens, 163
Motion, in asymmetrical diagrams, 178
Motivation/forces, in analysis patterns, 50
Multicolored lines, avoiding, 175, 176
Multiplicity, 190, 192

N

N-ary branch points, 113
N-squared Law of Group Interactions, 37, 38,
    45
    and recommended group size, 70
Navigational model, 84
Networked cultures, 39, 45
Notation, 6, 19
    ensuring uniformity in models, 81
Notebooks
    portability and durability of, 229
    use in recording information, 66–67
Notetaking, 66–67

O

Object diagrams, UML 2.0, 248
Object-Oriented Programming (OOP), 19
Objective Set, in Gestalt theory, 11
Objectives, in systems analysis, 19
Objects, in air travel domain model, 190
Oblique lines, 172, 174
    radial placement of elements with, 174
    vs. rectilinear lines, 172, 185
Observation, 29, 33–34
    dos and don'ts, 37
    environmental considerations, 43–44
    of groups, 37–38
    of individuals, 34–37

of legacy computer systems, 40–43
and organizational culture, 38–40
role of trust in accuracy of, 35
in scientific method, 24
Opposing colors, use in diagrams, 183
Organization, of research information, 66,
    75–76
Organizational culture, 38–40, 225–226
    and success of legacy software requirements
        discovery, 126
Organizational mapping, 47, 227
Orwell, George, 3–4
Overcrowding, 164
    confusion of figure and ground via, 158
    and loss of comprehension, 157
Ownership-based organization, 77

P

Package delivery service
    business workflow analysis example, 105
    flow chart *vs.* UML activity diagram, 112
    package sorter business case diagram,
        111
Package diagrams, 244
Past Experience, in Gestalt theory, 11
Pastel colors, 183
Pattern language, 50
Patterns, 155
    defined, 49
    modification of, 52
    and perception of beauty, 12
Pentagram shapes, relationships indicated by,
    180
People skills, 58
Perception, 13, 155–156, 164
    and diagrammatic reasoning, 160–164
    effect of context on, 10
    Gestalt theory of, 156–160
Perception field, 10
Perceptual constancy, 155
Performance steps, identifying through
        workflow analysis, 111
Performance testing, experimentation in, 75
PerlDoc, 136
Physical elements, distinguishing from
        functions, 51
Pivots, 83, 91, 180, 231
Plato's ideal forms, 7, 160–161
Pleomorphism, 52
Portable portfolios, presentation with, 194
Position, as common pivot, 83

Post-mortems, 228
Poster-size printouts, 194
Presentation, 189
   flow, 189–193
   session breaks during, 241
Presentation flow, 189–193
Presentation layer, 140
Presentation of information, xv
Presentation techniques, 193
   hard-copy printouts, 193–194
   observing, 197
   portable portfolios, 194
   printed *vs.* projected, 195
   screen projection, 193
   system architecture wall, 194
Previous knowledge
   discovery in research phase, 65
   use in analytical thinking, 49–50
Primary colors, 183
Principle of Closure, 159, 160
   and line styles, 175
Principle of Past Experience, 158, 160
Principle of Proximity, 159
Principle of Similarity, 159
Printed models, 195. *See also* Hard-copy
     printouts
Problem analysis patterns, 53
Problem statement, 50
Process approach, 17, 25–28, 28, 29
   positive/negative aspects, 28
Process diagram, for ticket printing, 146
Process questions, 68
Product questions, 106
   for interviews, 68
Production environments, 43, 146
   vs. development environments, 46
Programming languages, of legacy software
     code, 125
Progressive disclosure, 180, 189, 190, 195,
     240
   air travel domain model examples, 190,
     191
   in screen projections, 193
Projected models, 195. *See also* Screen
     projection
Proportion, 176
Prototype model, 13, 98
Proximity, in Gestalt theory, 11, 12
Publish-Subscribe view, 147
Purpose, in systems analysis, 19
Pythagorean Theorem, Euclid's half-area proof
     for, 162

R

Rapid-growth organizations, challenges in
     modeling, 119
Rational Unified Process, 107
Real-time operation environments, 44
Reasoning, 13
   models as central to, 9–10
Rectilinear lines, 172, 174, 176
   vs. oblique lines, 172, 185
RedHat Linux, 41
Reduction phase, in brainstorming, 72
Reference architecture, 99
Regularity of form, cognitive sensitivity to,
     172
Regulatory requirements, 107
Reinventing the wheel, 51, 57
Relationship building, 58
Relationship lines, 170
Repetitive tasks
   automation of, 37
   observation of, 35
Requirements analysis, 76
Requirements archaeology, 123–124,
     234–235. *See also* Software
     requirements
   deciphering and translation phase, 128–130
   interviewing for, 127–128
   investigation phase, 126–128
   preparation and discovery, 124–126
   public visibility issues, 130–131
Requirements base, 130, 131
Requirements management, 130
Requirements reengineering, support
     difficulties, 132
Research and investigation, 65–66
   beginning model construction during, 85
   experimentation in, 74–75
   group facilitation, 70–73
   importance to modeling efforts, 76
   independent investigation, 73–74
   interviews, 67–70
   organizing research information, 75–76
   recording information, 66–67
Restricted permission environments, 44
Retrospectives, 228
Review paralysis, 37
Review questions, 97
Review sessions. *See* Team reviews
Risk analysis exercise, 150–151, 238
Road signs, intuitive comprehension of,
     155–156, 156

Roles, 108
    key worker, 110
    vs. workers, 115
Rolled printouts, identifying with double titles,
      195, 196

S

Saturated color, 186
    avoiding, 183
Scale, 176
Schedule constraints, 238
Scientific method, 17, 24–25, 28, 29
    positive/negative aspects, 25
Screen projection, 193, 241
Scribe responsibilities, 71
    in review sessions, 96
Semantics, 6
    ensuring uniformity in models, 81
Senior management
    beginning observation with, 35
    communicating faulty business practices
      to, 119
Sequence diagrams
    antilock brake control unit example, 89
    UML 2.0, 255
    web-based authentication, 145
Service-oriented groups, 38
Service provisioning, example use case, 217
Services layer, 140
Services registries, frameworks for, 141
Shading, 181–184
    emphasis, 184–185
    and emphasis, 181
Similarity, in Gestalt theory, 11
Simulations, 95, 98, 100, 101, 232
Singleton pattern, 51
Six Sigma analysis, 34
    of business process stability, 107
Size variation, emphasis by, 182
Skill set, for business modeling, 227
Software architect, 148
Software architecture document template, 136,
      236–237
Software architecture modeling, 135–137
    alternate views, 146–148
    analytical framework, 136
    component view, 142–144
    deployment view, 145–146
    dynamic view, 144–145
    functional view, 137–138

implementation view, 142–144
    static structure view, 138–142
Software development
    embrace of analysis patterns by, 50
    functional decomposition in, 21
    visual models in, 83
Software fixes, *vs.* system enhancements, 127
Software project requirements, 54
Software requirements
    archaeology of, 123–124
    modeling with use cases, 70
    organizing with flows, 129
    rediscovery of lost, 123
    translation of, 133–134
Software requirements archaeology, 105
Software testing, scientific method in, 24
Solid lines, 170, 175, 186
Solution, in analysis patterns, 50
Solution bias, 69
Sound, use in models, 82
Source code, 127
    analysis for exception handling, 235
    for discovery of legacy software
      requirements, 125
    inaccessibility of, 131
    investigation tools, 74
    tools for rapid analysis, 136
    walking, 149
Space-based systems, 43
Stable problems, functional decomposition
      approach for, 24
Stakeholder needs, review questions, 97
State charts, inventory management, 140
State diagrams, 144, 193
    UML 2.0, 253–254
Static structure, 86, 91
    antilock brake control unit example, 88
    in model content, 88
    view in software architecture modeling,
      138–142
Static systems, 25, 26, 29, 33
Static view, 148
Strategic flexibility, and system knowledge,
      235
Strong colors, overuse of, 184
Structure diagrams, UML 2.0, 246–247
Subject matter experts, 44
    accessing via interviews, 67
    gaining access to, 226
    limited access to, 73
    validation of legacy documentation, 128

Subsystem descriptions, 141
    dependency map, 142
Subtractive color, 173
Surveys, 65, 73
Suspension bridge, 49
Swimlanes, 115, 145
    in business workflows, 114
Symbology, 6, 12
    difficulty in creating universally understood,
        239
    and model forms, 81
    recognition of, 155
Symmetrical balance, 178, 179, 186
    stability and harmony in, 178
Synergy, 29
    failure of functional decomposition to
        consider, 22
    in systems analysis, 19
System analysis model, UML 2.0, 258
System architecture framework, 55
    documentation of, 105
System architecture wall, 194
System behavior, 41, 45
    challenges for discovery of, 33
    classification of, 26
    data processing/storage in, 41
    investigating with user manuals, 75
System boundary, 19
System communications channels, 142
System components, 19
    class diagrams for, 141, 143
    discovery of, 105
    implementation diagram, 144
System enhancements, masquerading as fixes,
        127
System layer structure, 141
System replacement, 235
System requirements
    for customer care system example,
        217–218
    importance of, 131
    rediscovery of lost, 73
    translating to use case, 217–222, 236
System requirements framework, 55
    applicability to legacy systems, 56
Systematic approaches, 17–18
    formal systems analysis, 19–20
    functional decomposition, 20–24
    overview of, 18
    process approach, 25–28
    scientific method, 24–25

Systems analysis, 17, 19–20, 20, 28, 29, 224
    positive/negative aspects, 21
Systems integration, functional decomposition
        in, 22
Systems Modeling Language, 18

T

Tablet computers, use in research, 66
Task-based organization, 77
Task modeling, 35
Taxonomic organization, 77
Team behavior, 227
Team construction, 47
Team reviews, 72, 95, 100, 101, 232, 241
    active style for, 97
    for data validation, 95–97
Team support, systems models for, 37
Test-based verification, for data validation, 100
Test cases, 75, 237
Testing, 29, 95, 100
    in scientific method, 24
Testing environments, 43, 146
Text design, 239–240
Text manipulation tools, 235–236
Theoretical considerations, xv
Thinking. *See* Cognition
Threads, interactions between, 145
Time limits, for interviews, 69
Timing diagrams, UML 2.0, 256
Timing pressure environments, 44
Tools
    for analytical frameworks, 54
    for business modeling, 227
    for model creation, 91
    for software architecture modeling, 136
Top-down approach, 17, 28
    to modeling new systems, 135
    positive/negative aspects, 18
Topical organization, 77
Total Quality Management (TQM), 34
Tracing, avoiding close, 175
Trade-offs, 29
    in systems analysis, 19
Transitional cultures, 39, 56
Trust, role in accurate observations, 35

U

UML 2.0, 18
    activity diagrams, 252

business process model, 258
communication diagrams, 254–255
component diagrams, 250
composite diagrams, 249
database entity diagrams, 259
deployment diagrams, 251
interaction overview diagrams, 256–257
object diagrams, 248
package diagrams, 244
profiles/variations, 257–259
sequence diagrams, 255
state diagrams, 253–254
structure diagrams, 246–247
system analysis model, 258
timing diagrams, 256
use case diagrams, 245
visual software modeling in, 243–244
UML activity diagrams, 145
establishing workflow boundaries with, 111
Manage Trade Order, 139
package delivery service workflows, 112
ticket printing, 146
use in legacy software requirements projects, 126–127
UML analysis diagrams, 41
UML class diagrams, 149
UML connectors stereotype, 181
UML diagrams, 179
UML model forms, 169
appropriateness for presentation, 189
for system requirements and use cases, 221–222
UML Profiles, 18
Underanalysis, 56–57, 58, 59
Unified Modeling Language (UML), 6, 7, 81
facilitation of code-based analysis with, 74
Uniform Destiny, in Gestalt theory, 11
Uniform element size, 178
Uniform sizing, 178
Unix, 41
Usability, 220
in networked cultures, 39
Usability testing, 98
Use case analysis, 22, 45, 156, 218–222
in functional view, 137
legacy software requirements, 133–134
model form of, 85
pivots in, 83
stock trader example, 138
Use case diagrams, UML 2.0, 245
Use case rediscovery sessions, 128

Use cases, translating system requirements to, 217–222
User acceptance, 146
User activity audit trails, 129–130
User interaction flows, 22
User manuals, role in system behavior investigation, 75
Utility, validating, 95

V

Variables, holding constant in verification, 100
Vase/Profile illusion, 157
Verbalization, from diagrams, 162
Video recordings, 66
Visible system behavior, 40
Vision statement, 106
identifying, 105
Visual aesthetics, 183
Visual ambiguity, 157, 158
Visual attention, 180
Visual balance, 176–179, 186
Visual deduction, 164
Visual fatigue, 184
Visual grouping, 159
Visual models, 82, 160, 239
for deductive, inductive, analogical reasoning, 162
as information sources, 155
of mathematical proofs, 161
Visual noise, 172
Visual perception, 164
Visual recognition, by element position, 156
Visual software modeling, in UML 2.0, 243–244

W

Walkthrough reviews, 96
Wall diagrams, 241
Web-based systems, configuration weaknesses in, 43
Web server configuration, performance experiment for, 99
Weinberg, Gerald, xv
Whiteboard, use in group facilitation, 72
Wide-carriage printers, for diagram printouts, 194
WIKI electronic discussion boards, 236
Wire-frame models, 98

Worker roles, 233
    vs. person focus, 110–111
Workers
    as core of business processes, 34
    inter- and intra-actions, 36
Workflow boundaries, 111
Workflow documentation, 113
Workflows. *See also* Business workflows
    alternative and exceptional paths, 113

    crossover between, 113
    tasks as components of, 35
Worldview alignment, 5
Written surveys, 73

Z

Zachman Frameworks, 18
    in enterprise modeling, 81